ROUTLEDGE LIBRARY EDITIONS:
NUCLEAR SECURITY

Volume 19

THE NUCLEAR CONFRONTATION IN EUROPE

THE NUCLEAR CONFRONTATION IN EUROPE

Edited by
JEFFREY H. BOUTWELL, PAUL DOTY
AND GREGORY F. TREVERTON

LONDON AND NEW YORK

First published in 1985 by Croom Helm

This edition first published in 2021
by Routledge
2 Park Square, Milton Park, Abingdon, Oxon OX14 4RN

and by Routledge
52 Vanderbilt Avenue, New York, NY 10017

Routledge is an imprint of the Taylor & Francis Group, an informa business

© 1985 Jeffrey H. Boutwell, Paul Doty and Gregory F. Treverton

All rights reserved. No part of this book may be reprinted or reproduced or utilised in any form or by any electronic, mechanical, or other means, now known or hereafter invented, including photocopying and recording, or in any information storage or retrieval system, without permission in writing from the publishers.

Trademark notice: Product or corporate names may be trademarks or registered trademarks, and are used only for identification and explanation without intent to infringe.

British Library Cataloguing in Publication Data
A catalogue record for this book is available from the British Library

ISBN: 978-0-367-50682-7 (Set)
ISBN: 978-1-00-309763-1 (Set) (ebk)
ISBN: 978-0-367-52175-2 (Volume 19) (hbk)
ISBN: 978-1-00-305684-3 (Volume 19) (ebk)

Publisher's Note
The publisher has gone to great lengths to ensure the quality of this reprint but points out that some imperfections in the original copies may be apparent.

Disclaimer
The publisher has made every effort to trace copyright holders and would welcome correspondence from those they have been unable to trace.

The Nuclear Confrontation in Europe

A Research Volume from
The Center for Science and International Affairs
Harvard University

Edited by
Jeffrey H. Boutwell, Paul Doty
and Gregory F. Treverton

CROOM HELM
London & Sydney

AUBURN HOUSE PUBLISHING COMPANY
Dover, Massachusetts

© 1985 Jeffrey H. Boutwell, Paul Doty and Gregory F. Treverton
Croom Helm Ltd, Provident House, Burrell Row,
Beckenham, Kent BR3 1AT
Croom Helm Australia Pty Ltd, Suite 4, 6th Floor,
64-76 Kippax Street, Surry Hills, NSW 2010, Australia

British Library Cataloguing in Publication Data

The Nuclear confrontation in Europe.
   1. Nuclear weapons—Europe 2. Europe—
Strategic aspects
   I. Boutwell, Jeffrey H. II. Doty, Paul
   III. Treverton, Gregory
   358'.39'094 U264

ISBN 0-7099-2481-X

© 1985 Jeffrey H. Boutwell, Paul Doty and Gregory F. Treverton
Auburn House Publishing Company,
14 Dedham Street, Dover, Massachusetts 02030

Library of Congress Cataloging in Publication Data
Main entry under title:
The Nuclear confrontation in Europe.
   1. Europe—Defenses—Addresses, essays, lectures.
2. Nuclear weapons—Europe—Addresses, essays, lectures.
I. Boutwell, Jeffrey H. II. Doty, Paul. III. Treverton,
Gregory F.
UA646.N73 1985   355'.0217'094   85-14062
ISBN 0-86569-128-2

Printed and bound in Great Britain by Mackays of Chatham Ltd, Kent

CONTENTS

List of Abbreviations

Introduction *Paul Doty and Gregory F. Treverton*   1

1. Building NATO's Nuclear Posture: 1950-65
   Timothy Ireland   5

2. The Wilderness Years *Lawrence Freedman*   44

3. NATO Theatre Nuclear Forces: The Third Phase, 1977-85
   Jeffrey H. Boutwell   67

4. Theatre Nuclear Forces: Military Logic and Political Purpose
   Gregory F. Treverton   87

5. The Role of Third-Country Nuclear Forces
   Lawrence Freedman   113

6. Nuclear Weapons and NATO Politics *Jeffrey H. Boutwell*   141

7. The Soviet Theatre Nuclear Force Posture: Doctrine, Strategy and Capabilities *Stephen M. Meyer*   164

8. Nuclear Weapons and the Warsaw Pact *Condolezza Rice*   185

9. Whither the Nuclear Confrontation? *Paul Doty and Gregory F. Treverton*   203

Notes on Contributors   237

Index   239

LIST OF ABBREVIATIONS

ABM	anti-ballistic missile
ADMs	atomic demolition munitions
ANF	Atlantic Nuclear Force
ASMs	air-to-surface missiles
ASMP	*air-sol moyenne portée*
ASW	anti-submarine warfare
ATMs	anti-tactical missiles
AWRE	Atomic Weapons Research Establishment
C3I	command, control, communications and intelligence
CDU	Christian Democratic Union (FRG)
CEP	circular error probable
COMECON	Council for Mutual Economic Assistance (E. Europe)
CSU	Christian Social Union (FRG)
EDC	European Defence Community
EEC	European Economic Community
ERW	enhanced radiation weapons
ESECS	European Security Study
ET	emerging technologies
FBS	forward based systems
FRG	Federal Republic of Germany
GDR	German Democratic Republic
GLCM	ground-launched cruise missile
HLG	High-Level Group
ICBM	inter-continental ballistic missile
IISS	International Institute for Strategic Studies
INF	intermediate-range nuclear forces
IRBM	intermediate-range ballistic missile
JCAE	Joint Committee on Atomic Energy (USA)
KGB	*Komitet Gosudarstvennoi Bezopasnosti* (Committee of State Security, USSR)
LRA	long-range aviation
MBFR	Mutual and Balanced Force Reductions
MIRV	multiple independent re-entry vehicle
MLF	Multilateral Force
MRBM	medium-range ballistic missile
NATO	North Atlantic Treaty Organisation

NDVs	nuclear delivery vehicles	
NFU	no-first-use	
NPG	Nuclear Planning Group (NATO)	
NSC	National Security Council (USA)	
NTM	national technical means	
OMTs	other military targets	
OTK	*Obrona terytorium krajni* (Poland)	
PALs	permissive action links	
PCI	Italian Communist Party	
POCs	Programmes of Co-operation	
PSI	Italian Socialist Party	
PSOE	Spanish Socialist Party	
R&D	research and development	
ROAD	Reorganisation Objective Army Division	
SAC	Strategic Air Command (USA)	
SACEUR	Supreme Allied Commander Europe	
SACLANT	Supreme Allied Commander Atlantic	
SALT	Strategic Arms Limitation Talks	
SAM	surface-to-air missile	
SCG	Special Consultative Group	
SDI	Strategic Defense Initiative (USA)	
SHAPE	Supreme Headquarters Allied Powers in Europe	
SIOP	Single Integrated Operational Plan	
SLBM	sea-/submarine-launched ballistic missile	
SLCM	sea-/submarine-launched cruise missile	
SPD	Social Democratic Party (FRG)	
SRBM	short-range ballistic missile	
SRF	Strategic Rocket Forces (USSR)	
START	Strategic Arms Reduction Talks	
TNDVs	tactical nuclear delivery vehicles	
TNF	theatre nuclear forces	
TNWs	tactical nuclear forces	
UDF	*Union pour la Démocratie Française*	
WEU	Western European Union	
WP	Warsaw Pact/Treaty Organisation	

INTRODUCTION

Paul Doty and Gregory F. Treverton

When the first American cruise and Pershing II missiles began arriving in Western Europe in December 1983, the public furore surrounding those deployments had already dampened down. Although the issue of intermediate nuclear forces (INF) had remained on centre stage for over four years, by the end of 1983 much of the anti-nuclear movement in Europe was fatigued, plainly regarding the deployments as a *fait accompli*.

Yet the lull in public attention to the nuclear confrontation in Europe is likely to be temporary for a number of reasons. The beginning of the NATO deployments was followed by a series of Soviet 'counter' deployments, so announced, including the deployment of shorter-range nuclear missiles in Eastern Europe. One of the missiles in particular, the SS-22, with a range of 900-1,000 km, will pose much the same threat to Western Europe from bases in Eastern Europe as do the Soviet SS-20 missiles based inside Russia.

When the NATO deployments began, the Soviet Union made good its threat to walk out of existing nuclear-arms-control talks — both the INF and Strategic Arms Reduction Talks (START). The hiatus lasted through the American political campaign of 1984, and it was not until early 1985 that Moscow and Washington agreed to resume superpower nuclear-arms control. These talks will cover the range of systems from space-based to strategic to INF in Europe, and in the short run, will impel renewed attention to the nuclear confrontation in Europe; over the longer term, they may force NATO to make hard choices about future INF deployments and their relations to strategic nuclear forces.

This leads to a final reason why the nuclear confrontation in Europe will not pass from public attention in the way it did for the decade between the mid-1960s and the mid-1970s. No nuclear development by either superpower, including the Reagan administration's much heralded (and lamented) Strategic Defense Initiative (SDI) of 1983, will alter the essential fact of nuclear parity between the superpowers. That will remain a fact of life for the remainder of this century and beyond. In these circumstances, American military planners will continue to fret over this or that technical imbalance between the nuclear forces of the superpowers. That fretting, in turn, will deepen European concerns that run back to the beginning of the nuclear age: will the United States run the risk of using nuclear weapons in Europe's defence if need be? Will, as the old saying has it, an American President be prepared to trade Chicago for Hamburg? In the 1960s and 1970s, American nuclear superiority muted those questions, never mind that 'superiority' was hard to define in any meaningful way. But parity will keep these sensitive questions close to the surface. Efforts to sustain the credibility of the American nuclear commitment to Western Europe, such as the deployment of cruise and Pershing, will then raise the temperature of the nuclear issue in Europe: many Europeans will wonder if they are more protected than endangered by nuclear weapons.

The last few years have also underscored a second fact, also one that runs back to the beginning of the nuclear era. The future of NATO is bound up with the fate of the nuclear confrontation in Europe. In the wake of the cruise and Pershing deployments, old questions were once more in the air: should NATO reduce its reliance on nuclear weapons? Would new technologies for conventional defence enable it to do so? For some, particularly in Europe, the questioning went deeper, to a search for some alternative to NATO in its current form, with the degree of European dependence on the United States implied in existing arrangements. Many Europeans sought, vaguely, some more co-operative European defence arrangements that might at least diminish their dependence on Washington. If the United States pressed its European allies through calls by the administration or by Congress to 'bear more of the burden' of their own defence, that could well have the unintended effect of increasing Europe's irritation at its dependence.

This book addresses the tangle of issues in the nuclear confrontation in Europe. It outlines how we got where we are, and it provides benchmarks for thinking about the future — both of the nuclear confrontation in Europe and of the NATO alliance. Its first three chapters sketch the history of NATO nuclear doctrine and forces — from the very beginnings of NATO through to the current situation with the cruise and Pershing deployments under way.

The next three chapters sort out the mix of political and military issues at play in the nuclear confrontation. Chapter 4 looks at the relation — past and prospective — between military deployments and NATO's essentially political purpose of deterring the Soviet Union. Chapter 5 assesses the impact, both political and military, of the

Introduction

nuclear forces of 'third countries' — Britain, France and China. Chapter 6 then turns explicitly to the politics of nuclear weapons, looking at the principal European countries. It provides a guide to the nuclear debates of the last few years and hints about the future course of opinion in those countries.

Chapters 7 and 8 turn from West to East, looking first at Soviet doctrine and nuclear deployments, and then at nuclear issues within the Warsaw Pact. What the Soviet Union intends with its nuclear deployments directed towards Europe is both crucial to NATO decisions and impossible to know with any certainty, but Chapter 7 assembles what hints can be gleaned from the course of Soviet deployments themselves, from the writings of Soviet military leaders and from military exercises. Certainly, the Soviet Union and its allies have not debated nuclear issues in a way comparable to the Western alliance. Yet there were intimations of strain in the Warsaw Pact in the aftermath of the NATO cruise and Pershing deployments. There were rumours of public concern in the Eastern European countries nominated to host the Soviet 'counter' deployments, and East Germany visibly strove to protect its ties with West Germany despite the deployments, to the point that Moscow felt compelled, in the autumn of 1984, publicly to veto party boss Honecker's planned trip to the Federal Republic. Chapter 8 assesses these events in light of earlier suggestions of strain over nuclear issues within the Warsaw Pact.

The concluding chapter draws these strands of analysis together, and provides guidelines for thinking about the nuclear confrontation and the future of NATO. It begins by stressing the central point that nuclear weapons in Europe must be seen in light both of their essentially political purpose and of the broader strategic balance. The chapter then lays out a primer for INF arms control, briefly outlining the history of past efforts, then setting out the main issues that will confront future negotiations — whether these take place alone or in some relation to strategic and other nuclear forces. It concludes with nuclear weapons and the future of NATO, first sketching dramatic alternatives to existing arrangements, none of them probable, then hazarding predictions of more likely futures.

This book grew out of a study group on INF held during 1980-3 at Harvard's Center for Science and International Affairs and was supplemented by participation by some of its members in the series of workshops on European security held each spring at the Aspen Institute in Berlin. Initially, our purpose was to look hard at the considerations at play in events leading to NATO's 'double decision' of December 1979.

As we talked, our purposes broadened to look beyond the December decision to the basic shape and future of the nuclear confrontation in Europe. As our work proceeded, we drew in distinguished experts from beyond Harvard — like Lawrence Freedman, Professor of War Studies at King's College, London. Our goal, one in keeping with the Center's purpose of bringing the tools of different disciplines to bear on major questions of security and arms control, was to provide a complete analysis of the nuclear confrontation in Europe — weaponry, politics and strategy, West and East. Only the reader can judge whether we have succeeded.

1 BUILDING NATO'S NUCLEAR POSTURE 1950-65

Timothy Ireland

For seasoned observers, one question ran through the debates over intermediate nuclear forces (INF) of the late 1970s and 1980s: haven't we been through this before? In fact, to a considerable degree, we have. There was a similar debate in the late 1950s and early 1960s when doubts were raised about the credibility of the American commitment to defend Western Europe. Those doubts surfaced as a result of Soviet advances in ballistic missile technology that ended the traditional invulnerability of the United States and led to European fears that the United States would not be willing to risk nuclear devastation by employing its strategic forces to defend its allies. Then, as now, concerns that the US-USSR strategic balance was approaching parity also highlighted the threat posed to Western Europe by Soviet medium- and intermediate-range nuclear systems.

The period between 1957 and 1965 also witnessed a series of American and European efforts to resolve the security dilemma presented by the changed strategic environment. Those efforts included the stationing of American Thor and Jupiter intermediate-range ballistic missiles (IRBMs) in Europe, the flexible-response doctrine, independent European nuclear efforts, General Norstad's plan for a NATO medium-range ballistic missile force, and the Multilateral Force (MLF) proposal. Moreover, consideration of these plans required the alliance to deal with a number of political and military issues not unlike the ones being debated today.

This chapter looks back at this earlier stage in NATO's evolution, analyses the issues then at hand, and assesses what lessons — if any — may apply to the current situation. The chapter is divided into five sections: a look at the Atlantic alliance before 1957; the decision to station Thors and Jupiters in Europe and the evolution of the flexible-response doctrine; independent European programmes; collective force proposals; and reflections on the implications of this history for current discussions.

NATO Before Sputnik

Most analyses see the creation of NATO in the 'cold war' being waged between the United States and the Soviet Union. However, those analyses that concentrate on the cold war and the American desire to contain Soviet communism overlook a second goal of the American commitment to Western Europe through the Atlantic alliance: the restoration of Western Europe as a centre of economic, political, and *military* power capable of standing on its own (with limited American support) against threats from the Soviet Union.

That American policies aimed at the restoration of a balance of power in Europe was apparent throughout every stage of the evolution of the American commitment: the Marshall Plan, the Vandenberg Resolution, and the North Atlantic Treaty signed on 4 April 1949. Moreover, it must be remembered that the treaty itself was only a paper pledge designed to give *political* support for European economic recovery; a pledge that was backed by the United States' strategic nuclear bombing force but that did *not* include American involvement in continental defence efforts. In fact, it was not until the first Soviet atomic bomb explosion in August 1949 ended the United States' nuclear monopoly and the Korean invasion called into question the adequacy of European defence preparations that the United States substantially strengthened its forces in Europe and committed its own troops to the alliance. Even then the assignment of American forces to NATO was justified to a reluctant Congress only on the grounds that their presence would spur the Europeans to greater defence efforts, while administration spokesmen were careful to hold out the possibility of future reductions — and perhaps withdrawal — of American troops.

However, from the outset, the Truman administration's goal of restoring Europe as a centre of economic, political, and military power faced a complicating factor in the German question. Very soon after World War II, United States officials and Europeans such as Jean Monnet realized that if Europe were to recover from the effects of the war, the material and human resources of Germany, or at least Western Germany, would have to be revitalised and integrated into a larger Western European community. Of course, such a plan, coming so soon after the end of the war, quickly awakened memories of German domination and encountered strong European opposition, particularly from France. Moreover, by virtue of France's position as an occupying power, Paris was able to block any plans that did not take French security into account.

The United States realised that it had to offer France the sense of security needed to permit the weak Fourth Republic to merge the French occupation zone with the Anglo-American Bizonia and to allow Western Germany to participate in programmes for European recovery and defence. Washington found a solution for this in the Atlantic alliance.

Although potential West German might was the essential ingredient in the Truman administration's plan to strengthen the European balance of power against the USSR — and thereby reduce the need for an extensive American commitment to the continent — the need to offer France assurances against German domination helped give the Atlantic alliance a 'depth and permanence' not otherwise envisaged. It also meant that the subsequent unity of NATO would be closely connected with the complexities of the Federal Republic's relationship with a fearful Europe on the one hand and with the United States' interest in its returning to full European status on the other.[1]

The hallmarks of the Truman administration's plans to restore Europe militarily were to be found in the creation of the European Defence Community (EDC) and the NATO Lisbon force goals of February 1952. The EDC, by providing the framework for adding 12 German divisions to Western strength, made it possible for NATO to embrace both the 'forward defence' strategy (a defence as close to the inner-German border as possible) and the Lisbon objectives calling for 96 divisions (35-40 combat ready) and 9,000 aircraft by 1954, supposedly the year of greatest peril for the West. Thus, Western deterrence strategy could be based on two elements: the 'shield' of conventional forces largely supplied by the Europeans, and the 'sword' of the United States Strategic Air Command's nuclear striking power.[2] This strategy formed the basis of Eisenhower's thinking as well, and his administration looked forward to a united Europe of over 200 million people able to stand on its own without substantial dependence on conventional American forces.[3]

Unfortunately, both the European Defence Community and the Lisbon force goals turned out to be houses of cards. The EDC had been first proposed by French Premier René Pleven in October 1950 as a means for France to accept American pressures for a West German contribution to Western defence, but it went down to bitter defeat in the French Parliament in August 1954. It was not until the following year that British Prime Minister Anthony Eden proposed a successful solution to the rearmament question: the Federal Republic would become a member of both the Western European Union (WEU) and

NATO, and a reconstituted West German army (the Bundeswehr) would be integrated directly into the alliance's command structure. However, it was not until 1958 that German troops actually began to take the field in substantial numbers.[4]

Efforts to achieve the Lisbon objectives also failed. Realisation of those force goals would have placed an unbearable strain on European economies struggling to recover from the war. Moreover, the Lisbon meeting came at a time when France was facing a bloody conflict in Indo-China and the United Kingdom was re-evaluating its defence posture by placing more emphasis on strategic air-power and nuclear weapons and by decreasing conventional forces. The French were forced to divert money and men away from European defence to the war in South-East Asia, and in November 1952, Paris informed NATO that France would be unable to meet its pledge of 15 divisions.[5]

It was within this context of uncertainty over West German rearmament, the weakness of the EDC, and the erosion of the Lisbon force goals that the budget-conscious Eisenhower administration developed its 'New Look' strategy. In addition to concerns about failure to meet the Lisbon targets, the New Look fitted in with Eisenhower's belief that a strong economy was equally as important a weapon against the Soviet Union as a powerful military. As a consequence, the Eisenhower administration set in motion a historic change: it de-emphasised increased spending on large conventional forces — which was thought to be highly inflationary — and placed increased reliance on American nuclear superiority.

Moreover, because of new advances in nuclear technology, Western deterrence strategy could continue to rely on the long-range potential of the Strategic Air Command, while tactical (or battlefield) nuclear weapons could be deployed by the West in order to make up for manpower shortfalls on the continent.[6] In addition, the United States Army — frustrated by its experience in Korea and not wishing to fight a similarly frustrating conventional battle in Europe — viewed the tactical nuclear alternative as both the best deterrent to Soviet attack and as the most effective weapon should fighting actually break out.[7]

Accordingly, small numbers of tactical nuclear artillery weapons began to appear in Europe as early as the spring of 1952 (even before the New Look) and by October 1953 a National Security Council Document (NSC 162/2) instructed the Joint Chiefs of Staff to base their plans for European defence on the use of atomic weapons (both tactical and strategic) against large-scale conventional attacks. The essentials of the New Look strategy received widespread publicity

Building NATO's Nuclear Posture, 1950-65

through Secretary Dulles's 'massive retaliation' speech of 12 January 1954, and became official NATO doctrine at the end of the December 1954 alliance ministerial meeting, a meeting which also witnessed a downward revision of the Lisbon force goals. The new strategy was fleshed out by the arrival of the huge 280-mm atomic artillery shells in 1953, followed by Honest John, Corporal, Matador, and Regulus nuclear-capable tactical missiles in 1954 and 1955.[8] Meanwhile, the United States Army adopted the 'pentomic' division concept to improve its nuclear warfighting capability.

NATO's nuclear decision — based on an American desire to 'obtain maximum deterrence at a bearable cost' — was one of the turning points in alliance relations. Once the decision had been made to base Western defence on the United States' tactical as well as strategic nuclear fire-power, American calls for the Europeans to build large armies lost much of their force. As NATO began to rely on nuclear weapons possessed by the United States (and, to a lesser extent, Britain) the balance of allied responsibility and power shifted drastically toward the Americans. Thus, while the original purpose of the American commitment to European security had been to serve as a catalyst for increased allied defence efforts, the decision to 'go nuclear' meant that the allies were likely to do less, not more.[9]

America's chief concession to the changed environment was to amend the Atomic Energy Act of 1946, the so-called MacMahon Act. Its purpose was to protect what was then a United States monopoly of nuclear weapons by preventing the dissemination of information regarding the production, capabilities, and effects of atomic weapons. But eight years later the world situation had changed. The USSR had tested both atomic and hydrogen devices and the British had exploded an atomic weapon. Moreover, in addition to increasing European doubts about the need to maintain large standing armies, the New Look strategy generated European demands for greater control over American systems based in Europe.

However, the Eisenhower administration amended the MacMahon Act only to permit the sharing of information about the location, capabilities, and effects of those systems. The information provided would not be such as to help the Europeans design, produce, or operate their own atomic arsenals. It was designed to enable European military men better to understand the effects of nuclear warfare so they might better train, equip, and deploy their conventional forces for such a conflict.[10]

Clearly, the 1954 amendment to the MacMahon Act was limited in scope and did not go very far in aiding the Europeans either to play a direct role in nuclear decision-making within the alliance or to develop their own atomic capabilities. Eisenhower was a firm believer that European defence should ultimately be a European responsibility, however, and there are indications that he and Dulles retained open minds regarding aid to European nuclear programmes. Thus, the amended MacMahon Act, limited though it was, did help secure European support for the New Look and it established a precedent for future revisions.

From Sputnik to Flexible Response

Just as the New Look was being accepted as Alliance doctrine, however, studies appeared that challenged the thesis that atomic fire-power could substitute for large armies in modern warfare. In 1954-5 two wargames — Sagebrush in Louisiana and Carte Blanche in Western Europe — included the simulated use of nuclear weapons. The casualty estimates were so high that many military men believed that *more* rather than fewer ground troops would be needed for effective defence.[11]

Moreover, when the New Look defence policies were first prepared in 1953, they were based on an assumption that America's existing retaliatory capacity would be able to deter the Soviet Union well into the future. Yet it soon seemed clear that the Russians were beginning to stockpile thermonuclear weapons and vastly improving their ballistic-missile and jet-bomber technology. This emerging balance of terror made it less likely that either of the two rivals would risk using its nuclear forces to meet a small-scale attack, thus undermining the key assumption of the New Look.[12]

These Soviet advances were partly responsible for the development of a new defence doctrine: the so-called 'New New Look'. Instead of assuming continued nuclear superiority and conventional inferiority, the New New Look aimed at maintaining *sufficient* forces on both levels. To the Eisenhower administration, once each side had the absolute capacity to devastate the other (through possession of thermonuclear weapons and invulnerable strategy delivery systems), the relative strength of the opposing forces would no longer be the key to deterrence. But, once mutual deterrence had been achieved on the strategic level, the need for an increased capacity to fight 'limited wars' would have to be met.[13]

At first glance, sufficiency on the limited-war level implied the need to increase conventional force capabilities. However, the Eisenhower administration was unwilling to accept the budgetary implications of such an increase. Indeed, on 13 July 1956, the *New York Times* printed a report that Chairman of the Joint Chiefs of Staff Admiral Arthur W. Radford actually planned to reduce American armed forces by 800,000 men over the next three years, with 450,000 coming from the army alone.[14] And, as tactical nuclear weapons became more readily available, the idea of using them to meet limited aggressions gained favour within the government. Thus, the impact of the New New Look on America's conventional strength was minimal, as tactical nuclear weapons — albeit in a somewhat different mode — continued to be viewed as substitutes for more manpower.

The New New Look's impact on the strategic level was, however, more important. Because the new doctrine was based on possession of a *secure* retaliatory capacity, it was closely linked to developments in ballistic-missile technology which could provide that security. In July 1954, Eisenhower commissioned a panel of scientific experts headed by the president of Massachusetts Institute of Technology, James R. Killian, to analyse American technological capabilities to meet existing defence problems. One of the five objectives of the Killian panel was to assess the best technological means to strengthen America's retaliatory power as a deterrent against surprise attack and insurance against defeat should deterrence fail. In meeting that objective, the Killian report of February 1955 recommended that the development of intercontinental ballistic missiles should be given highest national priority and that intermediate-range ballistic missiles should 'be developed for strategic use'.[15]

The Killian panel's inclusion of a strategic function for IRBMs stemmed from the fact that, given existing missile technology, they would become operational long before ICBMs, which were not scheduled to be in place until 1962. Given the committee's belief that the country that developed ICBMs first would enjoy an enormous strategic advantage, IRBM development was seen as necessary to counter perceived Soviet advantages in ICBM technology.[16] As a result of the Killian report each of the three services pressed ahead with their own programmes: Thor (Air Force), Jupiter (Army), and Polaris (Navy). Since the development of the land-based Thor and Jupiter was ahead of the sea-based Polaris, negotiating European deployments for the land-based systems became a necessity. These efforts were already under way on a technical level in 1956 when they received additional political impetus from the Suez crisis.

In late October and early November 1956 British, French, and Israeli forces invaded Egypt in the hope of gaining control of the Suez Canal and toppling the government of Gamal Abdel Nasser. The Eisenhower administration took the lead in condemning what appeared to be a blatant return to imperialism, and Washington exerted strong pressures to force its allies to halt their invasion. The resulting crisis shook the alliance to the core as the British and, more pointedly, the French questioned the reliability of American support for allies acting in defence of their perceived vital interests. In the atomic age these concerns were even more real as London and Paris felt particularly vulnerable to the nuclear threats made by Soviet leader Nikita Krushchev when the Suez crisis was at its peak. However, while both Britain and France found cause to question the dependability of the United States, and while both drew as a lesson the need to develop and maintain national nuclear forces, each pursued a different path to that end: the British in co-operation with the United States; the French, ultimately, alone.[17]

The December 1956 North Atlantic Council meeting, coming on the heels of the Radford Plan, the New New Look, and the Suez crisis produced European calls for more extensive sharing of short-range nuclear systems on the part of the United States. These European calls were, in large part, motivated by a desire to reduce their conventional armies but, in the wake of the Suez crisis, also reflected growing doubts about the credibility of the American commitment to defend its allies. The weapons-sharing proposal was initiated by the British, who received support from the Germans, Dutch, and Turks. The French went even further, demanding that the atomic warheads themselves come under national and not exclusive United States control.[18] Because of Eisenhower's long-standing view that European defence should be primarily a European responsibility, his administration was generally receptive to European calls for nuclear sharing and supported liberalising the restrictive provisions of the MacMahon Act. The administration made its initial attempt following the Suez crisis of 1956.

But the members of Congress' Joint Committee on Atomic Energy (JCAE) had learned a lesson from the crisis that was quite different from the one learned in London and Paris: the French and, to a lesser degree, the British were unreliable allies who might take even more dangerous risks if they possessed their own atomic weapons. The JCAE promised intense opposition if Eisenhower and Dulles went very far in sharing missiles and warheads with the Europeans (as some American military men were prepared to do), and the 'dual-key' formula constituted the compromise worked out between the administration and the Committee.[19]

Under the dual-key system the European allies would purchase nuclear capable systems from the United States and station them with their own forces. However, the United States would retain physical custody over the nuclear warheads for the missiles. Thus, during April 1957 the Eisenhower administration announced that some short-range ballistic missiles, medium-range cruise missiles, and air-defence missiles would be made available to the Europeans under the dual-key formula.[20]

In requesting formal amendments to the 1954 Act, the administration wanted authorisation to provide the European allies with information about weapons design, nuclear propulsion for ships, and fuels for propulsion reactors. Administration witnesses presented arguments to the JCAE emphasising the political importance of restoring European confidence in the alliance by providing them with the most effective means to defend themselves. These witnesses also argued that co-operative information sharing would reduce the incentive for the Europeans to undertake costly independent programmes involving considerable duplication of effort.[21]

However, the JCAE remained opposed to substantial liberalisation of the MacMahon Act, and the 1958 amendments were highly limited in scope. Only Britain, because of its substantial progress in the development of atomic weapons, was given sophisticated information about weapons design. The other allies received only enough information to allow them to fit American-supplied nuclear warheads on their own delivery vehicles (purchased, of course, from the United States) and fire them should the need arise.[22]

More importantly, the spring of 1957 also witnessed an Anglo-American agreement on IRBM basing. At a Bermuda meeting in March President Eisenhower and Prime Minister Harold Macmillan (who had replaced Anthony Eden after the Suez debacle) agreed to deploy Air Force Thor missiles in the United Kingdom under a 'dual-key' arrangement; this arrangement both deepened Anglo-American co-operation and helped Macmillan counter domestic criticism that Britain could be drawn into a war against its will.

The Suez crisis had been a scarring experience for the British, largely because it demonstrated their inability to take independent action without American support. Therefore, one of the major themes of post-Suez British foreign policy was to reaffirm and strengthen the 'special relationship' with the United States. Moreover, the Bermuda agreements came at a time when British Minister of Defence Duncan Sandys was preparing the 1957 Defence White Paper, a document that placed increased reliance on a British nuclear deterrent. Clearly, information provided to British scientists through an amended MacMahon Act would aid the military and political justifications of such a policy. Moreover, the Eisenhower administration was just as eager as the British government to mend relations and was very conscious of the need to find European bases for its 1,500-mile-range IRBMs. Thus the Bermuda agreement provided an important vehicle for attaining both British and American political and military goals.[23]

The March arrangements were, however, not formalised and many of the details were put off to subsequent meetings between lower-level officials. This lack of urgency implies that the political considerations outweighed the military. Indeed, it was not until the launch of Sputnik in October of 1957 that the IRBM-basing decision gained much momentum.

In August 1957, the USSR tested its first ICBM and in October came the Russian orbiting of the Sputnik space satellite. These launchings appeared to confirm fears of a Soviet lead in ballistic-missile technology, of an increased vulnerability of the United States to an atomic attack, and further undermined sinking allied confidence in the credibility of the American nuclear guarantee. In addition, the USSR was beginning to deploy its own IRBMs (SS-4s and SS-5s) in the western reaches of the Soviet Union, a move that contributed to further allied uneasiness about their security.[24]

Both Suez and Sputnik added new urgency to a number of American programmes designed to bring the United States into the missile age and restore confidence in NATO. In November 1957, the United States announced that it would seek IRBM-base rights at the December meeting of the North Atlantic Council which, because of the implications of Sputnik, would be held at heads-of-government level in Paris.[25]

The motivations behind the decision to seek the basing rights were varied. The first reason was strategic. Once stationed in Europe, the intermediate-range Thors and Jupiters would be the American answer to Soviet-intercontinental ballistic missiles until America's own ICBMs and nuclear missile submarines could be deployed in the early 1960s.[26]

Moreover, because of their relationship to the US-USSR strategic balance, the Thors and Jupiters acquired an enormous political significance for the alliance. Proponents of the decision argued that European-based IRBMs would demonstrate the strength of America's commitment to European security. They maintained that as long as the Thors and Jupiters were so clearly related to the strategic balance, a Soviet attack on American IRBMs in Europe would also directly threaten American survival and trigger a massive American response.[27]

Another justification for the IRBM basing decision was the effect the Thors and Jupiters would have on the theatre balance in Europe. In this sense, the NATO Commander, General Norstad, viewed the missiles as a visible counter to the growing number of Soviet medium-range systems targeted against Western Europe. But in Norstad's eyes deployment of the Thors and Jupiters was only the first step in a more ambitious plan to make NATO itself the world's 'fourth nuclear power'. This plan will be discussed in more detail later, but it is important to note here that Norstad believed that the Soviet medium-range system posed a direct threat to European security and that he favoured both the IRBM-bases decision and a land based medium-range ballistic missile (MRBM) force for NATO as means to counter that threat.[28]

Given the fact that the Thors and Jupiters were supposed to help the alliance deal with a variety of military and political problems, the European reaction was very disappointing to the United States. The initial announcement that the United States was going to seek basing rights for the missile produced such a negative response from the continent that Dulles was forced to give prior reassurance to the allies that the US would not use the Paris meeting to force the IRBMs on any country. At the Paris meeting itself the final communiqué reported only that the alliance had agreed to the *principle* of European bases for the American missiles. Turkey was the only continental country quickly to accept the American offer, while further deployments had to await an assessment by SHAPE of the *military* requirements for the intermediate-range systems. The sceptical allies were reassured by the fact that such a study would undoubtedly include a survey of the *political* problems facing the European countries as they responded to the IRBM proposal.[29]

There were a number of European objections to accepting the Thors and Jupiters, virtually all of them presaging concerns expressed in the 1970s and 1980s. In the first place, basing the IRBMs on their territory would naturally earn the host countries the displeasure of the USSR. Indeed, Moscow launched a full-scale diplomatic offensive against the US missiles for Europe.

The Russian campaign began even before the 1957 NATO ministerial meeting and lasted until 1959. This campaign was unprecedented in intensity and scope and was aimed at dividing Western European governments, recalling old intra-European animosities, and driving a wedge between America and Europe. European neutralist and pacifist leaders were courted by Moscow in an effort to raise domestic opposition to the missiles; French fears of Germany and of Anglo-American dominance of the alliance were exploited; the Russians cautioned West Germany that accepting American missiles would have dire consequences for the cherished goal of reunification; Britain and Italy were warned that the United States might use their homelands to launch unprovoked attacks against other countries; Greece was threatened with potential economic sanctions; and the United States was constantly reminded of its responsibility for maintaining international peace and the dangers inherent in a diffusion of control over nuclear weapons.[30]

Other Soviet threats against the Europeans were more direct, and also prefigured tactics to be used two decades later. If war should break out, Moscow declared, those countries that accepted the American missiles would surely be targets for Russian nuclear weapons while those which rejected the IRBMs would be spared. The Soviets also advanced plans for 'nuclear-free zones' in the Balkans and Mediterranean in order to prevent Turkey, Greece, and Italy from accepting the Thors and Jupiters. These proposals were backed up by threats to deploy Russian missiles in Albania and the Warsaw Pact countries if the West rejected the nuclear-free zone idea.

Although precise assessments of the effect of the Soviet campaign are by nature impossible, it is safe to say that the Russian propaganda did add to the European public's sense of apprehension regarding bases for the Thors and Jupiters. The Soviet threat may have influenced Greece, Iceland, and the Netherlands not to accept the systems, but it certainly had little concrete effect elsewhere.[31] However, in addition to Soviet opposition, there were rising concerns in Europe and the United States that the characteristics of the missiles prevented them from fulfilling their basic mission of deterrence.[32]

Both the Thor and Jupiter were liquid-fuelled and based above ground in fixed positions. Given the lack of any protection, plus the necessity of long fuelling times, both missiles were regarded as highly vulnerable to Soviet pre-emptive attack. Moreover, since they would be based so close to the USSR, it was argued that the Soviets might view them as offensive rather than defensive systems and be tempted to launch a pre-emptive strike on them in times of crises. Thus, it was no surprise that many Europeans questioned the wisdom of placing the missiles on their territories.[33]

Finally, the Thor-Jupiter proposal raised fears that the United States was drawing a distinction between its own security and that of its NATO allies. Because the missiles were directly related to the overall US-Soviet strategic balance, yet were to be stationed in Europe, critics of the IRBM deployment argued that the United States was hoping to confine any potential nuclear conflict with the Soviet Union to European soil. This 'decoupling' argument reawakened fears of traditional American isolationism and increased European apprehension over the possibility of a nuclear war limited to Europe — fears found later in the debate over the Pershing II and ground-launched cruise missiles (GLCM).[34]

The general European reaction to the Thors and Jupiters was actually so negative that, in addition to Britain, only Turkey and Italy finally agreed to station the missiles on their territory. On the continent, Greece, Belgium, and Holland expressed interest, but domestic political pressures prevented positive action. Norway and Denmark had already articulated policies prohibiting the basing of nuclear weapons on their soil in peacetime, and Portugal was too distant from the Warsaw Pact to justify IRBM bases. The special cases of France and West Germany will be discussed later.[35]

Turkey was the country most eager to receive the American system, almost immediately agreeing to accept two squadrons totalling 30 Jupiters. The IRBM bases were especially important to the Turks because they helped bolster Turkey's status within NATO and helped strengthen bilateral relations with the United States. In Italy, negotiations dragged on until March 1959, when the Italians finally agreed to accept one squadron of 15 Jupiters. Here again, the positive decision was motivated by a desire to strengthen both Italy's standing within the alliance and bilateral relations with the United States.[36] The Jupiters in Turkey and Italy remained under American control.

Despite all the time, effort, and debate involved in the Thor-Jupiter decision, their stay in Europe was brief. By the time they were all deployed, their vulnerability and impending obsolescence were apparent. Moreover, as the new Kennedy administration challenged Eisenhower's defence policies and began to formulate its own strategic doctrine, the logic behind maintaining the IRBM force evaporated, and in the spring of 1962, it was decided to remove the Thors and Jupiters from Europe.

However, given the political significance of the Thors and Jupiters to the Turkish and Italian governments, American efforts to have the missile bases dismantled were interpreted as weakening the relationship between the United States and the host countries. Indeed, Turkish reluctance in regard to closing down their Jupiter bases may have placed the United States in a vulnerable position during the October 1962 missiles crisis.[37] At that time Krushchev pointed to the missiles in Turkey as an example of the type of American nuclear encirclement that justified similar Russian deployments in Cuba. Even after the missile crisis had ended, American efforts to have the IRBMs removed continued to encounter resistance in both Ankara and Rome.[38]

In retrospect, it is important to view the decision to dismantle the Thors and Jupiters in the context of the 'flexible-response' doctrine formulated by the Kennedy administration. Throughout the late 1950s, the wisdom of Eisenhower's defence policy — which relied so heavily on nuclear battlefield and INF weapons— was seriously questioned by many academics and professional military officers. Critics of the administration argued that Soviet possession of thermonuclear weapons and advanced delivery systems (long-range bombers and ICBMs) had erased the traditional invulnerability of the United States, creating a situation of nuclear parity, a condition that would deter the use of nuclear weapons except against the gravest threats to national security.[39]

The deployment of IRBMs in Europe as well as the Polaris programme helped the Army and Navy challenge the dominant position of the Strategic Air Command in formulating nuclear policy. Throughout the late 1950s SAC continued to increase the delivery capacity of its bomber force. According to David Alan Rosenberg, by 1959 'SAC had nearly 500 B-52s, more than 2,500 B-47s, and over 1,000 propeller and jet-driven tanker aircraft. Moreover, SAC's target list expanded from 2,997 in 1956 to 3,261 in early 1957'. According to Rosenberg SAC had developed and assigned priorities to over 20,000 targets by the end of the decade. However, because Navy leaders realised that the sea-based Polaris would be the most invulnerable delivery system in the American arsenal, they began to present their missile as a deterrent weapon and as an alternative to land-based bombers. Moreover, aided by Army planners who favoured improved limited-war capabilities, the Navy began pressing for modifications of US defence strategy so heavily reliant on strategic nuclear bombers.[40]

Those who challenged existing doctrine argued that in these new circumstances, it was unlikely that Washington would risk the destruction of American cities by responding with atomic weapons to all but the most direct threats to American vital interests. The problems created for United States policy-makers by parity were brought into sharper focus by communist pressures against exposed Western bastions such as Berlin and Taiwan and by Moscow's support for limited or unconventional wars of 'national liberation' in areas emerging from a history of European colonial rule. In order to prevent the United States from being paralysed by a 'suicide or surrender' dilemma, the Eisenhower administration's critics advocated a reversal of the New Look doctrine — that is, less reliance on atomic weapons, coupled with renewed effort to increase America's foreign policy options through both building up conventional forces and modernising American strategic systems. These analysts were opposed to the idea of matching Soviet ballistic missile capabilities on a system-to-system basis, and they argued that countering Russian missiles with American missiles based in Europe was unnecessary. Rather, the best guarantee of deterrence was the development of a secure retaliatory capacity: a strategic force that would include United States-based long-range bombers and ICBMs in hardened silos as well as ballistic-missile-launching nuclear submarines patrolling the seas.[41]

These views received a sympathetic hearing from Senator John F. Kennedy who, shortly after his inauguration as President in 1961, appointed a high-level committee under Acheson to study Atlantic alliance defence policy.[42] The Acheson committee's report drew on the expertise of a number of defence analysts and was submitted to Kennedy in March 1961. The report was quickly accepted by Kennedy, and its recommendation became official American doctrine in April 1961.

But the full detail of the administration's defence thinking was not presented to the alliance until the spring of 1962. At that time, Secretary of Defence Robert McNamara outlined the flexible-response doctrine in two speeches: the first was a classified briefing at the Athens meeting of the NATO Council in May; the second was a 'sanitised' version of the Athens talk delivered at the University of Michigan commencement in June.

As presented by McNamara, one of the first assumptions challenged by the Kennedy administration was the belief that deterrence derived from the mere possession of nuclear weapons. War, even atomic war, remained possible and, although the United States should make every effort to avoid conflict, she needed to be prepared should it occur. In McNamara's eyes, both the most effective deterrent and the best preparation for potential conflict was the development of a secure second-strike capability. That is, American strategic nuclear forces would be configured so as to enable them to absorb a Soviet first strike yet retain the ability to retaliate massively against the USSR. According to McNamara this capability was being achieved through deployment of

Polaris missile-launching submarines and Minuteman ICBMs in hardened silos, thus offering the Russians every incentive not to strike Western cities.[43]

However, even possession of a secure second-strike retaliatory capacity would not serve as an absolute guarantee against war. New advances in weapons technology meant that if war did break out, casualty and damage figures would vary greatly depending on how the opposing forces were used. Therefore, McNamara favoured a nuclear strategy that would more closely resemble a conventional war plan: American targets would be Soviet offensive forces not cities. Implicit in this policy was the assumption that deterrence could continue even after the first atomic exchange, and McNamara's aim was both to limit the scope of potential nuclear conflict and to retain post-attack bargaining flexibility. In order to be successful, McNamara argued that the new strategy required an 'indivisible' targeting system for the alliance and and 'unity of planning, concentration of executive authority, and central direction'.[44]

Because of the need to obtain such centralised control, McNamara came out strongly against small European national nuclear forces. These forces, he argued, would be highly vulnerable to Soviet pre-emption, would promote dangerous proliferation, and, if used independently of US strategic forces, would lead to national suicide. In order to reassure the Europeans of the American commitment and to encourage them not to pursue independent nuclear policies, McNamara told the allies that the United States was as much concerned about Soviet missiles aimed at Western Europe as it was with those targeted against America and that the new strategy simply meant that the United States had undertaken the nuclear defence of NATO on a global basis.[45]

Finally, McNamara addressed the question of conventional strength. While acknowledging Soviet superiority in non-nuclear arms, the Defense Secretary maintained that this superiority was not overwhelming and that the West had the collective strength to defend Europe against most conventional attacks. Moreover, McNamara pledged the Kennedy administration to call up 158,000 reserves as positive indication of America's commitment to the new strategy. The reserve call-up was also to serve as an incentive to the Europeans — especially the French and Germans — to increase their conventional forces so that the alliance could maintain the 30 combat-ready divisions believed necessary to offer effective resistance and give NATO military men more flexibility in dealing with potential threats from the Warsaw Pact.[46]

The impact of the flexible-response doctrine on US defence policy for Europe quickly became apparent. Under the Reorganisation Objective Army Division concept (ROAD), American forces in Europe abandoned the 'pentomic' battle group plan and returned to the 'triangular' division configuration that had been an integral part of the Army's organisation structure in World War II and Korea. This shift, coupled with the proposed increases in Army manpower, was a clear indication of the new doctrine's aim to conduct the initial defence of Europe on a conventional basis.[47]

The Kennedy Administration also moved to tighten controls over the tactical nuclear weapons based in Europe. These efforts included the installation of electronic 'permissive action links' (PAL) on dual-key tactical systems and reviews of the Eisenhower administration's plans to sell nuclear-capable tactical weapons to the Europeans.[48]

Nevertheless, the first years of the Kennedy administration did witness the deployment of a new generation of nuclear-capable tactical missiles in Europe. The 70-200-mile Sergeant replaced the Corporal; the 400-mile-range Pershing ballistic missile was an outgrowth of the obsolete and never deployed Redstone; Nike-Hercules replaced Nike-Ajax; and the Mace cruise missile, eventually capable of a range up to 1,350 miles, was a replacement for the Matador.[49]

Because of its long range, deployment of the Mace cruise missile presents an interesting parallel to the cruise-missile deployments in the mid-1980s. Ninety Mace As (650-mile range) began to appear in Europe during 1960 and were phased out in 1966. The longer-range Mace Bs were based in hardened shelters during 1963-4, and remained in Europe until 1969. Despite their long range, the missiles' deployment in Germany attracted little attention and did not provoke anything like the debate that accompanied the Thor-Jupiter decision. However, West German desires actually to possess Mace did provoke a small crisis in German-American relations.[50]

The major goals of both the IRBM-basing decision and the flexible response doctrine were to adjust NATO nuclear policy to a changed strategic environment and increase the credibility of the American commitment to Western Europe. However, it seemed to many Europeans that the United States was actually making a distinction between American and allied security, and the United States strategic nuclear forces were being decoupled from the rest of NATO's defence apparatus. Moreover, the flexible-response doctrine suggested that NATO was being compartmentalised: the United States taking responsibility for global security and nuclear strategy and the Europeans being relegated to the less glamorous regional tasks of maintaining conventional forces for continental defence.

Therefore, instead of seeing the allies fall into line with American strategic thinking, the American proposals of the late 1950s and early 1960s witnessed a growing split between the United States and Europe. One of the clearest manifestations of this split was the fact that both Britain and France challenged American thinking by steadfastly pursuing independent nuclear programmes, while the West Germans showed a desire to follow suit.[51]

Independent European Programmes

Of course, the development of European national nuclear forces was influenced by factors other than those related to the Soviet-American nuclear balance. Among the most important were prestige and alliance politics. Indeed, many Europeans saw possession of nuclear weapons as a military symbol of their restored economic vitality. Moreover, there were additional, purely national, reasons why each of the major allied powers wished to control atomic weapons.

For the British, a key element in their nuclear weapons programme involved their 'special' relationship with the United States. The history of Anglo-American co-operation in the nuclear field extended back to World War II when the British and Canadians participated in the Manhattan Project. Unfortunately for the British, many American officials viewed them as junior partners in the nuclear weapons programme, and after the war the Atomic Energy Act of 1946 ended the close wartime collaboration between the two allies. Nevertheless, the British proceeded alone and exploded their first atomic bomb during the summer of 1952. In 1954 the United Kingdom exploded its first hydrogen device and, after the Suez crisis of 1956, when both sides were anxious to mend fences, extensive US-UK nuclear collaboration resumed.

The breakthrough occurred at the March 1957 meeting between Eisenhower and Macmillan when the British agreed to accept 60 Thor IRBMs and the Americans promised to seek amendments to the MacMahon Act permitting information sharing with the United Kingdom. Thus, during the extensive debates in Britain over IRBM deployment Macmillan defended his position by arguing that the Thor deployment would only be temporary and that it would be replaced with a new generation of British systems developed with the help of American technology. In fact, the MacMahon Act Amendment of 1958 did lift restrictions on the British, and the close collaboration between London and Washington was confirmed in March of 1960 when the Eisenhower administration agreed to sell the British the Skybolt air-to-ground missile. This decision followed London's cancellation of their own Blue Streak silo-launched ballistic missile and was intended to extend the life of Britain's aging force of 'V' bombers. For its part, in a technically separate agreement, the Macmillan government agreed to open its Holy Loch naval base in Scotland to US Polaris submarines.[52]

While those agreements did offer continuing evidence of the special relationship, they also exposed British dependence on the United States and aroused the animosity of other European powers, especially France. Thus, when the Kennedy administration abruptly cancelled the Skybolt project in November of 1962, the very existence of an independent British deterrent was threatened. At the Nassau meeting the following month, it took a direct and eloquent appeal from Macmillan to move Kennedy to offer the Polaris missile as a substitute. And even then, there was a price: in line with the administration's opposition to national nuclear forces, the British submarines carrying the missiles had to be integrated directly into the NATO command, to be withdrawn only in case of extreme national emergency. Moreover, the spectacle of continued Anglo-American collaboration provoked a crisis with France.[53]

For the French, possession of nuclear weapons was symbolic of their return to the ranks of the great powers and equality with the Anglo-Saxons in NATO. These motives existed for much of the history of post-war France and were important reasons why the Fourth Republic made a secret commitment to embark on a nuclear weapons programme in early 1956.

Of course, the Suez crisis was the turning point for Paris. Humiliated politically, and angered by the appearance of the Anglo-American special relationship working against the interests of France, the French began to place more emphasis on an independent nuclear force. At the December 1956 NATO meeting, French leaders made public their decision to pursue a national nuclear policy, and in 1957 France led the effort to approve American IRBM deployments in principle only.[54]

When the time came for France to consider IRBM deployment, their demands were extreme. Not only would the weapons have to be stationed in France under the dual-key arrangement, but the French wanted both technical and financial support for their own atomic weapons programme. These conditions were expanded when, in June 1958, the Fourth Republic's inability to deal with the Algerian Crisis brought Charles de Gaulle to power as President of the Fifth Republic.

De Gaulle placed great importance on France's being the fourth country to join the select group of nuclear powers. Not only would possession of nuclear weapons add weight to the French voice in global politics, it would clearly strengthen France's leadership role on the continent, especially relative to West Germany. Therefore, after de Gaulle assumed office, he terminated France's participation in a joint French-Italian-German programme to develop 'modern weapons', and continued French requests for American technical assistance in atomic-warhead and delivery-vehicle design. Moreover, he refused to allow American IRBMs on French territory unless they came under the exclusive control of French officers, and he called for a French-American-British directorate of NATO.[55]

France, however, never enjoyed the same American trust and confidence as did the British, and the Eisenhower administration rejected both de Gaulle's terms for IRBM basing and his calls for a NATO directorate. This is not to say that there was no high-level American military and political support for the French force during both the Eisenhower and Kennedy years; it was simply outweighed by a distrust of French security procedures and a growing desire to prevent nuclear proliferation.

The final blow was Nassau. And, despite the fact that the Kennedy Administration quickly reversed its opposition to national nuclear forces and repeated the British offer to Paris, de Gaulle remained resentful of the Anglo-American special relationship, and he renewed his commitment to a purely national French force. Moreover, the following January he struck out at the special relationship by vetoing British membership of the EEC, and in 1963 moved toward his vision of a French-led continental bloc of European states through the Franco-German Treaty of Friendship and Co-operation.[56]

In the case of West Germany, the Federal Republic in 1954-5 had renounced the right to produce heavy armaments or atomic, bacteriological and chemical weapons. These promises were made by the FRG's first chancellor, Konrad Adenauer, and were designed to secure the integration of West Germany into both the European and Atlantic communities.[57]

However, the German renunciation of nuclear weapons was viewed as a natural consequence of the Federal Republic's need to earn the trust of its neighbours. There is speculation that Adenauer's pledge was a conditional one, subject to revision should international conditions change. Moreover, since one of the Chancellor's principal goals was to ensure that the Federal Republic be accepted on the basis of equality, his renunciation of nuclear-weapons production was viewed by some as relegating the FRG to second-class status within the alliance.[58]

Nevertheless, by 1957 Bonn had accommodated itself to the new strategy and pressed for German access to nuclear-capable tactical systems. While the Eisenhower administration was willing to sell such weapons to the Federal Republic, the Kennedy Administration's emphasis on centralised authority over nuclear weapons led to a series of misunderstandings between Bonn and Washington as the Germans chafed under the dual-key system. Although the West German government continuously denied that it would embark on an independent programme, that threat was always just beneath the surface. Moreover, given the British and French examples, there was cause for considerable concern in Washington.[59]

In addition to prestige, another factor leading to independent European nuclear weapons programmes was their relationship to conventional forces. Allied leaders were quick to recognise the potential for substituting nuclear fire-power for costly conventional forces. Indeed, it was the British (in the person of Air Marshall Sir John Slessor) who first brought the idea to the Americans in 1952.[60] The French, because of their troubles in Indo-China and later Algeria, were quick to follow suit. Eventually, so did the Germans. In fact, Adenauer's initial request that the Bundeswehr be equipped with nuclear-capable tactical systems came in September 1956, just after it became apparent that West Germany would not be able to meet its 500,000-man obligation to NATO by 1958.[61]

In addition to matters of prestige and economics, there were inescapable strategic reasons why the major European powers developed independent deterrent forces or, in the German case, sought increased control over American nuclear-capable systems in Europe. These strategic motivations included the emergence of a situation of mutual deterrence between the United States and the USSR and growing European concerns about Soviet intermediate-range systems targeted against their major cities. Actually, allied worries about the American willingness to engage in nuclear war to defend Europe surfaced even before the Soviet Union exploded its first atomic bomb, but it was not until about 1960 — when the United States itself was under the direct threat of Soviet long-range bombers and ICBMs — that these concerns moved to the forefront of alliance politics.

In Britain, the strategic rationale for maintaining an independent force first received considerable attention in the 1955 parliamentary debates over the Conservative government's desire to produce thermonuclear weapons. The government argued that not only would possession of thermonuclear weapons place the UK on an equal footing with the superpowers, but they would also be a powerful deterrent to Soviet aggression. Although the Conservatives proclaimed great faith in the reliability of American strategic forces, their arguments in favour of an independent deterrent contained growing doubts about the credibility of American guarantees in the unforeseeable future. In fact, as early as 1955, Winston Churchill suggested that the United States and United Kingdom might have different targeting priorities should war actually break out.[62]

Churchill's 1955 statement notwithstanding, British nuclear forces remained closely integrated with the United States Strategic Air Command, and British defence strategy actually mirrored that of the United States. Therefore, both the doctrines of massive retaliation and flexible response won quick acceptance in Britain, and because of the American willingness to support the British nuclear effort, no direct challenge to America's alliance strategy emerged from London. France, however, was another story.

Throughout the mid-1950s and early 1960s French military officers, led by Generals Gallois, Stehlin, Beaufre and Ailleret presented a series of critiques of NATO defence policy that led them to justify an independent French deterrent force. In analyses that sound very similar to those presented by advocates of INF modernisation today, French strategists argued that Russian advances in missile technology since 1958 had placed the United States and the USSR on an equal strategic footing and had created a situation of bilateral or mutual deterrence between the two superpowers. In those circumstances, the French wondered, what was the likelihood of the United States' acting to defend Europe against a Soviet attack when the result would be the destruction of the American homeland? Moreover, the French maintained that mutual deterrence on the strategic level neutralised the credibility of the American commitment to employ its strategic systems to defend Europe, and highlighted Soviet advantages both on the conventional level and in 'intermediate range strategic forces — aircraft and missiles — directly threatening Europe ...'.[63]

The French argued that neither reliance on tactical nuclear weapons nor an increase in conventional forces would provide an adequate deterrent to the USSR: short-range tactical weapons would only serve to confine wartime destruction to Europe while limiting damage to the

United States and the Soviet Union, and more conventional forces would present easy targets to Russian nuclear weapons.[64]

Instead, French Air Force officers maintained that only the threat of a strategic nuclear strike from Europe against the Russian homeland could serve as an adequate deterrent to Soviet aggression. While acknowledging that the Thors and Jupiters stationed in Europe were, at least in part, supposed to provide such a threat, French strategists challenged their credibility on the grounds of their vulnerability, and the fact that their launching depended on an American President located 3,000 miles away from the European continent.[65]

In justifying their own nuclear programme, French strategists embraced the idea of proportional deterrence, or sufficiency.[66] Instead of matching or even approaching the nuclear capabilities of the superpower, France's capacity to deter the USSR would rest on French ability to inflict a level of damage disproportionate to the gains the Soviets could secure by attacking France. The French forces would achieve deterrence through an explicit city-targeting strategy. Of course, such a policy was in direct contrast to the counter-force strategy inherent in the Kennedy administration's flexible-response doctrine.

The French were not, however, discounting Europe's continued reliance on American strategic nuclear forces. Even de Gaulle stressed this point in public addresses. Rather, the French perceived their own nuclear forces as coupling the American strategic arsenal to the defence of Europe. In this context, once France employed its nuclear weapons against important Russian urban and industrial targets, the strategic balance between the superpowers might very well shift and the United States would necessarily become involved. As General Stehlin wrote:

> I am convinced that the Soviets would be more cautious when faced with two allied but independent centers of decision, one of which would evaluate any offense on the basis of geographic, economic and above all, human considerations applying in the very area where such offenses are likely to be committed.[67]

None the less, the basic assumption behind France's desire to maintain an independent deterrent was that responsibility for French defence rested in Paris and not Washington. Moreover, as the British deterrent force stimulated the French national programme, many feared that the *force de frappe* would serve as a catalyst for similar German aspirations.

West Germany's 'Nuclear Weapons'

The Federal Republic's relationship to nuclear weapons was, of course, a complicated one. Because of West Germany's renunciation of nuclear-weapons production, NATO's nuclear decision put Konrad Adenauer and his ruling Christian Democratic Union (CDU) in a difficult political position. The alliance's acceptance of the New Look policy came in the midst of West Germany's rearmament debate and provided the opposition Social Democratic Party (SPD) (which opposed rearmament on the grounds that it jeopardised reunification with East Germany) with a powerful debating weapon. Adenauer based his rearmament arguments on two points: the creation of a West German army would be the final step toward full sovereignty for the FRG, and the integration of that army into NATO's forward defence strategy would be the best guarantee that West Germany would not become an atomic battleground. However, after 1954 the SPD maintained that because of its non-nuclear pledge, the federal Republic would be relegated to a second-class status within the alliance. Moreover, the results of Sagebrush and Carte Blanche indicated that it would be impossible to keep a war in Europe limited, and West German troops in NATO would actually be collaborating in a strategy that, if implemented, could only lead to the devastation of the Federal Republic.[68]

Adenauer's problems increased during the summer of 1956 when reports of the Radford Plan – which indicated possible American troop reductions in Europe and even more reliance on tactical nuclear weapons – received wide circulation. Because the 'Radford crisis' occurred at a crucial point in the West German debate on conscription, the Chancellor took the drastic step of labelling NATO's shift to atomic weapons a 'mistake' and urging continued reliance on conventional weapons.[69]

However, Adenauer's defence of conventional forces did not last long. Following much public criticism of his policies – much of it coming from the CDU's coalition partner, the Bavarian Christian Social Union (CSU) – the Chancellor announced that West Germany would not be able to meet its 500,000-man obligation by 1958, and that its 18-month conscription period would be shortened to 12 months. Moreover, by October 1956, Adenauer had reversed his position on nuclear weapons and had joined his aggressive young CSU Defence Minister, Franz Josef Strauss, in urging that the Federal Republic's forces be equipped with a tactical nuclear system (the warheads remaining in American hands) in order to make up for its manpower shortages.[70]

Bonn's subsequent drive to acquire the most modern nuclear-capable tactical systems took place at the same time as Soviet advances in ballistic-missile technology raised questions about the credibility of the US commitment and caused the Atlantic alliance to consider deploying US IRBMs in Europe. The Adenauer government supported stationing the Thors and Jupiters in Europe both in order to ease the 'missile gap' between the United States and USSR and as a counter to Soviet IRBM deployment aimed at Western Europe. However, there was never any sustained consideration given to basing the IRBMs in the Federal Republic. West German objections to the Thors and Jupiters were the same as those throughout Western Europe, but also included the fear that if the FRG took those missiles, reunification would become impossible. As a result of those considerations and Adenauer's sensitivity to them, the West Germans were not even asked to participate in deployment of the IRBMs.[71]

Nevertheless, despite the fact that no consideration was given to accepting the American IRBMs, both Strauss and Adenauer were very concerned about the European balance of nuclear forces and were most anxious to obtain tactical nuclear weapons under dual-key arrangements with the United States. In March 1958, Strauss returned from the United States and announced that he intended to equip the Bundeswehr with nuclear-capable Matador C cruise missiles and Nike-Ajax air defence systems. The Strauss announcement touched off one of the most bitter and vitriolic debates in German parliamentary history.

The government argued that acquisition of tactical systems was necessary to demonstrate West Germany's support for NATO's strategy and to maintain equality within the alliance. In addition to pacifist and general anti-nuclear arguments, the SPD (including the later Chancellor, Helmut Schmidt) countered that a nuclear armed West Germany would end all hopes for East-West disarmament and disengagement in Europe and would turn the FRG into a nuclear battleground. In the end, the government's position held, and during the remainder of the Eisenhower years the West Germans continued to receive short-range tactical systems with the United States retaining control over the warheads.[72]

Moreover, despite their refusal to accept the Thors and Jupiters, West German concerns about SS-4 and SS-5 deployments also led to a German willingness to have long-range systems stationed on the Federal Republic's territory. These systems included the Mace B cruise missile deployed by the US Air Force and support for General Norstad's proposal for a mobile medium-range ballistic missile force for NATO.

Therefore, due to its exposed position and because of the Federal Republic's difficult conversion to NATO's nuclear strategy in the late 1950s, the Kennedy administration's flexible-response strategy was a hard pill for Bonn to swallow. The emphasis on conventional forces and 'controlled escalation' suggested to many German officials that the United States envisaged the possibility of a large-scale conventional conflict fought on the Federal Republic's territory. Even more threatening was the fear that Washington might actually accept the loss of some West German territory rather than engage in a nuclear exchange with the Soviet Union. These fears were especially pronounced during the Berlin crises between 1958 and 1962. Finally, West German defence officials viewed the American desire to centralise control over nuclear weapons (both tactical and strategic) as threatening the Federal Republic's sovereign right to defend itself.[73]

In April 1961, shortly after Kennedy outlined flexible response to the North Atlantic Council, Adenauer journeyed to Washington to express German concerns and seek clarification of American strategic thinking. While in Washington, the Chancellor was assured by Kennedy that the United States remained prepared to use all methods necessary, including atomic weapons, to ensure the security of Western Europe. In fact, Kennedy pointed out that, far from being a departure from previous policy, the desire to increase conventional strength was merely a reiteration of the 30-division goal stipulated by MC-70 in 1957. Kennedy's assurances to Adenauer about the wisdom of the new doctrine launched the American 'education programme' that characterised transatlantic (and especially German-American) relations during 1961-2.[74]

The Kennedy administration's education campaign was largely successful in impressing the Germans with the strength of American deterrent forces and the continuing American commitment to Western European security. However, the questions raised in German minds by flexible response could not be resolved by assurances of the strength and credibility of American strategic forces. In Bonn's eyes, deterrence remained the key to its security, and deterrence could only be achieved by keeping the Soviets in perpetual doubt regarding NATO's willingness to use nuclear weapons to meet even limited acts of agression. Maintaining that doubt required removing Washington's veto over the use of nuclear weapons.[75]

It was not so much that the West Germans doubted the sincerity of American efforts and intentions. No matter how strong or secure American's strategic retaliatory forces, pressures on the American President not to use them would be great. Moreover, those pressures were likely to increase as Soviet nuclear capabilities improved. Therefore, the Adenauer government argued for continued delivery of nuclear capable tactical systems to the Bundeswehr, chafed against the electronic permissive action links, and mounted a concerted campaign in favour of increased control sharing over nuclear weapons.[76]

Bonn's lobbying for continued delivery of nuclear-capable tactical systems was successful on certain fronts. In addition to the Honest Johns secured during the Eisenhower years, the early 1960s saw the West Germans (and other NATO allies) equipped with Sergeant, Nike-Zeus, and Pershing missiles under tightened dual-key arrangements. However, an order of Mace cruise missiles for West German forces was cancelled by Washington. Although US officials denied it at the time, it appears that the United States wanted to keep the long-range Mace, capable of striking into the USSR, exclusively in US and out of West German hands.[77]

Throughout these debates, the most forceful and articulate advocate for control sharing was Defence Minister Strauss, who directly challenged the American position at the December 1961 meeting of the North Atlantic Council. While the German Defence Minister acknowledged the ability of American strategic systems to cover Russian IRBM/MRBM targets in 1962, he argued that the same would not be true in a few years when the USSR reached equality in ICBMs. Strauss made much the same argument as is heard today from advocates of INF modernisation: superpower equality in strategic systems would highlight Soviet theatre advantages and expose Western Europe to nuclear blackmail by decoupling US strategic forces from alliance defence.[78]

For these reasons, Bonn wanted medium-range missiles stationed in Europe. Moreover, as with the short-range systems, the FRG wanted as much control as possible over the longer-range weapons. Their decision to purchase Mace is a case in point. And, when they were denied that system, the Germans pressed for the development of a longer-range Pershing (700 miles) capable of striking the Soviet Union. In fact, Strauss's successor as Defence Minister, Kai-Uwe von Hassel, received an informal promise from Washington that the Germans would receive just such a missile in the late 1960s.[79]

Although Adenauer government officials were always careful to present their desire for increased control over atomic weapons in terms of control sharing within an alliance context, hidden just beneath the surface of their public statements was the threat of the Federal Republic's acquiring its own nuclear arsenal. For example, during his December 1961 speech to the North Atlantic Council, Strauss made a thinly veiled statement to the effect that if the idea of a NATO MRBM force was ultimately rejected, independent British and French nuclear programmes would surely find other European followers.

Indeed, it was fear of an independent German programme as well as concerns about Soviet medium- and intermediate-range systems in Europe that sparked the collective-force proposals of the late 1950s and early 1960s.[80]

Collective Forces

At the December 1957 NATO meeting, General Norstad outlined force requirements for the next five years. His plans (designated MC-70) called for a nuclear-equipped ground force of 30 divisions, a large stockpile of atomic battlefield support systems, and a mobile medium-range ballistic missile (MRBM) force for NATO. Norstad's plan for the establishment of a NATO MRBM force was to take place in three stages. The Thor-Jupiter deployments would constitute the first stage. The second stage would be a land-mobile version of the solid-fuelled Polaris missiles produced by a European consortium under licence from the United States. In the third stage the European-based NATO consortium would design and develop their own follow-up to the previous generation of missiles. In both the second and third stages, the missiles would be under the direct control of SACEUR.[81]

As SACEUR, Norstad, very popular with the Europeans, was sympathetic to their strategic concerns and growing desire to have a greater voice in Alliance nuclear strategy. He was also very sensitive to the balance of forces in Europe as the Soviets began to deploy their SS-4s and SS-5s during the late 1950s. Norstad had consistently maintained that NATO forces should have the means to answer the challenge posed by Russian systems targeted on Europe, and the primary purpose of his MRBM proposal was to give the Alliance such a capability. The new missiles would replace the aging interdiction aircraft that then constituted NATO's long-range theatre forces.[82]

The Norstad proposals did win the limited support of President Eisenhower, and some preliminary work was done on the consortium in Europe. However, de Gaulle quickly attached conditions designed to promote France's national nuclear programme. This French attitude raised State Department fears that the West Germans would soon make similar demands, and the Eisenhower administration backed away from the Norstad plan in the summer of 1960.[83]

The Kennedy administration's attitude was even harsher. Once in office the new administration accepted the advice of political analysts and strategic thinkers on both sides of the Atlantic who questioned whether Norstad's mobile MRBM was the best answer to the Russian challenge. Although the land-based version of Polaris missiles would be mobile and solid fuelled, many felt they would remain vulnerable to surprise attack and capture. In addition, the thought of those systems moving about on public thoroughfares in densely populated Europe raised logistic, safety, and security concerns for critics of the mobile-MRBM idea. Finally, because the number of missiles to be deployed under Norstad's plan was relatively small (700 at most) critics argued that the ability of the growing American strategic force to cover additional targets identified by SHAPE would render the MRBM force unnecessary. Given that the Kennedy administration was also opposed to the semi-independent role Norstad envisaged for SACEUR, the MRBM plan soon fell victim to the growing American desire to centralise control over nuclear forces. In 1962 the United States even went so far as to slow down its nuclear education programme and withhold information from the Europeans about Soviet intermediate-range systems for fear that such knowledge would regenerate West German calls for such a force.[84]

However, Kennedy was slightly more receptive to another collective-force idea developed in the last days of the Eisenhower administration: Robert Bowie's proposal for a sea-based, multilateral nuclear force. Bowie, a former director of the State Department's Policy Planning Staff envisioned the creation of the multilateral sea-based force in two stages. The first stage would be the assignment of some soon-to-be-completed American Polaris submarines (armed with Polaris missiles) to SACEUR who would have authority to launch these systems in case of a large-scale nuclear attack on Europe. In less definite cases of aggression, North Atlantic Council approval would be required. The second stage of Bowie's plan envisaged the assignment of additional ships and missiles directly to SACEUR; in this case, the crews would be multinational, made up of contingents from at least three different allied countries. The multinational basis of the crews would serve the dual purpose of giving the Europeans a real stake in the deterrent force (thus minimising the thrust for independence) and alleviating fears that one element of the crew could be able to commandeer the ship for its own purposes.[85]

The substance of Bowie's recommendations were presented by Dulles's replacement as Secretary of State, Christian Herter, at the December 1960 meeting of the North Atlantic Council. In Herter's plan the United States would assign five Polaris submarines with 80 Polaris missiles to NATO and would look favourably on the creation of a Multilateral Force of an additional 100 MRBMs stationed at sea. The creation of the Multilateral Force would be contingent on a European commitment to buy the missiles from the United States and to develop the political mechanisms to control launch procedures. Because of the already existing Norstad proposals, and because the Bowie/Herter plan was a product of the 'lame-duck' Eisenhower Administration, the MLF idea received only modest approval from the European allies.[86]

When Kennedy took office, much of the pressure on him to keep an open mind on the idea of a Multilateral Force came from the European experts at the State Department who felt that American support for a NATO nuclear force would strengthen the relationship between the United States and a revived and unified Europe. While the State Department was strongly opposed to national nuclear forces, it did support the idea of a Multilateral Force as a means both to promote European integration and to blunt national nuclear efforts.[87]

An early indication that Kennedy was prepared to keep the sea-based concept alive came in May 1961, when he addressed the Canadian Parliament in Ottawa. At that time, he pledged to commit five Polaris submarines (armed with Polaris missiles) to NATO as a prelude to the development of a truly multinational force.

However, Kennedy's support for the sea-based force was very limited and reflected the prevailing American desire to retain as much control as possible over nuclear weapons and strategy. In spelling out the details of his thinking, Kennedy attached a number of conditions to both the Polaris proposal and to the MLF concept. Before the five submarines could be assigned to NATO the alliance would first have to develop guidelines for use of the Polaris force that would be both responsive to the needs of *all* members and that would also present a credible posture in the event of an emergency. Moreover, the ships would remain under American control and would be assigned to SACLANT (an Admiral headquartered in Virginia) rather than to SACEUR. Kennedy's support for the European multinational force was even more conditional: before such a force could be considered the Europeans would have to determine the desirability and feasibility of the concept and again achieve a substantial build-up in conventional forces.⁸⁸

Nevertheless, even this highly equivocal support from the President was sufficient to keep the collective force idea alive within the State Department. While acknowledging that the Soviet development of a large stockpile of nuclear weapons and advanced delivery vehicles had created a shift in the superpower strategic environment, State Department officials believed that American and Western European security were so intertwined that American leaders would continue to regard any attack on NATO as an attack on itself. Moreover, they felt that the new flexible-response doctrine and America's new generation of strategic systems would serve as an adequate deterrent to any Russian attack. In fact, they had such faith in the ability of those strategic systems to cover targets in Europe that the need to counter Soviet theatre nuclear capabilities was not considered an important justification for the MLF.

The MLF 'cabal' at the State Department also acknowledged the fact that the changed strategic environment had generated European desires to play a greater role in their defence, especially where nuclear weapons were concerned. But, the State Department's analysts believed an even more important factor leading to independent nuclear programmes was the revival in economic strength and political stability that had taken place in Europe since the war. More than concerns about the nuclear balance, it was this new-found confidence in their revived strength that led to an inevitable desire for the allies to play a greater defence role.⁸⁹

The State Department's main fear about British and French nuclear programmes was that they would stimulate a similar effort by the West Germans. Since a strong justification for the French and British programmes was that no country would risk its own nulear devastation to defend another, it was unlikely that the Germans would view the French and British nuclear arsenals as credible deterrents against attacks on the Germans. Thus, the Germans would ultimately ask whether they too should possess a national nuclear force.⁹⁰

Given that one of the original purposes of the American commitment to NATO was to find a role for the Federal Republic in Europe that would be acceptable to the West Germans yet provide the necessary margin of safety for the European allies, the spectre of the FRG following France and embarking on a national nuclear programme was especially troubling to the State Department. Therefore, the MLF idea was presented as a political alternative to independent European efforts, as a means to satisfy whatever German nuclear aspirations existed, and as a means to promote European integration. Indeed, the MLF concept moved into the planning stages not as result of an increased sense of threat from the USSR, but rather as a result of a last ditch French effort to secure US aid for the *force de frappe*.

Staff work by the Navy on the collective-force idea began in the spring of 1962 and was completed in the late summer. Originally, it was thought that the backbone of the MLF would be the new Polaris submarine. But Admiral Hyman Rickover refused to allow foreign access to sophisticated American submarine technology. As it finally evolved, the MLF plan called for a fleet of 25 surface ships, each armed with 8 Polaris A3 missiles, and manned by crews of different nationalities. Although not as invulnerable as submarines, a sea-based force was still considered less vulnerable than land-based systems, and the range (2,500 miles) and accuracy of the missiles did give them a limited counterforce capability.

The outlines of the MLF were presented to the Europeans during the autumn of 1962 by Admiral Richard Lee and Gerard Smith of the State Department. They did not even visit Paris, and received at best a lukewarm reception in the other European capitals. The Germans were the most receptive, but even in Bonn there were serious concerns about the requirement that American as well as European consent would be necessary to launch the missiles. Moreover, when the two men returned home, Robert McNamara and the Defense Department launched a bureaucratic attack designed to scuttle the whole project. McNamara always was uncomfortable with the MLF idea because he viewed it as a challenge to his efforts to centralise command and control over nuclear weapons. He was supported in the Pentagon by many in the Navy who were protective of the Polaris system. In fact, it was only in the wake of Nassau, when de Gaulle vetoed British entry into the EEC and signed the Franco-German Treaty, that the MLF moved to the forefront of alliance politics.[91]

De Gaulle's actions blocked progress in the European unity movement, had removed the possibility of France integrating its nuclear force with NATO, and had fed concern over the possibility of an independent German nuclear programme. Therefore, in February 1963, Kennedy authorised the State Department to open talks with various European governments on the MLF proposal of the previous autumn. The configuration of the force would remain the same surface fleet previously described. The crews of each ship would consist of at least three nationalities with no group making up more than 40 per cent of the total. The force would be under SACEUR during peacetime, and during war a committee of MLF members would require a unanimous vote to launch the missiles. This implied American veto was to be removed only if the Europeans made substantial progress on European integration.

The MLF proposal dominated alliance relations for the next two-and-a-half years, but ended in failure. President Kennedy, smarting from de Gaulle's actions in January and highly sensitive to allied opinion, was reluctant to commit his prestige to another European project that might fail. Negotiations for an MLF treaty only got under way in October 1963, and it was not until April 1964 that Kennedy's successor, Lyndon Johnson, set a December deadline for a draft treaty. Moreover, powerful elements in Congress (especially in the JCAE) were highly sceptical of the project, and McNamara's Defense Department viewed the addition of 200 Polaris missiles as superfluous to the imposing American strategic arsenal. Finally, the United States was in the process of negotiating a Limited Nuclear Test-Ban Treaty with the USSR, and was susceptible to Russian charges that the MLF violated the non-proliferation motivations behind the test-ban agreement. Of course these pressures increased as negotiations for the Non-Proliferation Treaty itself began.[92]

In Britain, the Conservative governments of Harold Macmillan and his successor Sir Alec Douglas-Home expressed unenthusiastic official support for the project. However, Macmillan agreed to participate in the MLF negotiations after making it clear that the UK was not committed to participation in the force should the talks succeed. The idea of a sea-based multinational force was scoffed at by the Royal Navy, and many Britons feared that Britain's participation in a Multinational Force would undermine the United Kingdom's special relationship with the United States. Instead, the British favoured the idea of an Atlantic Nuclear Force (ANF) consisting of national nuclear forces committed to the Atlantic alliance but remaining under the control of the donating power.[93]

In France, de Gaulle remained committed to a purely national *force de frappe* and there was really no question of French participation in the MLF. While the French did show some interest in the ANF proposal, they did not participate in the negotiations designed to produce the MLF treaty and lobbied intensely against the project.

Of course, West Germany was the most enthusiastic supporter of the MLF project because of the promise it held for satisfying the Federal Republic's nuclear aspirations and desire to remain on an equal footing with the rest of the allies. However, even in the FRG, the veto over a decision to launch the missiles troubled the military. So too did the fact that the original submarine configuration had been scrapped in favour of surface ships. Moreover, de Gaulle exerted strong pressure on his political ally Adenauer not to allow West German participation in the MLF. Even after Adenauer was replaced by Ludwig Erhard, 'a confirmed Atlanticist', French pressures on the 'Gaullist' wing of the CDU were so great that the government could never throw its full weight behind the project.[94]

During the autumn of 1964, several events took place that sealed the fate of the MLF. In Britain the Labour Party won the October elections. While in opposition, Labour had argued that the viability of the American strategic nuclear guarantee was so great that European efforts, including the MLF, were wasteful and unnecessary. The new Prime Minister, Harold Wilson, maintained this position, and other European allies began to see the whole project as divisive in alliance and European relations.[95]

With British and European support clearly waning, and faced with mounting domestic concerns about negotiations for a non-proliferation treaty, Erhard publically expressed the hope that the United States and the Federal Republic of Germany would proceed with the MLF on a bilateral basis. While there was some support for this position in Washington, Erhard's call produced a storm of protest from Paris. Prime Minister Georges Pompidou charged that West German participation in the MLF would not be consistent with the Franco-German Treaty of 1963, and Adenauer, under pressure from de Gaulle, used his remaining influence with the CDU to help delay German participation.[96]

Faced with this array of declining European support for the project and aware that pressing the MLF would create a serious Franco-German rift, President Johnson shelved the scheme in early December. And after twelve more months of lacklustre negotiations, the MLF was formally dropped in December 1965.

Until the INF modernisation proposal began to develop in 1977, the MLF marked the last effort to address problems of European security and alliance politics through the introduction of long-range nuclear systems to Europe. During 1964, the United States did make good its promise to assign five Polaris submarines to NATO and SACEUR as a symbol of the American commitment to the alliance. Moreover, following the demise of the MLF, the United States sponsored the Nuclear Planning Group (NPG) in order to assure the Europeans (especially the West Germans) that American strategic nuclear forces were a credible deterrent to Soviet aggression. The NPG also allowed the allies to provide inputs into the planning process for the targeting of American strategic systems. To British analyst Alister Buchan, this mechanism offered the allies a measure of what the French call *contrôle* (translated by Buchan as examination, or verification, and the right to criticise) over NATO strategy, rather than direct control.

The establishment of a method whereby the United States and its NATO allies could engage in frank dialogue about nuclear strategy did go a long way in resolving West German and general European concerns about American intentions and plans. However, the French refused to participate, as de Gaulle preferred to pursue a purely national strategic nuclear programme, and France ultimately left NATO's military structure in 1966.

The turmoil generated by the MLF failure and French withdrawal did not lead to a period of anxious re-examination as might have been expected. This was largely due to the stability conferred on the scene by the rapid growth that had taken place in American strategic launchers: from 500 bombers in 1960 to the triad of 2100 diversified launchers in 1965. Soviet strategic launchers numbered only about 400 in 1965 but were destined to reach the American total by 1973.

Following the demise of the MLF, the maintenance and modernisation of long-range forces assigned to NATO has largely been an American responsibility. In 1971 the Polaris submarines assigned to NATO were replaced by more advanced Poseidons, and the United States has continuously stationed several squadrons of nuclear-capable land-based (F-111 and F-4) and carrier-based (A-6 and A-7) strike aircraft in the European theatre.

With nuclear weapons widely deployed in Europe and the strategic balance clearly favourable to the United States for some years to come, the passions and conflicts of the 1950-65 period in NATO subsided. Yet for a time a new doctrine to govern the use of this greatly enlarged nuclear arsenal would have to be hammered out, new weapons technology would require new decisions and the coming days of parity would demand reckoning.

The Shadow of History

This history of two decades ago can hardly be reassuring to advocates of the December 1979 modernisation decision. Just as in 1979, the previous decision to station long-range US missiles in Europe was supposed to demonstrate the credibility of the American commitment to European security. Indeed, the missiles were supposed to be visible manifestations of that commitment. However, as the Thor-Jupiter decision demonstrated, such systems evoked European fears that their security was actually being decoupled from American strategic systems. Indeed, the very visibility of the Thors and Jupiters made them appear as prime targets for pre-emption and stimulated widespread anti-nuclear protests throughout Europe. The vulnerability issue was also raised with Norstad's proposal for a mobile MRBM force. Moreover, to many in Europe, the IRBMs seemed to pose a first strike threat to the USSR. As a result, the only continental countries to accept the American IRBMs 25 years ago were Turkey and Italy, and even in those cases the desire to strengthen bilateral relations with the United States seems to have outweighed military considerations.

However, it is worthy of mention that some distinction appears to have been drawn between ballistic and cruise missiles. The deployment of the long-range Mace attracted little attention and was not a cause of serious debate either within the Atlantic alliance or with the Soviet Union.

It is also important to note that the decision to base Thors and Jupiters in Europe occurred in the context of a bitter inter-service dispute over the roles each branch of the armed forces would play in nuclear strategy. The Army was particularly anxious to assure itself a 'prestigious' strategic nuclear role in US defence planning, and viewed the production and overseas basing of the Jupiters as a means to that end.

Whatever European support did exist for earlier plans to station long-range systems in Europe appears to have been more a product of national desires to acquire the means to defend themselves and to increase their 'prestige' within NATO rather than enthusiasm for stationing American systems on their territories. The European impulse to possess the strategic means to defend themselves was an important one that caused severe strains within the alliance and witnessed France's departure from the military command structure. It may well be that NATO's inability to accommodate that impulse — either through acceptance of national nuclear forces (the British force being an exception) or the creation of collective forces — is at the root of many of the problems associated with TNF modernisation today. When the United States refused to accept the legitimacy of arguments supporting European national strategic forces, Washington was denying the rationale for whatever role those allied forces might have played. As a result, the effort to introduce new long-range land-based American systems has been taking place in absence of any long-standing alliance policy or doctrine, and it appears as something qualitatively different from 20 years of Western strategy.

Whether that European self-defence impulse will again manifest itself is another uncertainty. But the fact remains that even with the Pershings and GLCMs deployed, they will be, by choice of the European government concerned, under American control with the final decision to use them resting with the American President in Washington. And, if allied doubts about American leadership and intentions persist or grow beyond that reached in 1982 — regardless of the deployment of the new missiles — we may again witness renewed interest in independent or collective European nuclear-weapons programmes.

Notes

1. For a discussion of NATO's early years see Alan K. Henrikson, 'The Origins of NATO', *US Naval War College Review* (May-June 1980), pp. 4-39.
2. Robert Osgood, *The Entangling Alliance* (Chicago: University of Chicago Press, 1966).
3. US Congress, Senate Committee on Foreign Relations, *Executive Sessions of the Senate Foreign Relations Committee*, vol. V, p. 394.
4. Robert McGeehan, *The German Rearmament Question* (Bloomington, Indiana: University of Indiana Press, 1971).
5. Osgood, *The Entangling Alliance*, pp. 92-8; Andrew J. Pierre, *Nuclear Politics: The British Experience with an Independent Strategic Deterrent Force, 1939-1970* (London: Oxford University Press, 1972).
6. Samuel P. Huntington, *The Common Defense: Strategic Politics in Allied Defense* (New York: Columbia University Press, 1961), pp. 64-87; Glenn H. Snyder, 'The New Tools of 1953' in Winer Schilling, Paul Hammond and Glenn Snyder (eds), *Strategy, Politics, and Defense Budgets* (New York: Columbia University Press, 1966), pp. 379-524.
7. James Gavin, *War and Peace in the Space Age* (New York: Harper and Brothers, 1958).
8. Osgood, *The Entangling Alliance*, p. 107. Honest John and Corporal were both short-range (under 100 miles) surface-to-surface missiles, while the sea-based Regulus and land-based Matador were longer-range (over 500 miles) subsonic cruise missiles.
9. Ibid.
10. Catherine McArdle Helleher, *Germany and the Politics of Nuclear Weapons* (New York: Columbia University Press, 1975), pp. 132-4.
11. Ibid., pp. 39-42.
12. Hans Speier, *German Rearmament and Atomic War* (Evanston, Illinois: Row, Peterson and Co., 1957), pp. 182-93.
13. Huntington, *The Common Defense*, p. 92.
14. *New York Times*, 13 July 1956.
15. James R. Killian, Jr., *Sputnik, Scientists, and Eisenhower: A Memoir of*

the First Special Assistant to the President for Science and Technology (Cambridge: Massachusetts Institute of Technology Press, 1977), pp. 77-8.
16. Ibid.
17. Wilfred L. Kohl, *French Nuclear Diplomacy* (Princeton: Princeton University Press, 1971), p. 36.
18. John Steinbruner, *The Cybernetic Theory of Decision* (Princeton: Princeton University Press, 1974), p. 180.
19. Ibid., p. 181.
20. *New York Times*, 13 April 1957, p. 1.
21. U.S. Department of State, *Bulletin* (5 May 1958), p. 741. Testimony of John Foster Dulles.
22. Pierre, *Nuclear Politics*, p. 162.
23. Raymond Dawson and Richard Rosearance, 'Theory and Reality in Anglo-American Relations', *World Politics*, vol. 19, no. 1 (October 1966), pp. 21-51.
24. Steinbruner, *The Cybernetic Theory of Decision*, p. 159.
25. *The New York Times*, 17 December 1957.
26. Michael H. Armacost, *The Politics of Weapons Innovation: The Thor-Jupiter Controversy* (New York: Columbia University Press, 1969).
27. Henry A. Kissinger, 'Missiles and the Western Alliance', *Foreign Affairs*, vol. 39 (April 1958), pp. 383-400.
28. Steinbruner, *The Cybernetic Theory of Decision*, pp. 174-85. He also was anxious to replace the aging and increasing vulnerable fleet of fighter-bombers that formed almost the whole of the alliance's tactical interdiction force.
29. *New York Times*, 17 December 1957.
30. Armacost, *The Politics of Weapons Innovation*, pp. 198-202.
31. Ibid., p. 202.
32. Ibid. p. 179
33. Albert Wohlsteller, 'The Delicate Balance of Terror', Foreign Affairs, vol. 37 (January 1959), pp. 211-35.
34. Kissinger, 'Missiles and the Western Alliance', pp. 383-400.
35. Armacost, *The Politics of Weapons Innovation*, pp. 200-1.
36. Ibid.
37. Barton J. Bernstein, 'The Cuban Missile Crisis: Trading the Jupiters in Turkey?' *Political Science Quarterly*, vol. 95, no. 1 (Spring 1980), pp. 97-125.
38. *New York Times*, 21 January 1963.
39. Kissinger, 'Missiles and the Western Alliance', pp. 383-400.
40. David Alan Rosenberg, 'The Origins of Overkill: Nuclear Weapons and American Strategy, 1945-1960', *International Security*, vol. 7, no. 4 (Spring 1983), pp. 3-71.
41. Ibid.
42. Steinbruner, *The Cybernetic Theory of Decision*, p. 203.
43. *New York Times*, 7 June 1962.
44. Ibid.
45. Ibid.
46. Ibid.
47. John P. Rose, *The Evaluation of U.S. Army Nuclear Doctrine* (Boulder, Colo.: Westview Press, 1980), p. 76.
48. Kelleher, *Germany and the Politics of Nuclear Weapons*, pp. 161-2.
49. International Institute for Strategic Studies, *The Military Balance 1964* (London: IISS, 1964).
50. Kelleher, *Germany and the Politics of Nuclear Weapons*, p. 162.
51. Ibid., pp. 157-78.
52. Pierre, *Nuclear Politics*, p. 199.
53. Ibid., pp. 234-7.

54. Wolf Mendl, *Deterrence and Persuasion: French Nuclear Armament in the Context of National Policy, 1945-1969* (New York: Praeger, 1970), pp. 56-7.
55. Ibid.
56. Steinbruner, *The Cybernetic Theory of Decision*, pp. 238-9.
57. Kelleher, *Germany and the Politics of Nuclear Weapons*, pp. 22-6.
58. Ibid., p. 26.
59. Ibid., p. 180-3.
60. Andrew J. Pierre, *Nuclear Politics* (Boston: Houghton Mifflin Company, 1961).
61. Kelleher, *Germany and the Politics of Nuclear Weapons*, p. 48.
62. Pierre, *Nuclear Politics*, p. 93.
63. Paul Stehlin, 'The Revolution of Western Defense', *Foreign Affairs*, vol. 42 (October 1963), pp. 70-83.
64. Ibid., p. 76
65. Ibid., p. 77.
66. Pierre Gallois, *The Balance of Terror: Strategy for the Nuclear Age* (Boston: Houghton Mifflin Company, 1961).
67. Stehlin, 'The Evolution of Western Defense', p. 78.
68. Kelleher, *Germany and the Politics of Nuclear Weapons*, pp. 37-45.
69. Ibid., p. 45-9.
70. Ibid., p. 48.
71. Ibid., pp. 130-1.
72. Ibid., pp. 111-16.
73. Steinbruner, *The Cybernetic Theory of Decision*, p. 214-15.
74. Kelleher, *Germany and the Politics of Nuclear Weapons*, pp. 183-202.
75. Ibid.
76. Steinbruner, *The Cybernetic Theory of Decision*, pp. 214-15.
77. Kelleher, *Germany and the Politics of Nuclear Weapons*, p. 162.
78. Ibid., p. 86.
79. *New York Times*, 22 November 1964.
80. Kelleher, *Germany and the Politics of Nuclear Weapons*, p. 86.
81. Steinbruner, *The Cybernetic Theory of Decision*, p. 182-4.
82. Henry A. Kissinger, *The Troubled Partnership* (New York: McGraw Hill Books Company, 1961), p. 128.
83. Steinbruner, *The Cybernetic Theory of Decision*, pp. 188-90.
84. Ibid., p. 212.
85. Robert R. Bowie, 'Strategy and the Atlantic Alliance', *International Organization*, vol. 27, no. 3 (Summer 1963), pp. 709-33.
86. Steinbruner, *The Cybernetic Theory of Decision*, p. 189-91.
87. Ibid., pp. 223-5.
88. Ibid.
89. Bowie, 'Strategy and the Atlantic Alliance', pp. 709-33.
90. Ibid.
91. Steinbruner, *The Cybernetic Theory of Decision*, p. 234.
92. Ibid.
93. Pierre, *Nuclear Politics*, pp. 24-50.
94. Kelleher, *Germany and the Politics of Nuclear Weapons*, pp. 235-45.
95. Steinbruner, *The Cybernetic Theory of Decision*, pp. 287-91.
96. Ibid., p. 298.

2 THE WILDERNESS YEARS

Lawrence Freedman

Although deployed in quantity as early as the 1953-8 period, theatre nuclear forces (TNF) were the most neglected component of NATO's military capabilities. With strategic nuclear and conventional forces in the alliance 'triad', their position seemed comparable to that of the Holy Ghost in the Christian trinity and just about as difficult to explain. International attention concentrated on strategic and conventional weapons as providing the likely clues to the persistent conundrums of security policy, and as the weapons on the table at the main arms-control negotiations of SALT and Mutual and Balanced Force Reductions (MBFR). TNF were known as 'tactical nuclear weapons' (TNWs) until the mid-1970s and this term itself was widely taken to reflect the dubious nature of their military rationale. In fact, it was also accepted that the main reason for their being kept in Europe had little to do with military factors but was a consequence of the political value attached to these weapons by West Europeans as symbols of the American nuclear guarantee.

In the late 1970s there was a sudden surge of interest in nuclear weapons based in Europe. The existence of so many warheads dotted around the continent was revealed as the various proposals for their modernisation attracted notoriety. The 'nuclearisation' of Europe surprised many. There was a tendency to assume that the situation appeared so novel because it actually was novel — as if it had suddenly occurred to the superpowers to start moving forward nuclear weapons so that Europe could serve as the battleground while they stayed free of the consequences of nuclear confrontation. Instead of the controversy surrounding TNF being seen as a natural but more public extension of previous controversies, it was taken to herald a completely new stage in the arms race.

A quick glance at the strategic literature of the 1950s reveals just how much the debate of the early 1980s is following a well-trodden path.[1] The circularity of the debate may well result from the fact that in its early stages no destination was reached and the path just petered out. In Chapter 1, Timothy Ireland provides a full discussion of the debates within the alliance on theatre nuclear forces up to the mid-1960s when they ran out of steam, while subsequent chapters review

The Wilderness Years 45

the current controversies. My objective in this chapter is to consider the more tranquil period in the history of TNF — from the mid-1960s to the first stirrings over the neutron bomb.

This chapter does not look at all at the TNF-related issues such as security against terrorists or atomic demolition munitions (ADMs) or the vexed question of control. Nor is it concerned with the character of the decision-making or the composition of the stockpile. The main concern is with the doctrinal disputes that were subsiding in the mid-1960s but were reasserting themselves in the mid-1970s. What this analysis demonstrates is that, contrary to popular suspicions, NATO has never adopted a 'nuclear war-fighting posture'. That it gave this impression was largely a consequence of the processes of qualitative improvement of an ageing arsenal and the failure, when an opportunity presented itself, to trim the arsenal down to a size appropriate to the limited role assigned to it.

The Doctrinal Debate Subsides

The first half of the 1960s was a period of intense doctrinal debate within NATO. The debate was prompted by questions concerning the proper mix of conventional and nuclear forces, and of American and European contributions to these forces. It subsided in the second half of the decade. France's departure from NATO's integrated command opened the way for a doctrinal compromise among the rest of the allies. This emerged in 1967 with the adoption of the strategy of flexible response. By then it was clear that enthusiasm for the debate was waning. The NATO force structure seemed relatively fixed and the new strategy as good a way to rationalise it as any.

The fading of the nuclear debate was particularly marked. The great issues that had stimulated it had all reached some sort of conclusion: the partial Test-Ban Treaty had been signed; the British and French nuclear programmes were on course; schemes for a multilateral force had collapsed in confusion. With the Non-Proliferation Treaty and the superpowers moving towards the first strategic-arms accords in the early 1970s, there seemed even more reason to believe that the international community was learning to cope with 'the bomb'. Arguments now raged over conventional forces. Those who had protested so vigorously against nuclear weapons in earlier years turned their attention to Vietnam. Within NATO, the flexible-response debate had stemmed from European concern that increases in conventional forces would drain credibility from the American nuclear guarantee. This question now took on a different complexion as the competing pressures of Vietnam and Congressional demands for Europeans to look after their own defences raised the possibility of reductions in American conventional forces. Now the fear was that such a move would threaten the fundamental American commitment to the defence of Europe.

The circumstances were not conducive to debate on nuclear weapons: there was a desire not to reopen old arguments; there were no new initiatives to stimulate new arguments; and conventional forces provided ample scope for those who wanted to argue. But this respite from debate could only be temporary. The position at the end of the 1960s was well-described by Michael Howard who noted that only the 'sheer exhaustion of the participants' had curtailed a debate that had continued up to then with great vigour and in three languages.[2]

NATO's underlying problem of how to threaten convincingly the first use of nuclear weapons in the face of probable Soviet retaliation had not been solved — only shelved. Moreover, it was always likely that the argument would reappear. If arms control and disarmament prospered, then NATO's reliance on nuclear threats would soon appear anomalous and the European arsenal would come under the scrutiny of the controllers; with an arms race, the threats and the accompanying arsenal would soon appear dangerous. The question was when and how the issue would return to the fore, and whether this time NATO would be better prepared to cope.

The Nuclear Threshold and Conventional Force Posture

The analysis of the role of tactical nuclear weapons (as they were then called) during the 1960s within the Pentagon was largely a critique of the policies of the Eisenhower administration and its apparent readiness to raise TNWs to conventional status in order to save on the cost of proper conventional forces.[3] The critique relied on two propositions: first, that a war in which TNWs were used would be utterly different in kind to one in which only conventional forces were used and it would contain inherent tendencies to escalate out of control into uninhibited nuclear exchanges; second, that the difference in kind between conventional and nuclear war was so clear and obvious that a natural 'firebreak' existed between them.

The first proposition had occurred to many during the 1950s when TNWs were first being introduced and has remained at the centre of

The Wilderness Years

opposition to their deployment ever since. Keeping TNW use restricted to military targets and avoiding horrific levels of collateral civilian damage seemed impossible given both the inclination to achieve maximum military impact by attacking as many available military targets as possible in the first volley, and the probability of unrestrained Soviet retaliation. The most likely result of NATO's taking the nuclear initiative with TNWs, it was argued, would be massive destruction of civilian life and escalation to strategic nuclear exchanges without improving NATO's military position. Indeed, though advocates of reliance on TNWs saw this as the only possible compensation for the Warsaw Pact's comparative advantage in manpower, in practice TNWs could not provide such compensation. Their use would put an even higher premium on available reserves.

This made it prudent to take steps to ensure that TNWs were not used. Once the fateful threshold had been passed the destruction of the life, property and territory of those supposedly being defended would proceed with dreadful speed, to be followed, in all probablity, by escalation past the next threshold to the strategic nuclear level. For those working for United States Secretary of Defense Robert S. McNamara during the 1960s the only possible conclusion was that NATO's dependence on TNWs must be reversed and that the best method to do this was to strengthen conventional forces and so 'raise the nuclear threshold'.

As this seemed to be no more than the application of rigorous common sense, the Americans responsible were somewhat taken aback by the vigour of the initial European response. The Americans' understanding was hampered by the fact that this response was a jumble of anxieties, complaints and counter-arguments, not always internally consistent and usually wide ranging.

The Europeans, while perfectly well aware of the likely consequences of a resort to TNWs, were not so interested in the threshold between conventional and nuclear war and much more preoccupied by the threshold between peace and war. They were anxious that the Americans were not taking the risks and horrors of conventional war in Europe seriously enough. It was argued that any war would be catastrophic for Europe, so war itself, not just nuclear war, had to be deterred. If the best way of deterring war was to threaten nuclear use, then no steps must be allowed to diminish that threat. American anxiety to avoid passing the nuclear threshold, it was feared, would encourage the Soviet Union to remove from any calculations of the costs and benefits of aggressive actions the most crucial item on the debit side — the likelihood of passing this threshold. The American move seemed to suggest an interest in reducing the nuclear risk to the United States of fulfilling its responsibilities towards Europe, even if this meant increasing the likelihood of conventional war.[4]

The arguments that raged over an American desire to improve NATO's conventional options were similar to those that have developed more recently over the desire to improve limited nuclear options. They stemmed not so much from the military issues in which they were phrased, but from the differences in perception and interest resulting from the concentration of NATO's strategic assets in the country most distant from the likely location of any fighting. To Americans it is natural that their involvement in the defence of Europe is more plausible the lower the risk to their own homeland. A likely if limited response is more credible, and so more valuable for the purposes of deterrence, than a response much greater in magnitude but unlikely to be realised. For Europeans, to suggest to the Soviet Union that it can disregard the ultimate threat is folly. What appears limited and tolerable to the United States may also appear so to the Soviet Union, enabling the two superpowers, with some equanimity, to fight out their differences at Europe's expense. The main variation between the two debates was that whereas it was common ground in the 1960s that the threshold between tactical and strategic nuclear would be all too easy to slide over (a thought which encouraged the Europeans but worried the Americans) the possibility was raised in the 1970s that an effective demarcation line might be established. Again, however, the consensus that a fire-break would be difficult to establish is greater than is commonly supposed by the protagonists.

TNWs played an important role in the early 1960s debate, yet they were not central to its course nor unduly affected by its outcome. The approach of McNamara and his aides was to strengthen conventional options rather than to weaken nuclear options. The main reforms of NATO nuclear structure during the early 1960s was to try to accentuate the threshold between tactical and strategic weapons by removing the Thor and Jupiter IRBMs based in Europe and deciding against development and production of a new MRBM. As far as TNWs themselves were concerned, numbers were actually raised during the 1960s (especially 1963-6) from 3,500 to 7,000 warheads. There were also qualitative improvements, with the Sergeant, Pershing, Mace and Nike-Hercules missiles being introduced. The only force-improvement proposal that achieved real political notoriety was the MLF, which was viewed more in diplomatic than military terms, and suffered in the end from the incredibility of its political rationale.[5]

Despite their misgivings, McNamara's analysts in the Pentagon were still prepared to see TNWs as 'a desirable complement' to improved conventional forces. In part this was out of recognition that the firebreak argument had its limits. It would do no harm if the Soviet Union believed that a conventional invasion could lead to a nuclear war, and anyway there had to be some response available lest the Soviet Union be tempted to initiate nuclear use. Furthermore, until improved conventional forces were firmly in place, the intermediate option provided by TNWs might be needed. Most importantly, TNWs were extensively deployed and could not be removed without an enormous political fuss. Enthoven and Smith explain:

> Not only had the United States increased its own tactical nuclear forces in the area; it had also encouraged the European allies to buy nuclear delivery systems and had committed itself to stockpiling nuclear warheads in Europe for those systems. This was not a situation that defense officials could, or wanted to, change drastically at the time. To attempt to do so would have raised the specter of an imminent US withdrawal from Europe.[6]

Thus, despite the doctrinal arguments raging in the background in the first half of the 1960s, TNWs were left largely untouched. The European interest in TNWs did not extend much beyond keeping them on the continent and ensuring that their prospective employment would come earlier rather than later in a future war. The key feature of these weapons was not what they might achieve on the battlefield but that they were American and nuclear and so, in some physical manner, linked European defence to American nuclear weapons. The warhead stockpile had become a symbol of the American nuclear guarantee; so long as it was left undisturbed the guarantee was in place. There was little interest in the actual composition of the TNW arsenal. Uwe Nerlich has observed how the moves taken during the 1960s actually tended to make these forces more rather than less suicidal in nature.[7] The longer-range systems such as Thor and Jupiter, which were suitable for deep strikes and which did provide a close link with the American strategic arsenal, were removed. Meanwhile the shorter-range systems, ostensibly designed for battlefield support, were improved.

Europeans were unwilling to enhance the nuclear threat by making a possible early nuclear use easier. On the contrary the instinct pointed in the opposite direction. The Germans consistently refused to allow pre-positioning of atomic demolition munitions and the discussions surrounding the Athens Guidelines in 1962 on consultative procedures prior to nuclear use made it quite clear that Europeans did recognise the existence of a fire-break between nuclear and conventional war. Nor did Europeans exhibit the slightest interest, then or more recently, in proposals for making an early use of nuclear weapons more credible to the other side — for instance by announcing that weapons would be used quickly but only on NATO territory, and matching words with deeds by creating or preparing to create in wartime a depopulated zone along the East-West border. Domestic politics, especially in the Federal Republic, ruled these ideas out. Indeed, the disinclination to authorise an early nuclear use was evident in *all* allied governments, even if to many, this 'tactical nuclear allergy' and its institutional consequences were the main obstacle to a credible strategy.[8]

Europeans were aware that their interests would be even less well served if the fire-break was established between tactical and strategic weapons. Moreover, a fire-break at this level would be extremely difficult to establish. Once American weapons, whatever they were labelled, were attacking Soviet territory, Soviet risk calculations would be virtually the same. Simply because it was possible to establish the fire-break between conventional and tactical nuclear war there was anxiety that the USSR would be tempted to exploit evidence of an American unwillingness to pass this threshold.

In the late 1960s neither the United States nor its West European allies were putting much effort into developing an operational concept for TNWs or preparing ground forces to operate in a nuclear environment. There were no doubts about the awful consequences for Europe if these weapons were ever used and this in itself added unreality to proposals for controlled military employment. One outraged observer pointed to a 'general consensus' at the time in favour of ignoring the deficiencies in NATO's posture, with 'the Europeans refusing to entertain the notion of a purely local nuclear conflict, and the United States fearing that any attempt to redress these deficiencies would serve only to demolish once and for all the argument for a strong conventional option'.[9]

The Conditions of First Use

As the public debate of the early 1960s waned, it did leave one positive result in its wake — the Nuclear Planning Group (NPG), as Ireland noted. When the MLF sank, attention turned from 'hardware' to forms of communication. In December 1966 Ministers in NATO's Defence Planning Committee agreed to establish a permanent advisory committee for policy on nuclear defence for the alliance. The NPG has normally met with only seven or eight of the Ministers of the member countries in attendance although in 1979 it agreed that all eleven NPG countries could attend ministerial meetings.[10]

The NPG considers strategic nuclear issues, but the most regular item on its agenda has been TNWs. The first major NPG study concerned the political guidelines for the initial defensive tactical use of nuclear weapons. This was completed in 1969. The next year the NPG attempted to develop special political guidelines for the tricky subject of atomic demolition munitions, as well as to develop a concept for theatre nuclear strike forces. Thereafter the NPG returned to another awkward problem, that of guidelines for TNW use in deteriorating situations after initial use had occurred.[11]

My main concern is with the question of initial use. Michael Legge defines initial use as 'the first use of nuclear weapons at any level and against any target by either side'. This was therefore the first attempt to identify a method to fulfill the objective in the flexible-response document of 1967 (MC-14/3) to persuade an invading enemy 'to cease his aggression and withdraw'. The early studies on this subject were conducted by individual countries. In late 1968 it was agreed that Britain and Germany would prepare a joint paper to bring the various ideas together. The initiative was apparently taken by the then British Minister of Defence, Denis Healey, who was anxious both to maintain the momentum in the NPG in the absence of strong American leadership (McNamara had been replaced by Clark Clifford as Secretary of Defense at the start of 1968) and to establish a strategic relationship with Germany to counteract the latest French veto of Britain's application to join the EEC. At any rate the eventual paper, known as the Healey-Schröder Report after the two Defence Ministers, was 'the first and only time that a major paper on allied nuclear doctrine [was] undertaken without US participation'. It was ready by May 1969, while the new Nixon administration was still settling in in the United States.

According to Legge[12] the report's essential message was clear:

> Given that any initial use of nuclear weapons would result in a qualitative change in the nature of warfare, such use by NATO should have a fundamentally political purpose. It should be designed to confront the enemy with the prospect of the risks of escalation

consequent on a continuation of the conflict, with the aim of making him halt his attack and withdraw, thereby restoring the credibility of the deterrent. This did not imply that initial use should not have a military objective as a means of achieving its political aim, but it did suggest that such use would need to be carefully limited, and it therefore followed that it would be necessary to maintain the closest possible political control over such use.

The United States recognised that the questions of nuclear use in Europe, and in particular in Germany, were so sensitive that an American view would not be imposed. It made sense for the Europeans to take the lead. However, Americans had two reservations. Firstly, they were unwilling to rule out use on a substantial scale in order to achieve a military advantage as well as to make a political point; and secondly, they were not anxious to pass the nuclear threshold early in a conflict.

These reservations can be found in the memoirs of Henry Kissinger.[13] Kissinger records that the civilian analysts in the Pentagon, left over from the Johnson administration, saw no positive use for American nuclear forces based in Europe while at the same time viewing them as a dangerous source of escalation. Meanwhile, the allies 'urged both a guaranteed early resort to tactical nuclear weapons and immunity of their territories from their use'. He illustrated this with the views of Denis Healey, who visited Washington in February 1969 and presumably outlined the ideas that would be reflected in the Healey-Schröder report. As Kissinger described this approach, it presumed that NATO's conventional forces could only resist for a few days, so that early use of nuclear weapons was essential. Healey envisaged this early use as a warning to the Soviet Union that the West would prefer to escalate to a strategic exchange rather than surrender. A small number of tactical weapons might provide the warning while avoiding the devastation of Europe.[14]

Kissinger suggests that the British and West Germans succeeded in getting this view accepted by the NPG in the form of 'demonstrative use'. This involved 'setting off a nuclear weapon in some remote location, which did not involve many casualties — in the air over the Mediterranean, for example — as a signal of more drastic use if the weapon failed'. The NPG had certainly discussed 'demonstrative use'. In late 1968, the then Secretary of Defense Clark Clifford presented to the NPG 'a detailed outline of how demonstration-type nuclear bursts could be used to show an invading enemy the West was not afraid to resort to such weapons', based on the first American study for the group.

Kissinger indicates his own doubts about this concept. As the Soviet Union would probably anticipate a nuclear response if it decided to invade and if the response was no more than a demonstration, then that response probably would signal hesitation rather than determination and provide a spur to attack rather than a deterrent. According to Legge, there was in fact little support for this concept in the NPG, at least in its extreme form of the use of a single weapon over an uninhabited area. The main concern was that initial use would be a signal, designed to influence a perception of risk rather than inflict a defeat. This did not preclude a substantial strike. Equally, because a simple demonstration requires the minimum of advanced planning, it has remained a possibility.[15]

Kissinger's root suspicion was that the real objective of the allies was early use of strategic nuclear weapons 'which meant a US-Soviet war fought over their heads'. Although this is an interpretation few Europeans would endorse, it reflects no more suspicion over European motives than Europeans often exhibit over American motives. At any rate Kissinger could not accept any plan which made this possible. Strategic weapons had to be seen as a last resort. He suggests that the eventual document agreed at the November 1969 meeting of the NPG represented a 'temporary compromise' that 'in effect paper over the dispute', in that it kept open both 'demonstrative' and 'operational' uses of TNWs. Legge, on the other hand, while agreeing that ambiguities remained, suggests that the compromise was neither as even-handed as Kissinger suggests nor as temporary. The United States came down firmly in favour of the view that NATO's objective would be political; initial use would be selective. Furthermore, although the resultant document was entitled 'Provisional Political Guidelines for Initial Defensive Tactical Use of Nuclear Weapons by NATO', it turned out to be rather enduring. Paul Buteaux suggests that while the Americans made clear their preference for stronger conventional defences, Secretary of Defense Melvin Laird's realism as to the possibility of getting the Europeans to increase their defence spending meant that there was not much American pressure in this area.[16]

The NPG document did shift the emphasis in NATO from a general nuclear response to an escalatory use of TNWs. That is, initial use would involve tens of low-yield rather than hundreds of high-yield weapons. This would be accompanied by a clear declaration of restraint. Nevertheless, there remained disagreement over the form and nature of the escalation. The Americans were still anxious to delay any nuclear use but, when it became unavoidable, to hold on to the possibility of obtaining some military advantage even if this involved large-scale use.[17] The Europeans were prepared to see earlier use but only on a small scale with the political will of the enemy serving as the real target.[18]

In an attempt to resolve the issue subsequent NPG studies looked at the problem of follow-on use if the first volley failed to persuade the enemy to withdraw. In the first set of studies, conducted from 1970 to 1972, the problem was examined in alternative scenarios (including at sea) and for the various regions. The next stage, completed in 1974, drew together conclusions from the various analyses. The conclusions of these studies, with only a few limited and minor exceptions, pointed in the same direction: if the Soviet Union responded in kind without raising the stakes any higher, then neither side would have gained a significant military advantage. At best a pause in the fighting might result while both sides took stock and wondered once more about a political solution. At worst the Warsaw Pact would find itself in an even more favourable military position because it would be better placed to take advantage of its extra quantities of reserves and shorter reinforcement routes. According to Legge, the study was drawn to the conclusion that if the initial signal had failed adequately to convey the twin messages of NATO's determination to resist and the risks involved in continuing the conflict, then the signal would have to be repeated in a pre-emptory manner.[19]

This left NATO's TNW strategy perilously dependent on the success of the initial employment in persuading the Soviet Union to withdraw or at least not to retaliate.[20] If the invasion continued, then the only follow-on strategy was a better signal, conveying more forcefully a determination to resist. It was like attempting to communicate with an uncomprehending foreigner. If at first communication fails, then try again, only this time use simpler language and speak more loudly. Unfortunately experience warns that this is not always successful; what starts as an exercise in communication can end up with frustrated and mindless shouting.

NATO was in danger of becoming dependent on the strategic equivalent of a tantrum. The studies demonstrated that there was little prospect of turning the tide of war by a few or even many well-placed TNWs. So somehow the Soviet Union had to be convinced that nuclear escalation would take place even though there was no immediate practical military purpose. By controlled and deliberate initial nuclear use, NATO certainly would signal that it was willing to use nuclear weapons but not necessarily that it was enraged enough that deliberation and control would be forgotten, with escalation proceeding to a

The Wilderness Years

suicidal conclusion. By failing to take advantage of the opportunities to make maximum military advantage out of the 'first shots' — something that Soviet strategists have indicated that they would do — NATO could signal no more than that it was confused and not attempting to achieve a decisive military victory.

But, whatever NATO might think it was doing, could it really afford to try to communicate a warning of ultimate dangers rather than an attempt to exploit immediate battlefield opportunities? If the only circumstances in which nuclear use would be considered were those in which NATO was suffering conventional defeat, would it then be feasible to ignore any chance of reversing that defeat? The signal had to shock the enemy, so it could not be tentative. It had to hit military rather than civilian targets if it was not to escalate into wholly undesirable directions, so how discreet could it be? The image of 'the signal' as the first limited stage of a process of escalation might therefore be illusory. By any standards it could involve large-scale nuclear use. Otherwise it might fail to impress the enemy of a seriousness of intent while offering him the excuse to indulge in nuclear strikes according to his own theories. This point was made forcefully by those from the United States anxious to extract the maximum military utility from nuclear use. It was argued that preparations for widespread employment would have an imposing deterrent effect. Yet apart from European distaste at the prospect of becoming a nuclear battlefield, effective military use of nuclear weapons would have to come early on in the campaign while the enemy forces were still concentrated and not dispersed all over friendly territory, and this would contradict the other American objective of delaying first use.

The fact that a nuclear war-winning strategy appeared implausible did not make the signalling strategy convincing. It was, however, the only option that might make sense of the competing pressures on NATO's nuclear policy. It satisfied the need for a first-use option without appearing reckless. It could create uncertainty in Soviet perceptions even if it could provide no certainties for NATO planners. What it could not do was provide detailed operational guidance nor provide a definitive answer to all queries as to the quality of NATO'S position.

The Debate Renewed

NATO had now embraced a rather awkward and highly political concept to guide its initial use of TNWs. There was great uncertainty as to what might follow if this failed in application. A number of straightforward military options were available but none had straightforward military consequences. Meanwhile, the stockpile of 7,000 weapons remained in place.

In the early 1970s, out of the glare of public attention, there were definite stirrings in the American strategic community. Studies began to appear questioning the wisdom of existing deployments and the validity of NATO doctrine. In 1973 the Senate Foreign Relations Committee held hearings on the subject which served to draw attention to the ambiguities in NATO doctrine. All this reached a head in April 1974 when the United States Senate, at the instigation of Senator Nunn, asked the Department of Defense to prepare a report on the subject.

One reason for the renewed attention was change in the strategic environment. The Soviet achievement of numerical parity with the United States in strategic nuclear forces and its consolidation in SALT made all forces at lower levels seem more important. The start of MBFR talks in Vienna in 1973 focussed attention on to the composition of forces on the central front. In an atmosphere of détente, attention was being paid to all systems that could be deemed surplus to requirements. Furthermore, the discussion of alternative forms of targeting policy for American strategic forces, associated with Secretary of Defense James Schlesinger, encouraged discussion of how this might affect all nuclear weapons. However, the main stimulus to renewed debate appears to have been the wholly unsatisfactory nature of TNW policy.

By 1974 two distinct schools of thought had emerged in the United States. They reflected the alternative theories of deterrence by denial or by punishment. The first argued that the best form of deterrence was to deny to the Soviet Union the possibility of successful invasion. This could not be achieved by inferior conventional forces nor by an incredible strategic nuclear threat; hence the only answer was to bolster forward defences with nuclear fire-power. This nuclear fire-power need not suffer the disadvantages of the current stockpile in threatening to devastate the territory being defended if it were modernised to take advantage of new technologies of precision guidance and of small-yield, 'clean' and tailored nuclear munitions. So long as collateral damage could be kept to a minimum, it was assumed that Europeans would find a war-fighting option with these improved munitions acceptable.[21] The SACEUR, General Goodpaster, for example, while insisting in 1973 that political acceptability was necessary if new systems were to be introduced, also observed that 'the notion of an automatic and certain connection [between tactical and strategic nuclear weapons] such that any use would certainly be followed by use at the full scale — that concept of coupling — goes too far'.[22] This was hardly a statement likely to make the gaining of acceptability any easier.

The opposing view saw the existing stockpile of 7,000 warheads as excessive, and advocated reductions and rationalisation. The objective was to strengthen the fire-break by removing vulnerable forward storage sites and weapons, such as nuclear artillery, likely to blur the divide between conventional and nuclear forces. According to this view, TNWs were no substitute for a conventional defence; they could only serve to warn of escalation and to insure against a Soviet attempt to initiate nuclear war at this level.[23]

Within the American administration there were supporters of both schools. In the weapons laboratories work was well under way on new generations of smaller and 'cleaner' nuclear weapons designed to confine damage to a specific target area. Reports in 1972 suggested that Secretary of Defense Melvin Laird was inclined to move in this direction. In 1973 the United States Army initiated a study to 're-examine' nuclear warhead requirements for artillery projectiles with reduction of collateral damage as one objective.[24] In early 1974 the director of the Los Alamos laboratory, Dr Harold Agnew, was described as 'aggressively trying to influence the Defense Department to consider using these . . . weapons which could be very decisive on a battlefield, yet would limit collateral damage that is usually associated with nuclear weapons'.[25] Those of this persuasion criticised the NPG studies for failing to take account of the new technologies.

In particular, there was great interest in the prospects for enhanced radiation weapons offering, it was claimed, the ability to disable tank crews with a minimum of damage to the surroundings. In 1973 the Joint Committee on Atomic Energy had refused to authorise two new artillery warheads proposed by the Army on the grounds that the new nuclear warheads would just, rather expensively, reproduce the faults of those that they were replacing. Congress seemed to think that expenditure on TNWs was worthwhile only if it resulted in substantial qualitative improvements.[26] In practice there was pressure to introduce the means to implement the war-fighting concept irrespective of the adoption of the concept. Work on new generations of nuclear weapons had been under way, in low key, in the late 1960s and then more vigorously in the early 1970s. Those responsible now felt that this work should be exploited if for no other reason than that the existing stockpile was approaching obsolescence.

James Schlesinger, who became Secretary of Defense in late 1973, was if anything more inclined towards the second view — that the TNW stockpile was excessive and that its primary purpose was to threaten escalation. Press reports suggested that he did not believe that a clear threshold could be established between tactical and strategic weapons so as to make the war-fighting concept feasible, and that the existing disposition of weapons, including vulnerable storage sites and aircraft on Quick Reaction Alert, might encourage a premature and unnecessary step over the conventional-nuclear threshold.[27]

The difficulty was that neither option really appealed to the Europeans (or at least to those officials representing the European position) who by and large were far less dissatisfied with the status quo. In the continuing discussions concerning the pre-positioning of atomic demolition munitions and the unease over plans for use of nuclear artillery based on German soil (agreed only in 1974), the West Germans had indicated their distaste for any deployments that would make early nuclear use virtually automatic. As Laurence Martin explained: 'While many Europeans are happy to exploit the deterrent aura of nuclear weapons in peacetime, they do not necessarily prefer a nuclear defence to a conventional one if war comes.'[28]

In its 1976 Defence White Paper, the West German government confirmed that they were in no danger of being converted to a war-fighting view: 'The initial use of nuclear weapons is not intended so much to bring about a military decision as to achieve political effect.'[29] In a rehearsal for later arguments on the 'neutron bomb', active pro-disarmament groups in Europe had expressed concern about 'mini-nukes', and the American Ambassador to the Conference of the Committee on Disarmament at Geneva even went so far as to issue a statement that the United States would not develop a new generation of miniaturised nuclear weapons for use on a battlefield![30] However, the statement reflected a desire not to tamper with the nuclear fire-break more than real intentions with regard to weapons development.

Meanwhile Schlesinger himself showed an interest in breaking down the tactical-strategic threshold by developing limited options for central strategic systems that could be used to influence the course of events on the Central Front. He was tempted by the possibility of using the new technology of precision guidance for new generations of strategic weapons to attack targets relevant to a land war in Europe while new conventional weapons could deal more effectively than their predecessors with the initial stages of a Soviet attack. Furthermore, he was thinking very much in the tradition of 'demonstrative' attacks.[31]

Scheslinger was moving towards something that was in principle much more 'coupling' than previous doctrines by being prepared to offer a direct link to American strategic forces in the defence of Europe, without the intermediate stage of TNWs. Meanwhile, improvements in conventional forces would obviate the need to contemplate TNWs as alternatives to conventional inferiority. The need for nuclear weapons in Europe was therefore diminishing.

At this point, however, the other side of the European view came into play. The importance of TNWs was not what they signalled to the USSR about American intentions, but what they signalled to the allies about American intentions. The fact that the stockpile had reached 7,000 was irrelevant in itself. What mattered was that this number had become symbolic of the American commitment. Lower the number and the Europeans would see a lowered commitment.

It is unclear just to what extent European officials and leaders actually did think this way. The Dutch were already becoming unsure about the state of the nuclear arsenal in Europe. European strategic analysts were not wholly attached to the figure of 7,000 weapons and indeed had expressed doubts to McNamara while the arsenal was growing in the 1960s. The figure was far more than needed for signalling. There is little public evidence of any alarm at the prospect of reductions. Perhaps the recent experience with the Mansfield Amendment made Europeans suspicious of the motives of any proposals for reduced forces: each year since 1966, Senator Mike Mansfield had introduced proposals into the Senate calling for substantial reductions in American troops in Europe, and in 1971 his proposals came close to being adopted. Perhaps European officials, in the absence of any evidence of great interest from their political masters, reacted automatically. Perhaps —and this seems the most likely — the State Department anticipated European views without pushing very hard to see if they might be susceptible to change.[32] Early in the debate, in testimony to the Senate Foreign Relations Committee in April 1974, Secretary Schlesinger had said that the number of 7,000 warheads, while not 'immutable', was associated with 'diplomatic reasons'. At any rate, during the course of 1974 it soon became clear that the stockpile was not to be significantly altered. The December 1974 meeting of the NPG discussed the Congressional request for an examination of the TNW doctrine. A brief comment — '[Ministers] agreed on the continuing importance of such weapons within the NATO strategy of deterrence' —indicates the conservatism of the discussion.[33]

Secretary Schlesinger presented his report to Congress in 1975 on

60 *The Wilderness Years*

what had now become described as 'theatre nuclear weapons'. The report was a victory for the *status quo*. It gave little comfort both to the war-fighters and to the cutters. The report mentioned a series of improvement programmes already under way and indicated a readiness to modernise the arsenal, observing that its credibility for deterrent purposes would be enhanced 'if the targeting and characteristics of these weapons reduce collateral damage to civilian structures and population'. However this had to be 'without removing the ultimate deterrent value of the fear of escalation, involving US strategic forces'. The concept for initial employment reflected the established NATO guidelines of a political signal: 'First use should be clearly limited and defensive in nature, so as to reduce the risks of escalation. However, the attack should be delivered with sufficient shocks and decisiveness to forcibly change the perceptions of WP leaders and create a situation conducive to negotiations.' When it came to explaining the maintenance of nuclear weapons in Europe 'the most important reason' given was that they were 'a visible symbol to Allies and adversaries of the US commitment to provide for Europe's nuclear defence'.[34]

Beginning to Accommodate New Technologies

If the doctrine and the numbers were not to be significantly altered, then the only area for change was the composition and quality of the arsenal. With the obsolescence of the American arsenal becoming a problem and their own nuclear capable systems due for renewal, the Europeans could not object to an examination of how best to modernise the arsenal. In November 1973, after the flutter over the 'mini-nukes' and with pressure from within the United States to study seriously the potential of the new technologies, two NPG studies were authorised. Both were under American chairmanship with Britain leading the Military Implications Team and Germany the Political Implications Team. With all sorts of proposals being considered in Washington, the only way for the Europeans to keep NATO on the straight and narrow was to agree to a study of modernisation.

At the NPG meeting in June 1974, there was a 'preliminary exchange of views' on 'possible ways in which technological improvements might affect NATO's deterrent posture and defence capabilities', based on a briefing by Secretary Schlesinger.[35] After the December 1974 NPG meeting the British Secretary of Defence Roy Mason observed that 'Britain would go along with any American reassessment of the tactical nuclear stockpile in the interests of greater accuracy and warhead yield.'[36] In June 1975, in discussing the report to Congress on theatre nuclear forces, the NPG reviewed possible force improvements and this was taken up by Schlesinger's successor, Donald Rumsfeld, in 1976.

The conclusion of the Military Implications Team, which reported in November 1976, was that NATO should exploit the new technologies to prevent the Soviet Union from gaining a unilateral advantage, but the net result was unlikely to affect measurably the probable outcome of a European war. The Political Implications Team, reporting the next June, endorsed this view. Legge describes the main significance of the exercise as a further rebuff to the war-fighting school.[37] However, while not endorsing the views of the war-fighters, the studies did not argue against the introduction of much of the new weaponry required by this school. The point about signalling was that it provided few guidelines for the development of a total force structure. This awkward question of the relationship between doctrine and forces was taken up by the High-Level Group which was established at the June 1977 meeting initially to deal with the nuclear aspects of the Long-Term Defence Programme.

It is reasonably clear that the NPG had no authority over American theatre nuclear programmes. By the time that it got round to discussing the new technologies many of the relevant programmes had already been set in motion. The Senate Foreign Relations Committee had observed in 1973 that while United States military officers definitely favoured 'mini-nukes', the same NATO officials had told them that 'the United States had thus far sought to avoid serious discussion of the issue using the rationale that US policy and law precludes the discussion of new weapons before deployment is a practical possibility'.[38]

From the communiqués of the NPG it was not easy to identify exactly what was going on. However, certain criteria seemed to have guided its work. Firstly, there was no desire to lose the fire-break: 'the clear distinction between nuclear and conventional weapons should be maintained'.[39] Secondly, the NPG was keener to see work under way on problems of local security and vulnerability than on selective targeting options, or at least it sought to give that impression.[40] Thirdly, there seems to have been a greater willingness to push forward with improvements on shorter-range rather than the longer-range systems. Enhanced radiation weapons were very much part of this though they attracted slight publicity at the time.[41]

Much of the evidence for this is circumstantial; for example, the communiqués mention work on 'nuclear artillery systems' but little else.[42] More concrete evidence comes from the major initiative taken by NATO at this time — the so-called Option III put forward by the alliance in late 1975 at the Vienna MBFR talks. The idea of offering cuts in nuclear systems as a trade for substantial reductions in Warsaw Pact conventional capabilities had been around since 1972. In late 1974 the Dutch had advocated putting such a proposal on the table but found little support, partly because of how it might be read in the context of the current debate on NATO's overall TNF posture.[43] In December 1975 with NATO's policy apparently settled and MBFR in need of some stimulus, Option III was tentatively put forward. Specifically it offered cuts of 54 nuclear-capable F-4 Phantom aircraft and 36 Pershing short-range missile launchers, along with 1,000 warheads, from American forces in Germany if a Soviet tank army of 68,000 men and 1,700 tanks was removed in return.

Our interest here is not in this proposal as arms control but for what it reveals about thinking in NATO. The 1,000 warheads were widely recognised to be assigned to Honest John missiles and other systems that were due for removal. NATO was storing substantially more warheads than it could actually use. More significant was the offer on delivery systems because, although it was not as restrictive as it first seemed, it did envisage the removal of key systems from a relatively limited component of the total force structure. Furthermore, these were not systems designed to meet the 'tank threat' that the Warsaw Pact was being asked to reduce, while no limitations were being asked for on comparable Soviet systems which were then already being improved. The assumption appeared to be that because the Soviet Union seemed to find these forces threatening they might give up something in return. The Soviet Union had always identified the F-4s as part of the American strategic threat. Lothar Ruehl suggests that, while the USSR may have been impressed by this threat, NATO was less impressed. Improvements in Soviet forces were raising doubts as to the survivability of these systems and the ability of the F-4 to penetrate air defences.[44] When coupled with the fact that the only system withdrawn without replacement since the early 1960s was the 2,000-km Mace cruise missiles (in 1969), and with the stress on survivability in official documents, there is a clear indication of a disposition to phase out the larger, and therefore less mobile, ground-launched systems.

It is of note that the only action on longer-range systems was 'the idea of committing more Poseidons to NATO, recognising the unique

The Wilderness Years

survival characteristics of the submerged systems'.[45] This was mentioned in Schlesinger's 1975 report. Towards the end of our period a second measure was taken when it was announced in October 1976 that a second wing of F-111 strike aircraft was to be based in Britain. By now the involvement of European-based systems in SALT[46] and the growth of the Soviet long-range theatre force with SS-20s and Backfire bombers was forcing this question onto the agenda.

New Stirrings

In 1977 a completely new phase in alliance decision-making on TNF began. Official discussions became more intensive and policies bolder, while the broad issues connected with the basing of nuclear weapons in Europe moved to the centre of public debate. Theatre nuclear forces moved out of the political wilderness.

The analysis in this chapter suggests that the years in the wilderness had not been particularly profitable. The set of compromises enshrined in 1967 in the doctrine of flexible response were reinforced, and an unwarranted amount of symbolism was allowed to become attached to a stockpile of weapons whose military role remained uncertain. The only source of change was the ageing of the arsenal and the availability of new designs.

The main research work had been on improvements to the short-range systems, such as nuclear artillery. This had important consequences. Firstly, it drew attention to the dangers of blurring the conventional-nuclear fire-break. Despite their previous distrust of this concept, Europeans found themselves anxious to see it sustained. Secondly, the preoccupation with short-range systems led to a neglect of the long-range systems. The tendency to put more emphasis on sea-based systems meant there was little preparation for the post-1977 requirement for ground-launched long-range TNF.

In 1974 there had been an opportunity for a radical restructuring of NATO's theatre nuclear forces but it was not taken. One of those participating wrote at the time how some of the alternatives proposed were 'politically naive and totally unaware of the domestic, political environment of the NATO allies'.[47] Yet the circumstances of the mid-1970s were more propitious than those later in the decade. Public, as opposed to official, anxieties over the role of nuclear weapons was not yet in evidence, forestalled by relatively cheerful East-West relations and prospects for arms control, especially SALT II. Yet relative calm also meant a lack of urgency. The aimless debate continued until external events redirected it. When they did, what seemed naive was the presumption of the mid-1970s that the nuclear issue would remain a debate among the ingrained orthodoxies of the responsible national officials.

Notes

1. See L. Freedman, *Evolution of Nuclear Strategy* (London: Macmillan, 1981). Section 3.
2. Michael Howard, 'The Classical Strategists' in Alastair Buchan (ed.), *Problems of Modern Strategy* (London: Chatto & Windus, 1970), p. 62.
3. This critique is developed with the greatest clarity in Alain C. Enthoven and K. Wayne Smith, *How Much is Enough? Shaping the Defense Program 1961-1969* (New York: Harper & Row, 1971), pp. 124-32.
4. Although this is presented here as a 'European' viewpoint, it is best expressed by an American, Bernard Brodie, in *Escalation and the Nuclear Option* (Princeton: Princeton University Press, 1969).
5. See Chapter 1. Mace was removed in 1969.
6. Enthoven and Smith, *How Much is Enough?* p. 128. Michael Legge, however, suggests that the Europeans were, if anything, concerned over the growth of the stockpile under McNamara rather than the prospects for its contraction: see J. Michael Legge, *Theater Nuclear Weapons and the NATO Strategy of Flexible Response*, R-2964-ff (Santa Monica:The Rand Corporation, April 1983), p. 32.
7. Uwe Nerlich, 'Theatre Nuclear Forces in Europe' in Kenneth A. Myers (ed.), *NATO: The Next Thirty Years* (Boulder, Colo.: The Westview Press, 1980).
8. See, for example, Colin Gray, 'Deterrence and Defence in Europe: Revising NATO's Theatre Nuclear Posture', *Journal of the Royal United Services Institute* (December 1974): 'NATO's military commanders are fully aware of the fact that in the event of war their political masters must be expected to go to almost any lengths to avoid nuclear use.'
9. Richard Hart Sinnreich, 'NATO's Evolving Nuclear Strategy', *Orbis*, vol. 19, no. 2 (Summer 1975), 466.
10. The permanent members of the NPG were Germany, Italy, the United Kingdom and the United States with Belgium, Canada, Denmark, Greece, the Netherlands, Norway and Turkey rotating as members on an eighteen-monthly basis. Portugal left the NPG in the sensitive period just after its 1974 revolution. For background see Legge, *Theater Nuclear Weapons*, and Paul Buteaux, *The Politics of Nuclear Consultation in NATO* (Cambridge: Cambridge University Press, 1983).
11. Harvey B. Seim, 'Nuclear Policy-Making in NATO', *NATO Review*, no. 6 (Winter 1973).
12. Legge, *Theater Nuclear Weapons*, p. 19.
13. Henry Kissinger, *The White House Years* (London: Weidenfeld & Nicolson, 1979), pp. 218-20.
14. Healey was saying similar things in public at the time. See Denis Healey, 'NATO, Britain and Soviet Military Policy', *Orbis*, vol. 13, no. 1 (1969), pp. 48-59.
15. Legge, *Theater Nuclear Weapons*, pp. 18-19. In a curious episode in 1981 Secretary of State Haig confirmed the existence of 'contingency plans in the

NATO doctrine to fire a nuclear weapon ... to demonstrate to the other side they are exceeding the limits of toleration in the conventional areas – all designed to maintain violence at the lowest possible level'. His colleague, Secretary of Defense Caspar Weinberger then told a Senate Committee: 'There is absolutely nothing in any of the plans that I know of that contains anything remotely resembling it – nor should there be.' In supporting Haig's interpretation a British Foreign Office spokesman used language that mighthave been taken directly from a submission to the NPG in 1969, observing that NATO plans embraced actions that 'would be intended to halt hostilities as quickly as possible by demonstrating to the aggressor that the West was determined to resist and that further aggression would have dire consequences', (see *International Herald Tribune*, 6 November 1981). The most charitable explanation of Weinberger's ignorance is that he had been made so aware of the sensitivity of public opinion to notions of limited nuclear war during a recent visit that he was anxious to play the issue down – even if this meant denying what had been taken in NATO circles to be the 'European' approach to TNW employment.

16. Legge, *Theater Nuclear Weapons*, p. 20; Buteaux, *Politics of Nuclear Consultation*, p. 102.

17. See, for example, the testimony of SACEUR, General Andrew Goodpaster, to the hearings of the Subcommittee on Military Applications of the Joint Committee on Atomic Energy, *Military Applications of Nuclear Technology* (29 June 1973). 'Those nuclear weapons that carry the highest escalatory effect are the ones that one would be most reluctant to use,' p. 126.

18. Wolfgang Heisenberg, *The Alliance and Europe. Part 1: Crisis Stability in Europe and Theatre Nuclear Weapons*, Adelphi Paper, no. 96 (Summer 1973), p. 3. See also M. Leitenberg, 'Background Materials in Tactical Nuclear Weapons' in Stockholm International Peace Research Institute, *Tactical NuclearWeapons: European Perspectives* (London: Taylor & Francis, 1978).

19. Legge, *Theater Nuclear Weapons*, p. 27.

20. In 1973 when Senator Symington asked if 'the Soviets in all probability would not respond to nuclear weapons' used by the United States in Europe, General Goodpaster replied: 'I would not go so far as to say in all probability ... I think there is an appreciable possibility that they would not.' (Subcommittee on Military Applications of JCAE, *Military Applications of Nuclear Technology*, p. 101.)

21. An early statement of this view is found in two articles by Robert M. Lawrence, 'On Tactical Nuclear War', in *Revue générale militaire*, January and February, 1971. See also General James Polk, 'The Realities of Tactical Nuclear Warfare', *Orbis* (Summer 1973).

22. Subcommittee on Military Applications of JCAE, *Military Applications of Nuclear Technology*, p. 120.

23. See testimony of most of the non-official participants (Stanley Hoffmann, Morton Halperin, Alain Enthoven) in hearings before subcommittees of the Senate Foreign Relations Committee, *Nuclear Weapons and Foreign Policy* (7 March, 14 March and 4 April 1974). Also Jeffrey Record, *US Nuclear Weapons in Europe – Issues and Alternatives* (Washington, DC: The Brookings Institution, 1974).

24. Sherri L.Wasserman, *The Neutron Bomb Controversy: A Study in Alliance Politics* (New York: Praeger, 1983), pp. 30-1.

25. William Beecher, 'Over the Threshold: "Clean" Tactical Nuclear Weapons for Europe', *Army* (July 1972); Walter Pincus, 'A New Generation of Weaponry – Why More Nukes', *New Republic* (9 February 1974).

26. S.T. Cohen, *The Neutron Bomb: Political, Technological and Military Issues* (Cambridge, Mass. Institute for Foreign Policy Analysis, Inc., November 1978),

pp. 32-4.

27. See Leitenberg, 'Background Materials', pp. 38-9.

28. Laurence Martin, 'Theater Nuclear Weapons and Europe', *Survival*, vol. 16, no. 6 (November/December 1974), p. 271.

29. *White Paper 1975/76* (Ministry of Defence, Government of the FRG, 1976), p. 38.

30. This story arose out of a story in *The Times* (London) on 7 May 1973. It was a matter of definition, but weapons with an extremely small yield had been around for some time (i.e., the Davy Crockett bazooka).

31. This interpretation of the 'Schlesinger doctrine' has been developed in Freedman, *Evolution of Nuclear Strategy*, pp. 377-87.

32. This appears to be Legge's view.

33. *NATO Nuclear Planning Group Communiqué* (Brussels, 10 December 1974).

34. Report to Congress by Secretary of Defence James Schlesinger, *The Theatre Nuclear Force Posture in Europe*, reprinted in *Survival*, vol. 17, no. 5 (September/October 1975), pp. 235-41.

35. See Johan Jorgen Holst, 'Flexible Options in Alliance Strategy', in Johan Jorgen Holst and Uwe Nerlich (eds.), *Beyond Nuclear Deterrence: New Aims, New Arms* (London: Macdonald & James, 1977), p. 270. Holst noted that the NPG had become 'the repositors of orthodox position' and added: 'Should the policy assessments be confined to the somewhat cumbersome procedures of the NPG, strong propensities would be operating in favour of changes that are at best marginal, natural extensions of existing capabilities . . . ' p. 271.

36. Quoted by Leitenberg, 'Background Materials', p. 57.

37. Legge, *Theater Nuclear Weapons*, p. 31.

38. United States Congress, Subcommittee on US Security Arrangements and Commitments Abroad of the Senate Committee on Foreign Relations, *Report on US Security Issues in Europe: Border Sharing and Offset, MBFR and Nuclear Weapons* (12 December 1973), p. 22.

39. *NATO Nuclear Planning Group Final Communiqué* (London, 18 November 1976).

40. For example, see Richard Shearer, 'Nuclear Weapons and the Defence of Europe', *NATO Review* (December 1975). Shearer was then NATO's Director for Nuclear Planning.

41. Wasserman, *The Neutron Bomb*, p. 33. In November 1976 President Ford signed a bill approving a report by ERDA to fund research and development of enhanced radiation weapons.

42. *NATO Nuclear Planning Group Final Communiqué* (Oslo, 20-21 May 1976).

43. For background see Buteaux, *Politics of Nuclear Consultation*, pp. 148-9.

44. Lothar Ruehl, *MBFR Lessons and Problems*, Adelphi Paper, no. 176 (London: IISS, 1972), pp. 15-17.

45. Shearer, 'Nuclear Weapons', p. 14.

46. The involvement of European systems in strategic arms control during this period has been discussed in Freedman, 'Negotiations on Nuclear Forces in Europe, 1969-1983' in Hans-Henrik Holm and Nikolaj Petersen (eds.), *The European Missile Crisis: Nuclear Weapons and Security Policy* (London: Frances Pinter, 1983).

47. Shearer, 'Nuclear Weapons', p. 13.

3 NATO THEATRE NUCLEAR FORCES: THE THIRD PHASE 1977-85

Jeffrey H. Boutwell

Coping with Parity

In 1977, the NATO alliance entered a third phase regarding the role of theatre nuclear forces (TNF) in the Western deterrent strategy. The quiescence of the previous decade, the product of the adoption of flexible response as NATO doctrine and of the East-West détente of the 1970s, was about to be shattered. TNF were set to 'come out of the political wilderness' with a vengeance.

Ironically, the two major security issues before the alliance in the first six months of 1977 gave little inkling of how important the complex of TNF issues would become. Firstly, the Carter administration was preoccupied with strategic arms control, as evidenced by the Vance deep-cut SALT proposals of March 1977. Secondly, there was the NATO initiative on conventional-force improvements, inaugurated in May 1977 as the Long-Term Defence Programme. Both of these suggested that the alliance would continue to focus most on the two extremes of the deterrence spectrum, strategic nuclear and conventional forces, with TNF remaining as an amorphous 'grey area' somewhere in between.

Within a matter of months, however, both strategic nuclear and conventional-force issues were overshadowed by two of the most contentious issues ever to face the alliance: enhanced radiation weapons (ERW) and intermediate nuclear forces (INF). From 1977, when the neutron bomb issue first appeared, until well into the 1980s, when hundreds of thousands of West Europeans and Americans were protesting against the deployment of Pershing and cruise missiles in Western Europe, these two issues were the centre of heated debate within the alliance.

Yet initially both of these theatre nuclear force issues had their origins in debates that focused on these extremes – strategic nuclear and conventional forces. At the upper end of the TNF spectrum, the modernisation of INF, decided upon in December 1979, was seen as strengthening the coupling of NATO forces to American strategic forces, a coupling that, many argued, had been called into question by the onset of US-Soviet strategic parity. From at least the late 1960s, when the Soviet Union began to reach that parity with the United States, there was growing concern within the alliance that parity would neutralise American strategic forces, thus decoupling Western Europe from the United States.

At the lower end of the spectrum, enhanced radiation weapons were touted as providing a useable nuclear capability that could offset what was generally perceived to be a Warsaw Pact superiority in conventional forces. Given that the neutron bomb might be effective against Soviet tank formations while causing limited collateral damage, it was thought that ERW deployment could compensate for NATO's chronic inability to greatly strengthen its own conventional forces.

Gradually, however, the debate over ERW and INF widened to include a broader range of TNF issues. Indeed, it was only after these two issues had propelled the entire TNF question out into the open that the members of the alliance began seriously to consider the very rationale of TNF in NATO strategy. As a result, by the 1980s general questions — NATO nuclear doctrine, public fears of limited nuclear war, and the NATO strategy of possible first use of nuclear weapons — had overshadowed the specific ERW and INF issues. In this climate, there were numerous proposals in the early 1980s for strengthening NATO conventional forces in order to reduce, if not eliminate entirely, NATO's reliance on theatre nuclear weapons.

In essence, the NATO doctrine of flexible response, with its central component of possible first use of nuclear weapons, had become the centrepiece of the debate. Although narrowly focused deployment and arms-control considerations surrounding ERW and INF were the focuses of attention in the late 1970s, the emphasis in the early 1980s had shifted to the core issue — the utility of theatre nuclear weapons in alliance strategy. No longer were issues of force structure (ERW and INF) pushing NATO doctrine. By the mid-1980s, the relationship between doctrine and force posture was reversed. To a great extent, the debate touched off by ERW and INF had, within the space of a few years, widened to encompass the strategy of flexible response on which the alliance had been relying since the 1960s.

Thus, there was a silver lining to the considerable internal divisions brought on by the ERW and INF issues. No longer were individual TNF systems promoted as providing military solutions to the political dilemmas inherent in NATO strategy. That strategy itself had become open to discussion. To be sure, there had been some questioning of flexible response even during the 'years in the wilderness', as Lawrence

NATO TNF: The Third Phase, 1977-85

Freedman noted in Chapter 2. In 1974, for example, Defense Secretary James Schlesinger had initiated a wide-ranging review of the implications of Soviet strategic parity for NATO's TNF posture.

This theme was picked up in May 1977 when West German Chancellor Helmut Schmidt pointedly referred to the implications of superpower parity in a speech given at the NATO heads-of-government meeting in London. In private remarks that were later made public on Schmidt's insistence, the Chancellor emphasised how the onset of strategic parity had ushered in a third phase in East-West military relations. No longer, Schmidt argued, could the alliance rely on the deterrent capabilities of superior American strategic forces, as in the 1950s, or on the flexible-response strategy of the 1960s and 1970s. Rather, Soviet attainment of strategic parity had brought on this third phase, 'making it necessary during the coming years, at least within the Atlantic and European framework, to reduce the political and military role of strategic nuclear weapons as a normal component of our defense and deterrence . . .'[1]

Schmidt was certainly not the first to recognise the importance of Soviet strategic parity for the NATO deterrent; de Gaulle and Adenauer had appreciated its significance as early as the 1950s (see Chapter 1). Nor was he the last. In September 1979, Henry Kissinger also scathingly criticised the viability of the American nuclear guarantee to Western Europe. In a speech to a high-level gathering of political and military officials in Brussels, Kissinger maintained that NATO could no longer rely on the 'ladder of escalation' inherent in the flexible-response strategy. The only option left to an American President once a conflict escalated to the strategic level would be to choose between annihilation and capitulation: 'Of course, the US president will threaten massive destruction in a crisis, but will he do it? We must face the fact that it is absurd to base the strategy of the West on the credibility of mutual suicide.'[2]

Although Schmidt's remarks in 1977 received nowhere near as much publicity as Kissinger's, they were none the less as important, coming as they did from a European head of government. The Chancellor's statement that 'the strategic nuclear component will become increasingly regarded as an instrument of last resort, to serve the national interest and protect the survival of those who possess these weapons of last resort'[3] presaged Kissinger in dismissing the utility of American strategic forces to provide anything other than deterrence of a Soviet strike against the American homeland. To offset this decline in the ability of the United States to provide extended deterrence, Schmidt initially stressed the need for establishing a conventional-force balance in Europe, through both force modernisation (the Long-Term Defence Programme) and arms control (at the MBFR talks in Vienna). Later, in his now famous speech given at the International Institute for Strategic Studies in London in October1977, Schmidt pointed as well to the dangers of superpower strategic parity for the European theatre nuclear balance.

The Neutron Bomb and the Euromissiles

Whatever chance there might have been for re-examining NATO's flexible-response strategy in the spring of 1977 soon disappeared, however, as the alliance found itself caught up in the furore over the neutron bomb. Less than a month after the NATO summit in London, a story in the *Washington Post* on 5 June 1977 reported that the Carter administration had given the go-ahead to the Department of Energy to begin producing enhanced radiation warheads for short-range tactical nuclear delivery systems.[4] Designed primarily for use in the European theatre against massed Soviet tank formations, the neutron warhead was seen by many as providing a needed corrective to NATO's conventional-force deficiencies.

Although President Carter had made no firm decision to proceed with full-scale production of neutron warheads, preferring first to gain European acceptance for their deployment, the news that ERW components were being produced sparked off a massive debate first in the United States, then in Western Europe. The fact that ERW are designed to limit blast effects while increasing prompt nuclear radiation, led many Europeans, as well as the Soviets, to portray them as the ultimate capitalist weapon: one that would kill people while leaving property intact. Egon Bahr of the West German Social Democratic Party called the weapon 'a perversion of human thought',[5] while the German weekly news Magazine *Der Spiegel* ran a cover story on ERW satirically entitled 'Neutron Bomb: America's Wonder Weapon for Europe'.[6] In West Germany and the Netherlands especially, hundreds of thousands of demonstrators took to the streets to protest against what many regarded, naively, as an American attempt to find a means of limiting any future nuclear war to Europe.

Ultimately, the political difficulties of deploying ERW led President Carter in April 1978 to defer production of ERW components,[7] and the neutron warhead issue faded from view. Yet it surfaced again in the summer of 1981 when the Reagan administration decided to proceed with production of ERW components, but to stockpile them in the United States, not Western Europe.[8]

In looking back at the ERW debate of 1977-8, it is ironic that, so soon after the alliance had declared its intention to bolster its conventional forces through the Long-Term Defence Programme, the major issue should have become the means (ERW) by which NATO could substitute nuclear weapons precisely to make up for its conventional-force deficiencies. Not until 1982 could the alliance again concentrate on the central issue of strengthening its conventional deterrent, spurred in large part by the issue of 'no first use' and the possibilities for raising the nuclear threshold in Europe.

By the time the furore over ERW had subsided in 1978, the alliance was already in the process of deciding its next major theatre nuclear weapons issue, that of modernising its intermediate-range nuclear systems (INF). Here again, political concerns were paramount, not least because of the intra-alliance strains produced by the ERW episode. Having backed away from deploying ERW in the face of a massive Soviet propaganda campaign, alliance leaders, especially in Washington, did not want to flinch again. In addition, the vehement Soviet propaganda campaign against possible NATO deployment of ERW convinced many in the alliance of the need to demonstrate unity and resolve.

At the same time, the steady Soviet deployment of its new SS-20 intermediate-range ballistic missiles was cited as providing the main military rationale for NATO's acquiring a similar long-range INF capability. Specifically, the Carter administration regarded NATO INF modernisation as one way to respond to the concerns voiced by Chancellor Schmidt in his IISS speech. In that speech, Schmidt had criticised American negotiating strategy in the SALT II talks for neglecting European security concerns. In particular, the Chancellor was upset over possible restraints in providing NATO with American cruise missiles, while the SS-20 and the new Soviet Backfire bomber were left unconstrained. Accordingly, Schmidt criticised the codification of superpower parity in SALT II as magnifying 'the significance of the disparities between East and West in nuclear tactical and conventional weapons[4] . . . ' adding that 'we in Europe must be particularly careful to ensure that these [SALT] negotiations do not neglect the components of NATO's deterrent strategy'.[9]

Schmidt's remarks, delivered as they were in a highly visible public forum, crystallised alliance attention on the INF issue. To be sure, the alliance itself had recognised the need for some TNF modernisation at its London summit in May, when it included TNF as point 10 of its

Long-Term Defence Programme. At that time, however, the TNF issue took very much a back seat to the overall emphasis on the need for conventional-force improvements. The TNF modernisation under discussion was limited to the possibility of deploying a more accurate Pershing missile, without, however, extending the Pershing's range.

Thus, although the alliance's Nuclear Planning Group (NPG) had been given responsibility for studying the TNF issue, there was little movement on the issue in the summer of 1977. By the time of the NPG meeting in mid-October in Bari, Italy, however, European concerns about the need for a more serious study of the issue prompted the NPG to create a special body, the High-Level Group (HLG), to study the issue.[10] Consisting of eleven military experts from the NATO member states, and chaired by David McGiffert, US Assistant Secretary of Defense for International Security Affairs, the HLG had only been in existence for a few weeks prior to Schmidt's speech at the IISS. Yet the fact that the HLG was created before that speech indicated how pressures within NATO were building for some type of alliance response to Soviet TNF deployments.

The added visibility that the Chancellor gave to the TNF issue only served to heighten the urgency of the task laid before the HLG. Having met three more times prior to the NPG meeting of April 1978, the HLG recommended a 'need for an evolutionary adjustment in NATO's TNF which would provide more *in-theater* long-range capability than at present'.[11]

That same month, the end of the ERW affair contributed an added sense of urgency to the deliberations of the HLG, and the Carter administration itself worked on a high-level study (PRM-38) concerning NATO's long-range theatre nuclear force options. By the end of the summer, agreement within the HLG had been reached that, for political and military reasons, the alliance should adopt both a deployment and arms-control approach to re-establishing a NATO land-based missile INF capability that the alliance had not had since the 1960s. At the same time, however, the HLG rejected any attempt at establishing strict parity in Euro-strategic weapons, as this might abet perceptions of decoupling that had prompted concern over the INF issue in the first place. In contrast to those Europeans who saw NATO INF as an American means for limiting any future nuclear conflict to Europe, the HLG proposed that NATO did not have to match Soviet INF deployments equally. What was needed, however, was a convincing alliance response that would both induce the Soviets to negotiate seriously over INF systems, while providing NATO with a credible INF military capability.[12]

In carrying the American proposals to the HLG in the autumn of 1978, McGiffert laid out the various choices open to the Alliance for modernizing its nuclear forces, including: the ground-launched cruise missile (GLCM), a modernised version of the Pershing IA (The Pershing IIXR) with increased accuracy and extended range; a new MRBM, called 'Longbow' which would utilise the existing Mark 12A warhead; sea-launched cruise missiles (SLCM); and the FB-111H, an improved version of the FB-111A based in the United States. In considering these choices, the HLG was working by early 1979 under the following guidelines:[13]

1. INF modernisation should not entail any increase in the role of nuclear weapons in allied defence or any change in the strategy of flexible response.
2. There should be no change in the overall total of nuclear weapons in Western Europe.
3. There was no need for a direct matching capability to the SS-20; instead, the alliance should create an offsetting caability that provided a 'credible response'.
4. The weapon systems themselves should have as much visibility as possible, to enhance the force's deterrent value (thus a preference for land-based systems).
5. The weapons systems should strive for survivability (e.g. mobility), penetrability and accuracy.
6. There should be a mix of systems, for 'synergistic' effect (e.g., to complicate Soviet defence planning and increase NATO targeting options).

Given these guidelines, it soon became apparent which systems were preferable. The lack of visibility (and thus tangible evidence of political commitment), and expense, argued against the sea-based cruise missile. Both the F-111H and the 'Longbow' could not be operational until the mid-1980s, so the need for a timely response argued against these systems. By the spring of 1979, then, it was becoming apparent that the preferred systems were the GLCM and the Pershing IIXR. Although some in the Pentagon favoured the deployment of as many as 2000 systems, the HLG recommended a total deployment of 572 (108 Pershing II and 464 cruise missiles), which was then incorporated into the NATO INF double decision of December 1979.[14] At the same time, the NATO Brussels INF communiqué called on the Soviet Union promptly to join in arms-control negotiations on these systems.

NATO's Theatre Nuclear Force Structure

Although public attention in the late 1970s and early 1980s was focused mainly on ERW, Pershing and cruise missiles, other elements of NATO's TNF were also changing. The following summary of these systems, including both delivery vehicles and warheads, presents a general picture of alliance (including French) nuclear capabilities during the period 1977-85.[15]

Nuclear Capable Aircraft

For more than 15 years prior to the deployment of the first Pershing and cruise missiles in late 1983, the only NATO systems capable of reaching the Soviet Union (other than the American SLBMs assigned to NATO) were nuclear-capable aircraft. Although the alliance had deployed land-based missiles that could strike Soviet targets in the 1950s and 1960s (the Thor and Jupiter IRBM/MRBMs and the Mace B cruise missiles), these had all been withdrawn by the late 1960s.

In the early 1970s, the Soviet Union had attempted to include these NATO aircraft (the so-called forward-based systems, or FBS) in the SALT I talks, on the premise that any nuclear system that could reach Soviet territory should be considered 'strategic'. The FBS issue was a contentious one between the United States and USSR, but the Soviets finally dropped their demand, while reserving the right to include FBS in subsequent SALT negotiations.

At issue primarily was the American F-111 E/F strike fighter, capable of all-weather nuclear bombing: 75 of these were first deployed in Great Britain in 1969. In 1977, the Carter administration deployed an additional 91 of these aircraft in Britain, bringing the total number deployed to approximately 150.

While the F-111s constitute the main part of NATO's air-based INF, there were also 56 FB-111A strategic bombers based in the United States which could be redeployed for use in the European theatre. In addition, it was reported in October 1979 that the United States was planning to assign some 80 B-52s to NATO.[16] These would continue to be based in the United States, but could operate from European staging airfields, such as the RAF Markham airbase in the UK. At the time, it was stressed that these B-52Ds would be used in a conventional role: with each aircraft capable of carrying 20-30 tons of conventional bombs, they could increase NATO's conventional bomb delivery by some 50 per cent. This same report noted, however, that 'the aircraft have a nuclear weapons delivery capability that could add to the Alliance's theater nuclear force'. While another source has claimed that 75 B-52s have been assigned to SACEUR, there is no reason to consider these B-52s as being a part of NATO's direct nuclear capability.[17]

The comparable British intermediate-range theater bomber since 1960 has been the Vulcan. Once the centrepiece of Britain's independent nuclear force, the Vulcan bombers were assigned to SACEUR in 1970, when the UK Polaris submarine force became operational. Up to 1981, NATO could call on 56 Vulcans, 48 of which were operational. Beginning in February 1982, the Vulcan force began to be phased out, to be replaced by the multi-role but shorter-range Tornado.

The French Mirage IVA bomber, though not officially part of NATO's nuclear force, is none the less counted by the Soviets in their tabulations of the European nuclear balance. In service since 1964, there were 28 Mirage IVA bombers deployed as of 1984. In 1976 a programme was begun to extend their operational life until 1985, at which time 15 of these aircraft will be assigned to tactical roles while others will be redeployed for reconnaissance missions or taken out of service. In its tactical role, the Mirage will carry the ASMP (*air-sol moyenne portée*) standoff nuclear missile.[18]

In addition to these intermediate-range aircraft, the Alliance has a number of shorter-range dual-capable aircraft, with combat ranges extending from 150 to 1,500 km. The two primary aircraft, in service with American and allied forces, have been the F-4 and F-104, both of which were first deployed in the early 1960s. As of 1984, there were 96 F-4s deployed with American forces in Europe and a total of 131 F-4s were deployed with West German and Turkish forces. In addition, there were a total of 281 F-104s deployed with West German, Greek, Italian, Turkish and Dutch forces.

Beginning in the early 1980s, these two aircraft began to be replaced by the American F-16. As of 1984, there were 72 F-16s deployed with American forces and 178 with Belgian, Dutch, Danish and Norwegian forces.

Furthermore, the RAF in 1984 had 25 ageing Buccaneer fighter-bombers. Like the Vulcan, the Buccaneer will gradually be replaced by the Tornado, although it is possible that some aircraft will continue to be operational after 1985.[19]

Total production of the multi-role Tornado (a joint British-German-

Italian project) is expected to reach 400 aircraft, rather than the more than 500 originally envisaged. The Tornado, which can serve as either a low-level fighter-bomber or an air-superiority fighter plane, has been plagued with higher than usual cost-overruns, and the production schedule has been stretched out accordingly, to 1988-9. Britain has ordered 123 of the aircraft, West Germany and Italy have ordered 109 and 102 respectively, and the remaining aircraft will be sold on the export market. As of 1984, there were a total of 223 Tornado aircraft deployed with British, Italian and West German forces.

Finally, as of the early 1980s the French had 45 Jaguar aircraft and 30 Mirage IIIE, although both were scheduled to be replaced by the new Mirage 2000, some 200 of which were expected to be assigned a nuclear role in the 1990s.

In addition to land-based aircraft, there were some 68 A-6 and A-7 nuclear-capable ground-attack aircraft deployed on the two American Sixth Fleet aircraft carriers in the Mediterranean. Beginning in 1985, the A-7 will be replaced by the dual-capable F/A-18, and by the 1990s it is projected that the F/A-18 will comprise all United States Navy light attack squadrons.

In addition, there were some 36 French Super-Etendard nuclear-capable aircraft, based on French aircraft carriers, although it is believed that only 12 of these were available for service in the European theatre.

In evaluating NATO nuclear forces, it must be remembered that not all of the systems which are nuclear-capable are necessarily configured for a nuclear role. Thus, although there were more than 1,200 NATO and French aircraft which were designated as capable of carrying nuclear weapons, it is likely that only about 50 per cent of these were actually outfitted to do so. Thus the 1981 Defence Estimates of the United Kingdom put the number of land-based aircraft (NATO and French) that were configured for delivery of nuclear weapons at 700.[20] In 1982, this document excluded French forces, and put the number at 650, which is comparable to the figure of 600 given by NATO documents. The number of nuclear gravity bombs available to land- and sea-based NATO aircraft is reportedly well over 2,000.[21]

Short-Range Theatre Nuclear Forces

As with dual-capable aircraft, it is exceedingly difficult to determine exactly how many of the thousands of short-range (under 100 km) systems available to NATO were configured for a nuclear role. Until 1982, the only official figure for these short-range artillery and missile

Table 3.1: NATO Nuclear Capable Aircraft

System	First Deployed	Combat Radius (km)	Mach Speed	Number 1985	Deployed 1989
Long Range Aircraft					
F-111 E/F (US)	1969	1,900	2.5	150	150
Mirage IVA (FR)	1964/85	1,600	2.2	28	15
			Subtotal	178	165
Medium Range Aircraft					
F-4 (Allied)	1962	750	2.4	227	100
F-104 (Allied)	1958	800	2.2	281	0
Buccaneer (UK)	1962	950	0.95	25	0
Tornado (Allied)	1982	925	2.0	223	334
Jaguar (FR)	1974	720	1.4	45	0
Mirage IIIE (FR)	1964	600	1.8	30	0
Mirage 2000 (FR)	1980	800	2.2	0	200
F-16 (Allied)	1980	925	2.0	250	400
			Subtotal	1,081	1,034
Carrier Based Aircraft					
A-6E (US)	1963	1,000	0.9	20	0
A-7E (US)	1966	900	0.9		0
F/A-18 (US)	1984	950	2.0	48	48
Super-Etendard (FR)	1980	560	1.0	36	36
			Subtotal	104	84
			TOTAL	1,363	1,283

Note: It is likely that no more than 50% of the above aircraft are capable of carrying nuclear weapons and that an even smaller percentage are actually pre-assigned for nuclear missions. For instance, few if any of the F-104 Starfighters are thought to be designated for nuclear roles.
Source: *The Military Balance 1984-5* (London: International Institute for Strategic Studies, 1984), pp. 130-7 and author's projections for 1989 deployments.

systems in the NATO inventory, including France, was that of 1,200 supplied in the 1981 United Kingdom Defence Estimates.[22] These systems included the 203 mm and 155 mm artillery pieces, and the Honest John, Lance and Pluton missiles.

In 1983, however, the United States Defense Department published more precise figures on the types of nuclear warheads to be matched with these short-range systems. Of the approximately 6,000 nuclear weapons available to NATO in 1983 (prior to the planned withdrawal of 1,400 warheads agreed upon by the alliance in October 1983), some 1,670 were reported to be artillery shells, with another 1,190 warheads for the Honest John, Lance and Pershing I surface-to-surface missiles.[23]

In discussing these short-range systems, it is worth noting that modernisation of short-range nuclear warheads continued in the late 1970s and early 1980s, despite the furore over the neutron bomb. In October 1978, President Carter authorised production of some of those components needed for an enhanced radiation warhead, while in 1981 President Reagan extended that to the production of all enhanced radiation components, without, however, proceeding to final assembly. Since the late 1970s, there has also continued a parallel modernisation of the more traditional nuclear warheads.[24] For instance, warheads for the Lance surface-to-surface missile scheduled for production from 1981 to 1983 were to be capable of incorporating enhanced radiation components, although it has been reported that this might involve a one-third loss of destructive power.[25] Similarly, Walter Pincus reported in the *Washington Post* in late 1981 that production was proceeding of new shells for the 155 mm and 203 mm artillery pieces that would result in both increased range and more flexible yield selection.[26]

The short-range delivery systems themselves included the Lance surface-to-surface missile, with a range of 110 km; the Honest John missile, which is being phased out by the mid-1980s; and the French Pluton missile, which will be replaced by the longer-range Hades in the early 1990s. As of late 1984, there were 92 Lance and 54 Honest John launchers deployed with NATO forces, and 44 Pluton launchers with French forces.

NATO artillery pieces included the M-110 203 mm howitzer (936 systems) and the M-109 155 mm artillery piece (1,686 systems). While it is impossible to determine how many of these are configured for a nuclear mission, most analysts assume that roughly one-third to one-half are nuclear-capable, with an even smaller number actually designated for nuclear use.

In addition, the NATO nuclear stockpile in the early 1980s also included a number of maritime nuclear weapons (such as nuclear

Table 3.2: NATO Land-based Nuclear Systems

System	First Deployed	Combat Range (km)	Number 1985	Deployed 1989
Long Range				
Pershing II (US)	1983	1,600	48	108
GLCM (US)	1983	2,500	64	464
		Subtotal	112	572
Medium Range				
Pershing IA (US & FRG)	1962	160-720	132	72 (FRG only)
Short Range Missiles				
Lance (Allied)	1974	130	92	92
Honest John (Allied)	1953	40	54	0
Pluton (FR)	1975	120	44	44
		Subtotal	190	136
Short Range Artillery				
M-110 203mm (Allied)	1962	14-29	936	900
M-109 155mm (Allied)	1964	16-29	1,686	1,600
		Subtotal	2,622	2,500
		TOTAL	3,056	3,280

Note: It is thought that few of the 155mm artillery pieces are designated for nuclear roles.
Source: *The Military Balance 1984-5* (London: International Institute for Strategic Studies, 1984), pp. 130-7 and author's projections for 1989 deployments.

depth-charges, torpedos, and anti-ship and anti-submarine missiles), as well as atomic demolition munitions (ADMs). These latter weapons are designed for pre-emplacement along the inner-German border and elsewhere before a Warsaw Pact attack so as to hinder the advance of Soviet and East European tank formations. While some 370 small-yield ADMs have been stored in the Netherlands and West Germany for many years, it has proved difficult politically to gain agreement on how and when such weapons might be pre-chambered in selected locales in a time of crisis.

Finally, the NATO nuclear stockpile also included a total of 644 Nike-Hercules surface-to-air missiles for anti-aircraft defence. By the early 1980s, however, it had been decided to phase out this system in favour of the conventionally-armed Patriot SAM.

Thus, of the total of 2,400 nuclear warheads to be withdrawn from Europe (1,000 following the 1979 NATO INF decision, and the additional 1,400 decided on in 1983), it seemed likely that these would include approximately 600 Nike-Hercules warheads, many of the 370 ADMs, as well as outdated artillery shells, gravity bombs and maritime nuclear weapons.[27]

Questioning NATO's Nuclear Doctrine

By December 1981, the debate on the role of nuclear weapons in NATO strategy had spread well beyond the alliance's politico-military establishment to the publics of the United States and Western Europe. In the United States, the nuclear freeze movement was gathering momentum, while in Western Europe, there were massive demonstrations in the autumn of 1981 involving hundreds of thousands of people protesting against NATO deployment plans for the Pershing and cruise missiles (see Chapter 6 for further discussion).

To a large extent, however, the INF issue was but a lightning rod for public anxieties over deteriorating US-Soviet relations and general fears of nuclear war. While the INF systems were appropriate symbols for these fears, and although early Reagan administration rhetoric further stimulated European anxieties, anti-nuclear sentiments in both the United States and Western Europe in the early 1980s were as much the product of superpower tensions over such issues as Afghanistan, the Polish crisis, the Middle East and Latin America.

Indeed, nuclear anxieties had been on the rise since late 1979, when the Soviets invaded Afghanistan and the SALT process was aborted. In addition, there had been a growing American domestic debate, which increased greatly during the Carter-Reagan presidential race, over American defence policy and the state of the superpower strategic balance. The American public debate in 1978-9 over the perceived vulnerability of American land-based missiles (the so-called 'window of vulnerability') served to increase the concerns voiced by Schmidt in 1977 about the viability of extended deterrence. As noted at the time, the ICBM vulnerability debate fed 'European concerns over the implications of parity, psychologically if not analytically, by suggesting another reason for American caution if Europe alone [were] attacked by Soviet nuclear weapons'.[28]

Then, during the American presidential campaign in 1980, the Carter administration made public what many Europeans took to be a marked departure in American nuclear strategy. Known as Presidential Document no. 59 (PD-59), the 'counter-vailing strategy', made public by Defense Secretary Harold Brown in August 1980, was interpreted by many in Europe as an American shift away from deterrence and towards a war-fighting strategy. In reality, the 'counter-vailing strategy' was but an evolutionary refinement of American nuclear policy that was aimed at strengthening deterrence against a wider range of possible threats.[29] It was not, as some Europeans argued, predicated on the idea that the United States could fight and win a nuclear war. None the less, the appearance of PD-59, and American plans for acquiring more accurate strategic systems (the MX and Trident D-5 SLBM missiles) that could be used for nuclear pre-emption, served to increase public unease in both Western Europe and the United States.

European dissatisfaction with American policy increased again when, following Reagan's election as President in November 1980, he and members of his administration both belittled previous arms-control efforts and advocated American strategic superiority as a national goal. To make matters worse, several officials of the administration, including the President, were quite careless in remarking on the possibilities of limited nuclear war. For example, Secretary of State Haig noted, in congressional testimony that NATO might consider the use of a 'nuclear warning shot' during a conventional conflict in Europe, while President Reagan told a gathering of newspaper editors that it was impossible to rule out the prospect of a nuclear war limited to Europe: 'I could see where you could have the exchange of tactical weapons against troops in the field without it bringing either one of the major powers to pushing the button.'[30] Administration officials tried to limit the political damage caused by the President's remark by saying that Reagan had only been speculating hypothetically, and that the President in no way endorsed the concept of limited nuclear war. None the less, the harsh anti-Soviet rhetoric of the administration, coupled with its hardline arms-control policies, continued to focus public attention on the limited nuclear war issue. As previously noted, the administration's decision of August 1981 to proceed with production of neutron warheads further fuelled public apprehension over NATO nuclear-weapons policies, especially in Europe.

By the spring of 1982, then, public debate centred on American and NATO nuclear strategy in general, and not just on individual TNF issues such as ERW and INF. The debate was then given added impetus by the appearance of an article in *Foreign Affairs* magazine urging NATO to evolve toward a policy of 'no first use' of nuclear weapons.[31] Written by four influential former American policy-makers (McGeorge Bundy, Robert McNamara, George Kennan, and Gerard Smith), the 'no-first-use' article questioned the central premise of the alliance strategy of flexible response. In effect, the article asserted that NATO's threat to initiate the use of nuclear weapons was no longer credible, and could well be militarily disadvantageous to the alliance. Moreover, such a strategy was no longer politically acceptable, as it was losing the support of those citizens it was supposed to defend.

While their call for increasing NATO conventional capabilities so as to reduce NATO reliance on nuclear weapons elicited considerable public support, it also made a number of West European policy-makers nervous. Especially alarming was the prospect that such a policy could decouple the NATO nuclear deterrent from the American strategic deterrent, and thus increase the risk of a European limited war. In voicing the concerns of those Europeans who took issue with the 'no first use' policy, a West German rejoinder in the autumn 1982 issue of *Foreign Affairs* claimed that the ambiguity inherent in the flexible-response doctrine enabled NATO to deter all conflict, not just nuclear conflict.[32] For many, both in Europe and the United States, an attempt by NATO to rely too heavily on conventional deterrence would increase the risk of a non-nuclear conflict, which could be tremendously destructive in and of itself, and still result in the use of nuclear weapons. Europeans in particular had no stomach for contemplating a repeat of World War II.

Sparked by this debate over 'no first use', a number of studies were undertaken in 1982 and 1983 to promote the concept of conventional deterrence. For his part, the NATO Supreme Commander, General Bernard Rogers, said that NATO could greatly strengthen its conventional forces, and thus reduce its TNF deployments, if the alliance members could increase their defence spending by 4 per cent in real terms annually.[33] Given the already severe economic constraints on governmental budgets, there seemed little prospect of NATO meeting the 4 per cent goal. None the less, Rogers's support for greatly strengthened conventional forces added further impetus to the issue. Analyses from the European Security Study (ESECS) and the Brookings Institution, as well as other organisations and individuals, sought to show how the Alliance could at least begin to move toward revising its flexible-response strategy.[34]

In many ways, then, the focus of the debate in 1982-5 had returned to the issues raised by Chancellor Schmidt and others in 1977: namely, how the alliance could use both the arms-control and the force-modernisation processes to re-establish conventional parity in Europe and thus strengthen deterrence. In the interim, of course, questions of conventional deterrence had been overshadowed by the ERW and INF debates, and the latter was still at the forefront of the public debate in the early 1980s. The peace movements in Western Europe kept up their opposition to the deployment of the Pershing and cruise missiles, while major political parties like the British Labour Party and the West German Social Democrats turned increasingly anti-nuclear. The INF arms-control talks in Geneva limped along with little prospect of success, and they finally collapsed in November 1983 when the Soviets made good their threat to walk out of the talks once the first Pershings and cruise missiles arrived in Europe. Although the United States and the Soviet Union resumed their arms-control dialogue in March 1985, the fact that INF systems were now being discussed along with both strategic offensive systems and space weapons suggested no imminent breakthroughs.

While it remained unclear how this third phase in NATO nuclear strategy would ultimately be played out, there were at least encouraging signs that both policy-makers and the general public were seriously examining the flexible-response doctrine. No longer were individual nuclear weapons systems given paramount importance as technical 'fixes' to the inherent political dilemma of NATO's nuclear strategy. While the ultimate resolution of the INF issue, and the prospects for INF arms control, remained in doubt, there was the realisation within NATO that the alliance's nuclear forces were badly in need of restructuring. The October 1983 decision to withdraw an additional 1,400 warheads, as well as plans for creating special nuclear weapons units that could be held back from the front lines (so as to avoid the 'use 'em or lose 'em' dilemma) testified to a growing appreciation within the alliance that unnecessary pressures for an early use of nuclear weapons in a conventional conflict were bad strategy and bad politics.

To what extent the Alliance would also be able to afford, both economically and politically, the sacrifices necessary to strengthen conventional forces and raise the nuclear threshold remained in doubt. Whatever the long-term outcome, however, there seemed little chance in the mid-1980s that NATO nuclear-weapons issues would return to the wilderness of NATO policy circles, and that continued public and élite debate would continue to prod, if not push, the alliance toward a fundamental revision of the flexible-response strategy that had helped dampen the nuclear weapons debate two decades earlier.

Notes

1. For the text of Schmidt's remarks, see 'The North Atlantic Summit Meeting: Remarks by Chancellor Helmut Schmidt, May 10, 1977', *Survival* (July/August 1977), pp. 177-8.
2. Kissinger's speech can be found in Kenneth A. Myers (ed.), *NATO: The Next Thirty Years* (Boulder, Colo.: Westview Press, 1980).
3. 'The North Atlantic Summit Meeting', p. 178.
4. *Washington Post*, 5 June 1977.
5. Proponents of this view not only simplified the issue (e.g., that blast and thermal radiation of ERW would still destroy buildings, especially when used in heavy concentrations), but often conveniently passed over the converse of their claim: that standard battlefield nuclear weapons would both kill people and destroy property. For more on the technical characteristics of enhanced radiation weapons, see Fred Kaplan, 'Enhanced Radiation Weapons', *Scientific American* (May 1978).
6. See *Der Spiegel*, 18 July 1977.
7. For an insightful analysis of the politics of President Carter's ERW decision, see Lothar Ruehl, 'Ein Lehrstück der Verworrenheit', *Die Zeit*, 14 April 1978, p. 3.
8. At a meeting of the National Security Planning Group on 6 August 1981, President Reagan decided to proceed with production of enhanced radiation warheads for the Lance missile and the 203 mm howitzer, despite the objections of Secretary of State Haig that the decision would only complicate the INF issue in Europe. See *New York Times*, 9 August 1981.
9. For the text of Schmidt's speech at the IISS, see *Survival* (January/February 1978).
10. For the text of the communiqué issued by the Nuclear Planning Group following its meeting in Italy, see *Europa Archiv* (10 April 1978).
11. Stephen Hanmer, 'NATO's Long-Range Theater Nuclear Forces: Modernization in Parallel with Arms Control', *NATO Review* (February 1980).
12. See 'The Modernization of NATO's Long-Range Theater Nuclear Forces', a report prepared for the Subcommittee on Europe and the Middle East, Committee on Foreign Affairs, US House of Representatives (Washington, DC: US Government

Printing Office, 1980).

13. See Klaas de Vries, 'General Report on the Security of the Alliance — The Role of Nuclear Weapons', prepared for the North Atlantic Assembly (Brussels. November 1979), pp. 9-10.

14. For instance, the Joint Chiefs of Staff reportedly favoured deploying 2,000 cruise missiles in Europe on the theory that 572 systems would not meet military requirements.

15. Except where noted, all data regarding NATO theatre nuclear forces are taken from International Institute for Strategic Studies, *The Military Balance 1984-1985* (London: IISS, 1984), pp. 130-7.

16. *Aviation Week and Space Technology* (15 October 1979).

17. Anthony H. Cordesman, 'Europe's Quiet Profile is Courage', *Armed Forces Journal International* (June 1981).

18. An excellent source on French nuclear-weapons systems is 'Rapport d'information par la commission de la défense nationale et des forces armées, Assemblée Nationale, L'état et la modernisation des forces nucléaires françaises, 1979-80 session' (Paris, May 1980), often referred to as the Tourrain Report.

19. *Aviation Week and Space Technology* (4 June 1984).

20. *Statement on the Defence Estimates, 1981*, Cmnd 8212-1, p. 12.

21. These US. Defense Department figures were published in the *New York Times*, 15 November 1983.

22. *Statement on the Defence Estimates, 1981*, Cmnd 8212-1.

23. *New York Times*, 15 November 1983.

24. For descriptions of the various nuclear warheads available to American and NATO forces, see Thomas B. Cochran, William M. Arkin and Milton M. Hoenig, *Nuclear Weapons Databook. Volume One: US Nuclear Forces and Capabilities* (Cambridge, Mass.: Ballinger Publishing Co., 1984), especially pp. 38-79.

25. US Department of Defense *Annual Report for Fiscal Year 1981* (Washington, DC: US Government Printing Office, 1981), p. 146.

26. *Washington Post*, 27 October 1981.

27. For more on how NATO could restructure its TNF force posture, see William Kaufmann, 'Nuclear Deterrence in Central Europe' in John D. Steinbruner and Leon V. Sigal (eds.), *Alliance Security: NATO and the No-First-Use Question* (Washington, DC: The Brookings Institution, 1983).

28. Gregory Treverton, 'Nuclear Weapons and the "Gray Area" ', *Foreign Affairs* (Summer 1979), p. 1080.

29. See Walter Slocombe, 'The Counter-vailing Strategy', *International Security* (Spring 1981).

30. *New York Times*, 22 October 1981.

31. McGeorge Bundy *et al*, 'Nuclear Weapons and the Atlantic Alliance', *Foreign Affairs* (Spring 1982).

32. Karl Kaiser *et al*, 'Nuclear Weapons and the Preservation of Peace: A German View', *Foreign Affairs* (Summer 1982).

33. General Bernard W. Rogers, 'Greater Flexibility for NATO's Flexible Response', *Strategic Review* (Spring 1983).

34. See especially the report of the European Security Study, *Strengthening Conventional Deterrence in Europe: Proposals for the 1980s* (New York: St. Martin's Press, 1983) and Steinbruner and Sigal (eds.), *Alliance Security*. See also, John Mearsheimer, *Conventional Deterrence* (Ithaca: Cornell University Press, 1983); Eckhard Lubkemeier, 'Problems, Prerequisites and Prospects of Conventionalizing NATO's Strategy' (Bonn: Friedrich Ebert Stiftung, 1983); and Joshua M.Epstein, 'On Conventional Deterrence in Europe: Questions of Soviet

Confidence', *Orbis* (Spring 1982). Finally, the winter 1983-4 issue of *International Security* contained four quite different approaches to the subject of conventional deterrence, under the heading, 'Alternative Non-Nuclear Strategies'.

4 THEATRE NUCLEAR FORCES: MILITARY LOGIC AND POLITICAL PURPOSE*

Gregory F. Treverton

This chapter begins from two presumptions. The first is that the role of theatre nuclear forces in NATO strategy is primarily a political question. Weapons matter but politics is decisive. Put differently, the political arrangements in which weapons are imbedded count for more than the weapons themselves. The credibility of NATO strategy — and of the role of TNF in that strategy — turns, finally, on political confidence and cohesion. Deterrence is, after all, as much a political as a military concept, a fact we forget at our peril.

Yet if narrow military considerations are not decisive, they are hardly irrelevant. One lesson stands out sharply in NATO's nuclear history: military measures designed to serve political purposes will fail to do so if they do not make sense on technical grounds to the ostensible military experts. That was the lesson of the Multilateral Force (MLF) misadventure of the 1960s.[1] NATO's decision of December 1979 to deploy 572 long-range cruise and Pershing II ballistic missiles in Western Europe is being implemented and thus may yet have a happier outcome than MLF, but there were disturbing parallels between the two. The military rationale for the December 1979 decision was stronger than the case in the 1960s for the MLF, but that rationale was neither obvious nor simple, a fact that bedevilled the public debate in Europe over the decision and casts a shadow over the deployments now under way.

This chapter examines the military considerations surrounding TNF in the decade ahead; inevitably, however, the line between military and political blurs. It begins with background to how NATO's TNF posture became the haphazard affair it is; then it outlines the specific problems of that posture; then it looks more broadly at TNF and the declining

---

*This chapter draws on but extends the analysis in my *Nuclear Weapons in Europe*, Adelphi Paper no. 168 (London: IISS, Summer 1981). It was first written during a pleasant and productive stay at the Rockefeller Foundation's Villa Serbelloni in Bellagio, a debt I happily acknowledge.

credibility of NATO's doctrine of flexible response; and finally it sketches military guidelines for a future-oriented TNF posture, both in making weapons choices and in framing approaches to arms control.

Making the Muddle

The process that has produced NATO's existing theatre nuclear posture was haphazard at best, as this book's first two chapters detail. The NATO Council made the initial decision to introduce tactical nuclear weapons in 1954, but the actual weapons choices were hardly driven by clear determinations about the role of nuclear weapons in NATO doctrine. The total number of 7,000, then 6,000,[2] warheads seems to have been as much related to the production capabilities of the American weapons laboratories as to anything else. The arsenal that resulted was a grab-bag of yields, ranges and types of weapons, but it was, and is, heavily tilted toward short-range systems. The 6,000 warheads in the inventory in 1983 were many more than NATO had systems to deliver; many of them were so obsolete as to be essentially unusable.

The vagueness about the role of TNF meant that from the beginning Europeans and Americans have viewed the weapons differently. For Europeans, who live in the potential battleground, 'pure' deterrence has been the key, hence they have emphasised TNF as the trigger to a quick resort to American strategic nuclear weapons, seeing that as the way to ensure that the Soviet Union is not tempted to begin *any* war in Europe. That has meant, implicitly at least, relatively less interest in conventional defence and a lower 'threshold' for the use of nuclear weapons.

By contrast, Americans have tended to stress the importance of presenting Soviet leaders with credible forces at each level of violence through to a strategic response. Their incentives run to the latest possible use of nuclear weapons — thus delaying the spectre of a strategic nuclear exchange striking the American homeland — hence to a high nuclear threshold and an effective conventional defence. While Europeans have emphasised the symbolic effect of TNF, Americans have focused on the military utility of the weapons. Those diverging tendencies were clear in recent discussions of the enhanced radiation warheads (ERW).

Decisions about longer-range TNF appear especially haphazard.[3] NATO deployed medium-range American nuclear missiles in Europe in 1959 — 60 Thors in Britain and 45 Jupiters in Italy and Turkey. NATO's Supreme Commander at the time, General Norstad, advocated a force of NATO medium-range ballistic missiles (MRBM) in addition to the Thors and Jupiters, and for the next few years there were a variety of schemes for some form of NATO nuclear force. Of these the most famous, now infamous, was the MLF, which was to be a fleet of 25 NATO surface ships, manned by sailors of different NATO nations and carrying nuclear missiles whose firing was to be subject to an American veto.

The debate over NATO's nuclear role, especially in longer-range theatre forces, subsided rather than ended with the withdrawal of the Thors and Jupiters by 1964 and with the demise of the MLF in 1965. The strategic rationale for those actions was that land- and sea-based missiles from the central American strategic arsenal could by then cover all targets of interest deep into the Warsaw Pact, including the Soviet Union. In the 1950s the United States had given equal emphasis to the development of intercontinental ballistic missiles (ICBMs) and to intermediate or medium-range ballistic missiles for deployment in Europe. Yet from the start, the IRBMs were viewed by Americans primarily as a hedge against technical problems in the ICBM programme. By that logic, the sooner ICBMs could cover all the Soviet targets of interest, the sooner the need for IRBMs would fade.

The debate at the time recognised some of the arguments for European-based forces — they would disperse the retaliatory forces and provide more flexibility for limited wars, in addition to whatever value they had in providing political reassurance to Europeans. However, the counter-arguments seemed overriding, in American eyes at any rate: politically, the interest in centralised command and control seemed imperative, as Americans worried about independent European nuclear forces; moreover, effective ICBMs were at hand, while a second generation of more survivable IRBMs appeared to be years away.[4] Psychologically, the rapid American build-up of strategic forces in the early 1960s — and the parallel realisation that the so-called 'missile gap' was a myth, with Soviet ICBM forces growing at a snail's pace — were crucial. American nuclear superiority, never mind that it became increasingly difficult to define that 'superiority', seemed to mean that it did not matter much that Europe became in some sense 'hostage' to Soviet IRBMs targeted against it — some 700 SS-4s and SS-5s by the early 1960s.

It is, above all, the emergence of strategic parity (some would say worse) between the United States and the Soviet Union that has put, and will continue to put, pressure on NATO's TNF posture. In purely military terms, it can be argued that not much has changed, at least not in the last 15 years. As long ago as that the United States lost 'superiority' by the clearest and most significant definition: it lost any credible threat to disarm the Soviet Union in a nuclear first strike. The United States homeland had become vulnerable, and the Soviet Union had achieved a kind of 'minimum deterrence'. Then, as now, deterrence in Europe rested on the confidence that the United States would respond with nuclear weapons if need be, despite the risk to its own cities.

Yet, more recent implications of strategic parity do matter in military terms. One is the theoretical vulnerability of American land-based ICBMs to a Soviet first strike. That is vastly overrated as a general problem for American strategic forces; it is, however, a specific concern in extending deterrence to Western Europe. In an escalating nuclear exchange, the United States may want to make selective strikes against military targets in the Soviet Union. ICBM forces, despite their vulnerability, would be attractive for this role, given their accuracy, flexibility in retargeting and relatively secure control. Yet their use for such missions would compete with the need to withhold warheads of all types for the ultimate deterrent — assured destruction of the Soviet Union. ICBM vulnerability sharpens that conflict of interest, and an American President might therefore be reluctant to spend these forces for a European contingency, especially early.

More generally, assuming the vulnerability of ICBM, the United States might be reluctant to resort to the use of nuclear weapons based in the continental United States lest the Soviet Union retaliate by destroying (remaining) ICBMs. That poses the risk that the United States might try to contain a nuclear war in Europe without committing its strategic forces, or even that NATO might never use American nuclear weapons at all, even in a losing conventional war.

The strictly military considerations slide into political and psychological ones. Somehow, Europeans felt that so long as the United States remained superior in nuclear terms to the Soviet Union, by however loose a definition, they could be tolerably confident that it would respond to a Soviet attack on Western Europe with nuclear weapons if need be. Now, with parity, they can no longer be so confident. That surely was the meaning of Helmut Schmidt's words in 1977 to the IISS in London: 'SALT neutralises . . . strategic nuclear capabilities. In Europe this magnifies the significance of the disparities between East and West in nuclear tactical and conventional weapons.'[5]

TNF: Military Logic and Political Purpose 91

In the 1950s and 1960s, perhaps, NATO could afford to be vague about TNF. Europeans could emphasise them as a link to American strategic systems, while Americans could stress them as a complement to conventional defence if need be; and both could reiterate that American nuclear systems remained the ultimate deterrent. Yet now that vagueness will no longer do. Strategic parity will continue to impel doubts over American nuclear responses, and ICBM vulnerability will give those doubts some analytic justification. European publics will worry that existing theatre systems make them vulnerable more than they protect them, and they will continue to raise hard questions.

If ICBM vulnerability were diminished, that would reduce pressure on TNF somewhat. It would make Americans more confident in their own strategic posture which, in turn, would reassure Europeans, who always tend to care less about the military details of nuclear forces than about whether or not Americans are happy with those forces. Yet, as the strategic decisions of the Reagan administration made clear, there is no early solution to ICBM vulnerabilty, and perhaps none at all. Even if there were, by the time it were implemented, the prospect of more general vulnerability of nuclear forces could well be on the horizon. Nuclear parity is likely to be a continuing fact of life. For that reason there are no quick fixes or once-for-all solutions to the problems of NATO's TNF posture. The December 1979 decisions and the deployments now under way can be a beginning to sorting out that posture; they hardly are an end.

Problems of NATO's TNF Posture

The specific deficiencies in NATO's theatre nuclear posture were examined in Chapter 3 and need only be rehearsed briefly here; the next section will draw their implications.

The problems at the longer-range end of the TNF spectrum have been the focus of recent attention. Until the cruise and Pershing II deployments began, NATO had no land-based missiles in Europe with enough range to reach the Soviet Union (with the exception of the 18 French SSBS S-2s, and France does not participate in the integrated NATO military command). By contrast, there are well over 1,000 warheads on the Soviet SS-4s and SS-20s. With regard to nuclear-capable strike aircraft, the Soviet numerical advantage is less marked — perhaps about a third — as the inventories of Chapter 3 show. But special uncertainty surrounds this estimate because nuclear-capable planes can be modified to carry nuclear weapons, and because superior Soviet air defences may cause greater attrition for NATO.

The submarine-based component of NATO's longer-range TNF presents a different set of difficulties. None of the systems — the French MSBS M-20 submarine-launched ballistic missiles (SLBMs), the British Polaris force or the 400 American Poseidon warheads assigned to NATO and targeted by the Supreme Allied Commander, Europe (SACEUR) — has anywhere near the accuracy imputed to the Soviet SS-20, although they are certainly accurate enough to strike 'soft' military targets in the Soviet Union, like airfields, of which there are a great many.[6] Each Poseidon missile carries between ten and 14 warheads, which would make 'small' attacks difficult, and single missile launches could reveal the location of the boat. Moreover, communication lags make battle management difficult.

More important, the fact that SLBMs are the least vulnerable of nuclear forces argues for their being withheld as instruments of ultimate deterrence, not used for theatre purposes relatively early in a nuclear conflict. The argument for withholding would be reinforced by the difficulty of communicating quickly with submarines under water, by the inability to retarget SLBMs rapidly, and by the fact that if French and British systems are to have any meaning as independent national systems, they would have to be withheld for last-ditch retaliation, not used for NATO purposes earlier in a war.

At the lower end of the range spectrum, the preponderance of existing NATO TNF is of very limited range: as many as 2,000 American and European artillery pieces capable of firing nuclear rounds, but with ranges under 10 miles, compared with under 150 Pershing IA missiles, 400 miles in range. In many cases the nuclear yields are relatively large. Aircraft are vulnerable to pre-emption, all the more so if their ranges require them to be based forward. Even the Pershing I and II missiles and cruise missiles, in form mobile, are cumbersome to move and must be fired from a limited number of pre-surveyed sites, thus raising questions about their survivability. The much larger Soviet inventory of short-range ballistic missiles (about 1,400) is being modernised by deployments of SS-21s, SS-22s and SS-23s.

Worse, most of NATO's 6,000-odd tactical warheads in Europe are stored at some fifty sites; according to a recent estimate, NATO presents no more than 70 TNF targets in peacetime and only 200-300 once weapons are dispersed for war.[7] Storing tactical warheads in the United States, as the Reagan administration decided to do with enhanced radiation warheads in 1981, solves some problems but creates more. Moving

TNF: Military Logic and Political Purpose

them to Europe in a crisis would compete for scarce airlift and would be likely to be regarded by political leaders as provocative only deepening existing doubts about whether NATO would actually use to advantage that warning time of an impending attack it could expect. Much of the current NATO posture does, as one analyst put it several years ago, beg the Soviet Union to pre-empt, and perhaps even makes it possible to do so with conventional weapons.[8]

Procedures for securing release of weapons, dispersing them from stockpiles to be mated with launching systems, and applying the codes to unlock the weapons would take hours, even days in the case of the older weapons. The development of so-called permissive action links (PALs), now generally electronic rather than mechanical as in the past, to activate warheads diminishes the risk that terrorists could detonate a bomb even if they could steal one. Still, there is inherent tension between interests in storing weapons in a small number of very secure sites to protect them from terrorists and dispersing them widely to make them less vulnerable to pre-emption, and between making weapons hard for terrorists to activate but quick for NATO forces to make ready in the event of war.

Finally, any NATO TNF posture would put a tremendous burden on arrangements for command, control, communications and intelligence (C31), but those arrangements are particularly dubious for the existing posture and doctrine. Soviet strikes on some ten C31 centres in Europe could 'blind' the alliance. In the customary scenario of a tactical nuclear response to a losing conventional war, it is not clear that NATO would be able to use nuclear weapons at all; the imperative of control would collide with the requirements of timely use for military purpose. By the time the American President authorised release and approved targets, presumably in consultation with his fellow NATO leaders, and the weapons were physically prepared and triggered, they could well have been overrun or their use have otherwise become inappropriate. This is not to say, however, that NATO leaders would have to 'use 'em or lose 'em'. That notion, a caricature, is all too frequent in writings about nuclear weapons. In fact, as Thomas Schelling pointed out, there would be no choice: NATO would simply 'lose 'em'. They could not be fired by an enemy, and NATO would still retain lots of nuclear options. In those circumstances, no American President or European leader would be stampeded across the nuclear threshold by the prospect of losing a few weapons.

The Decision to Go Nuclear

Most presumptions about how NATO would use nuclear weapons in Europe are simply wide of the mark, illustrating how vague thinking about TNF has been. Explicit in NATO's doctrine of flexible response and implicit in most discussions is the notion of an escalation ladder: the first nuclear weapons to be used would be short-range battlefield systems; these would be followed by deeper strike theatre systems if need be; and eventually, in the extreme case, American central strategic systems would be employed.

Yet, to use the hardest case, what would ensue if NATO actually were losing a conventional war and its leaders decided the time had come to face the great abyss of a first use of nuclear weapons? It is hard to imagine that battlefield weapons actually would be used, for a number of reasons. Most obvious, the Soviet Union now has an array of short-range systems of its own, from nuclear artillery up through the latest generation of shorter-range missiles, the SS-21, -22 and -23 (though there remains uncertainty about whether and to what extent the Soviet Union deploys nuclear warheads in Eastern Europe during peacetime). More than a decade of NATO studies, referred to in Chapter 2, have shown that if NATO used short-range weapons and the Soviet Union responded in kind, it is far from obvious that NATO would be the net gainer in purely military terms.

Secondly, using short-range systems in a losing conventional war would mean using them on NATO's own territory. A German Chancellor who agreed to an American use of nuclear weapons — and it is hard to conceive that the United States would use them, at least initially, without such agreement — surely would add a condition to his agreement: not on German territory, West, and probably East as well. NATO's Carte Blanche wargame in 1955 had a lasting impression on Europeans, for good reason. That game, held in Germany, the Low Countries and northern France, simulated the use of 355 atomic bombs and resulted in 5.2 million prompt civilian casualties, leaving aside longer-term effects.[9] A German Chancellor or British Prime Minister who agreed to use nuclear weapons might also add a second condition: not fired from German or British territory. That is reasonable enough: who wants to invite nuclear retaliation on their own heads?

Finally, there would be no automatic decision to go nuclear, far from it; the decision would be the most agonising one political leaders have ever made, and they would give great emphasis to those nuclear systems which are most controllable. The American President certainly would want to approve every release of a nuclear weapon and every single target; he could hardly do less. Yet that suggests that he would be extremely reluctant to release short-range weapons for battlefield use at the subsequent discretion of commanders on the scene. Nor would existing army procedures give political leaders much assurance that the use of battlefield weapons would be limited, much less calibrated for political purposes. Understandably, American Army doctrine emphasises military utility, not political signalling. Corps commanders are to propose pre-planned packages of 100 to 200 weapons, 'sufficient to alter the tactical situation decisively and to accomplish the mission'.[10]

So were would that leave NATO a few minutes after its leaders began to face nuclear war? A strike on the Soviet Union itself probably would be ruled out for the time being as too escalatory, and NATO leaders would be likely instead to look at targets in Eastern Europe.[11] They would look no doubt at military targets, but the intended effect would be more political than military. And they would quickly move to discussion of 'offshore' systems as the best launch vehicles. No one could be sure that the Soviet Union would respect *any* categories in framing its response, but using 'offshore' systems at least would make more difficult the Soviet decision about how, and where, to respond. Thus, for NATO a limited, demonstrative Poseidon strike against targets deep in Eastern Europe could turn out not to be one of the last 'rungs' on some notional escalation ladder, but the first.

NATO's customary assumptions may be more tenable in the contingency of a selective Warsaw Pact nuclear attack on military targets in Western Europe. In that case, NATO would want to have a broad range of nuclear options with which to respond and to select the most limited option commensurate with the attack. Yet given that even a 'limited' Soviet attack would cross the nuclear threshold, with all its awesome implications, it is hard to imagine such a strike except as part of, or as an immediate prelude to, a Soviet conventional attack. NATO might then want to respond with TNF, but the same inhibitions on the use of short-range weapons would apply.

There is no easy way around these uncomfortable implications. One way that has often been suggested, strategies for nuclear defence, is not politically feasible, no matter how tempting it might be in technical terms. Since its inception, NATO could logically have solved its defence dilemma by acknowledging frankly that no convincing conventional defence of Western Europe is possible within foreseeable levels of NATO spending, given Soviet conventional capabilities. The alliance would then have built its defence around the threat to use nuclear weapons at the very start of any conflict. Its forces would be structured accordingly, and might be much smaller and cheaper than at present.[12] Such strategies would explicitly decouple the American strategic arsenal from the immediate defence of Europe. They would aim to deter attack by presenting unacceptable odds on the ground, not by the risk of escalation.

NATO has never accepted such strategies, and they were specifically abandoned when the doctrine of flexible response was formulated in the early 1960s. Yet they persist. The growing Soviet arsenal of short-range systems, coupled with the conclusion that NATO could well be worse off after an exchange of battlefield nuclear weapons would appear to make such strategies less and less attractive on military grounds. However, a nuclear defender dispersed for nuclear combat could retain some of the advantages of the defence, and a variety of means of making the early use of nuclear weapons credible have been suggested, for instance by creating or preparing to create in time of crisis a depopulated border zone on the intra-German frontier with nuclear mines in place or readily deployed.

However, responsible political leaders in the West simply will not authorise the use the nuclear weapons early in a conflict (unless the other side fires them first), or delegate responsibility for firing weapons to *anyone else* (much less to field commanders). Politics in NATO are strained enough by current nuclear issues. They could not bear the weight of strategies that relied on the early and extensive release of nuclear weapons, even if those strategies had the virtue of a clarity that current NATO doctrine does not.

No Alternative to Flexible Response

To many on both sides of the Atlantic, the doctrine of flexible response looks meaningless at best, dangerous at worst. Yet for the foreseeable future there will be no alternative to something akin to flexible response, by whatever label. Neither politics nor technology will permit once-for-all military solutions to NATO's nuclear dilemma. That dilemma is rooted in geography and cannot be made to go away: the bulk of NATO's ultimate deterrent, American strategic forces, is located an ocean away from the likely point of attack or pressure in

Europe. Now, as in the past, there is only one real resolution of that dilemma: if Europeans doubt that the United States would press the nuclear button, then they need buttons of their own, with weapons to match. But that is ruled out for political reasons: for the Federal Republic to have nuclear weapons of its own would be a solution worse than the problem.[13] Similarly, an independent European nuclear force could not be credible without direct German participation but is not politically possible with it. So the best that can be done is to manage the dilemma, through measures that make both military and political sense.

From the beginning, flexible response was as much a political compromise as a military strategy. As Lawrence Freedman put it, flexible response involved 'an inadequate conventional defence backed by an incredible nuclear guarantee'.[14] In the realm of TNF it has amounted to little more than the hope that the Soviet Union would be deterred because it would be at least as uncertain how NATO would behave in a crisis as the alliance itself was.

The existing muddle of flexible response may in fact deter the Soviet Union, but it can no longer reassure us. It may deter because, in the first half of the theorem attributed many years ago to Denis Healey, even a small probability that the United States might come to Europe's defence with nuclear weapons probably is enough to deter the Soviet Union. Yet, as Healey had it, even a large probability of such a response will not suffice to reassure American allies in Europe.

The current TNF posture reassures neither American hawks nor European doves. It does not reassure hawks because they insist on looking at ladders of escalation in a purely mechanical way: for them, deficiencies at the top of the ladder, for instance ICBM vulnerability, make any use of nuclear weapons unthinkable. Worse, current arrangements are the opposite of reassuring to doves because those arrangements look both mindless and unpredictable, making the West seem as likely to ignite nuclear catastrophe as the East, hence as dangerous. Thus, hawks and doves reinforce each other on a number of points: growing East-West tension is increasing the risk of a confrontation between the superpowers, new technology will unsettle the strategic balance, and the security interests of Europe and the United States are not identical.

The weakest point in the doctrine of flexible response is the threat to use nuclear weapons first if need be. That is so because the doctrine brought together but could not integrate two different concepts of deterrence. One was deterrence through denial, physically preventing the

Warsaw pact from occupying Western Europe, the classical strategy of defence. In accepting flexible response, the European NATO members genuflected in the direction of conventional defence but remained unwilling to improve forces to match intentions.

The other concept is deterrence through punishment, the threat to wreak unacceptable damage on the other, not necessarily in areas adjacent or related to the point of aggression, the kind of threat that has been at the centre of nuclear deterrence since nuclear weapons were invented. This notion of deterrence can be rational only if the side making the threat is superior to its opponent in the sense of being more able to stand punishment. It can be credible though not rational if the other side believes the stake which occasions the threat is so important that the threat might actually be carried out despite the irrationality of doing so. In this sense, the Soviet Union may believe that Western Europe is so important that the United States and its allies would go nuclear to prevent it being overrun even if doing so was tantamount to committing suicide.

TNF stand right at the intersection of these two notions, with Europeans and Americans looking at them through the lenses of different concepts of deterrence. It is harder and harder to escape the conclusion that, with respect to the specific question of the role of TNF, Europeans have been right and Americans wrong, even if the Europeans have been unwilling to accept the implications of their own analysis. Nuclear weapons, by their nature, can deter through the threat to punish, not by their role in physical defence. In a time of nuclear stalemate between the two superpowers, that means that nuclear weapons primarily can deter other nuclear weapons. They *may* also have a role as last-ditch uppers of the ante. That latter threat may be credible if the Soviet Union believes our stake is so important to us, yet since the threat is irrational, there will always be doubts about its credibility, perhaps more to us than to the Soviet Union.

Both these roles for TNF are essentially political, not military. Indeed, to push the point further, it is hard to conceive of any military role for TNF.[15] That conclusion is not fundamentally altered by the impact of new technology. Technology will not solve NATO's nuclear dilemma. The most that can be said about enhanced radiation warheads, for example, is that under certain specific, and transitory, battlefield conditions, they would be marginally more effective against Soviet tank formations than NATO's existing tactical nuclear weapons.[16] That marginal gain hardly outweighs the problems with their use. ERW are, after all, nuclear weapons, with all the inhibitions surrounding their use. To make a military difference, they would have to be used early and in large numbers. Even if we could convince West Germans that ERW could be used on *their* territory without devastating it, they would not be convinced that the Soviet Union would play that game. Indeed, the Soviets would have every reason not to do so. And given the fragility of C3I arrangements, especially in Europe, no one could have any confidence that a nuclear war could be contained once dozens of even 'small' nuclear weapons were being exchanged.[17]

Similarly, no technological breakthrough is visible on the horizon that would restore a kind of American nuclear superiority which could, in turn, make fully credible a threat to use nuclear weapons other than to deter nuclear weapons. The recent history of the MX basing problem is instructive in that regard. There simply is no technical solution to the problem of ICBM vulnerability now, certainly not one that can be afforded; by contrast, hardened silos provided such an elegant solution in the 1960s. So it is likely to be with anti-ballistic missile systems. They will be further off or less effective than their current proponents hope, or they will be deployed by both sides in a way that gives decisive advantage to neither. To expect technology to solve our dilemma is to delude ourselves. The problem is not in our technology but in our concepts, and it is there that answers must be found.

Nor will conventional defence provide a way out of NATO's nuclear dilemma, though doing better on that score is an important part of managing the dilemma. The logic of conventional defence appears compelling: if deterrence through the threatened resort to nuclear weapons is less and less credible, then raising the nuclear threshold through better conventional defence is preferable. Yet there are a number of reasons why that logic cannot be made operational.

One is that NATO has preached its inferiority in conventional forces for so long it has come to believe it; hence confidence, especially among defence analysts and attentive publics, that NATO can rely less on nuclear weapons will be slow in coming. Moreover, given the uncertainties that surround any reckoning of the balance in central Europe, prudent military planners can hardly avoid making worse-case estimates, and those will never be comforting. Improvements in conventional defence are not only costly, but they also run up against the shortage of personnel which most Western armed forces will experience in the latter part of the 1980s, especially as commitments beyond Europe expand to make more demands on fewer men of age for military service.

Nor will new technologies — like precision-guided weapons for deep interdiction strikes behind the front lines — or new tactics — such as recent enthusiasm for manoeuvre defences — sever the dilemma.[18] They will turn out either not to be cheaper than existing arrangements or to imply changes, such as a NATO posture with more 'offensive' capabilities for counter-attack, that are politically unacceptable.

Even if NATO could markedly improve its conventional forces and convince its publics that it had, it would still confront the clashing European and American perspectives. For understandable reasons, Europeans have an abiding horror of a conventional war in Europe: in their eyes, if better conventional defences make a resort to nuclear weapons less likely, the Soviets may in a crisis be *more* tempted to risk such a conventional war.

Guidelines for TNF Posture

For the next decade or more, dramatic alternatives to flexible response are unlikely. There will be no escaping the nuclear dilemma. But managing it will require more clarity about TNF than has been the case in the past. In military terms, the first watchword is survivability: so that NATO can retain some credible nuclear options; so that it does not invite pre-emption; and so that its nuclear weapons do not seem more frightening to the people they are intended to protect than to would-be adversaries.[19] A second watchword is flexibility. Happily, we have no precedent for nuclear war in Europe, so the only thing we can predict about one should it occur is that it would be unpredictable. But the analysis of this chapter underscores two propositions: if NATO leaders are forced to the awful choice of using nuclear weapons, their choices probably will not reflect the conventional wisdom of the time. And they are likely to look to relatively limited, largely demonstrative strikes which pose to the Soviet Union the most awkward retaliatory options.

Against those criteria, the first need for NATO is sharply to reduce its nominal reliance on short-range TNF. These systems have little value in military terms; reliance on them distorts military planning, and the large numbers are handy objects of anti-nuclear protest. At the time of the December 1979 decisions, NATO agreed to withdraw 1,000 warheads — and then withdrew them so quietly it got no public credit for having done so —and in October 1983 NATO leaders promised to withdraw 1,400 more. It should be possible to go further. Consider a recent inventory after the 1,000 warheads referred to above were removed (Table 4.1).

Table 4.1: NATO Nuclear Weapons in Europe, including French and British Weapons (1982)

Weapon	Quantity
Atomic demolition munitions (ADMs, or mines)	300
Artillery shells	2250
Surface-to-surface missiles (Honest John, Lance Pershing I, Pluton)	550
Gravity bombs	1900
Surface-to-air missiles (Nike-Hercules)	700
Maritime weapons	400
Total	6100

Source: Adapted from Jonathan Alford, 'Tactical Nuclear Weapons in Europe', *NATO's Fifteen Nations*, 2 (1981), p. 80.

The Nike-Hercules systems is scheduled to be replaced by a conventional air defence in any case, and with the exception of some possible uses on NATO flanks, it is hard to imagine any reason for keeping atomic mines.

Similarly, most of NATO's current dual-capable aircraft should be reconfigured as conventional only, along with most of the dual-capable artillery. While the artillery systems are numerous, hence relatively survivable, while most of their nuclear yields are relatively low, and while they permit many allies to share in the nuclear mission, the arguments against retaining many are formidable. Longer-range NATO systems should suffice to deter the Soviets both from using shorter-range systems of their own and from massing their conventional forces as they might if they had no fear that nuclear weapons would be used against them.

The shift away from short-range systems would have several happy consequences for the alliance. In military planning, it would free nuclear-capable aircraft and artillery pieces which are badly needed for conventional roles in the defence of Europe. At present, the nuclear and conventional roles for such weapons compete directly. If field commanders believe nuclear use is likely, then they should withhold systems, probably just at the point in the conventional battle when they would be most needed. Or if they do the opposite and commit such systems to the conventional battle, they may be reluctant later to pull them back in reserve for nuclear use lest that signal the adversary that nuclear war is imminent.

As important, by reducing numbers of nuclear weapons, especially those that seem in popular image the weapons most likely to be used, reducing reliance on short-range systems should diminish opposition to nuclear weapons among publics in Western Europe. It now looks to many Western Europeans that despite the reductions underway, NATO is simply piling up weapons beyond reason, and that it is dangerously trigger-happy to boot. Fewer total numbers of weapons and more clarity about their purpose would hardly satisfy all the nuclear critics in Europe, but it would help.

The second guideline is related to the first. It is the need to continue to modernise NATO's TNF posture in the direction of longer-range, hence more survivable, systems. Again, the point is not to develop a better 'war-fighting' capability. It is to sustain the credibility on which NATO's essentially political purpose – deterrence – rests, and to do so with numbers and configurations of weapons that do not scare NATO's citizens more than they worry the Soviet General Staff. If weapons are survivable enough, numbers do not have to be large. For example, William Kaufman estimates that there are about 1,600 military targets for nuclear weapons in Eastern Europe, of which less than half would be mobile company-sized units.[20] Yet even if the targets were military it is important to recognise that the intent of the targeting would be essentially political: to deter the Soviet Union from going nuclear or, if need be, to dramatically up the ante.

Longer-range systems are less vulnerable to pre-emption because they can be based further back in NATO Europe even if their targets are not deep in the Warsaw Pact. For example, NATO has been considering a successor to the Lance, which has a range of 70 miles. Systems slightly longer than that in range would also make sense by permitting a broader range of basing options, while perhaps not evoking the public emotion of systems that can strike the Soviet Union. Newer missiles will have more flexiblity in targeting mobile forces, to the extent NATO desires. If missiles do not have the requisite flexibility, Kaufman has suggested substituting helicopters carrying nuclear rockets, deployed back and dispersed in peacetime, for the existing reliance on nuclear-capable aircraft.

Targeting the Soviet Union with missiles based on the ground in Western Europe will remain a sensitive issue for NATO. Striking targets inside the Soviet Union would have little effect on the course of a ground battle in Central Europe, but that is not the point of NATO's TNF. Everything we know about Soviet thinking indicates, as Chapter 7 notes, that the Soviet Union *does* make a sharp distinction between the territory of its allies and its own homeland, never mind how discomforting that must be to allies. Thus, *some* European-based capability to strike Soviet territory is a powerful indicator of NATO resolve, and it underscores the essential symmetry, as NATO sees it, between SS-20s in Russia targeted on Western Europe and similar missiles in Western Europe that can strike Russia.

At the same time, there are arguments against *too* many missiles in Europe targeted on the Soviet Union. As I suggested above, in a war NATO probably would not want to use those missiles early on anyway; in peacetime, NATO wants to avoid a force big enough to seem to decouple Europe from the American strategic deterrence deterrent, which, after all, has plenty of capability to strike the Soviet Union. Most important, Europeans will be sensitive about striking the Soviet Union from their territory. Moscow will argue that such capabilities are tantamount to first-strike threats, and that argument will find a resonance in Western Europe.

In any event, there are grounds for avoiding too much preoccupation with land-basing. There are strong military arguments for sea-basing: mobility, hence relative invulnerability to pre-emptive destruction, and the lack of obvious retaliatory options against European territory inherent in land-based systems.

Command and control of sea-based systems would remain a problem but perhaps less of a one under the approach to TNF outlined here, since NATO would plan relatively limited strikes for political purposes, rather than precise, highly co-ordinated attacks on a scale large enough directly to affect the land battle. There is no reason why sea-based cruise missiles should be less accurate against military targets than ground-based versions, and the next generation of SLBMs will be more accurate than current systems. Moreover, some of the political controversy which surrounds the stationing of nuclear weapons on European territory could be avoided, and the escalatory distance to strategic sea-based systems reduced.

However, NATO's December 1979 decision excluded sea-based systems, apparently for three reasons.[21] Land-based missile technologies seemed to be more readily availble. Cost was also crucial: sea-based systems would be more expensive, either directly if new submarines (or fast surface craft) were built as launch platforms, or indirectly if existing submarines were converted to the cruise-missile role. Second, the Nordic NATO governments apparently opposed sea-basing for fear that NATO submarines would seek the protection of their inland waters, thus exposing them to Soviet retaliation. There was also the widely held view that only the visibility of deployment on land could demonstrate NATO's resolve to the Soviet Union, reassuring Europeans that the American President would not be tempted to fail to respond to a Soviet attack on Western Europe. Alas, there is more than a hint that Europe and America were caught in a game of mirrors, with the United States arguing that only ground-basing would assuage European fears and the Federal Republic in particular sensing an American preference for land-based systems.

Again, however, political symbolism alone should not be allowed to dominate military considerations; if it is permitted to dominate, the original political purposes will not be served. One of the ironies of the debate over the December 1979 decision is that European doves and American hawks were joined in deprecating the 572 missiles: what looked unnecessary and dangerous to the former seemed too few to matter and of questionable survivability to the latter. If sea-based systems are attractive on technical and strategic grounds, they will need to be considered more seriously in the future.

Almost unnoticed in the public debate, the Reagan administration has accelerated previous plans to deploy cruise missiles aboard attack submarines and surface ships, in both anti-ship and land-attack missions.[22] It should not be beyond the wit of the alliance to give many of those a theatre mission, and to concoct ways to connect them with Europe, for instance by assigning them to NATO and perhaps basing a portion in Europe. Similarly, it might be possible to give American B-52s with cruise missiles a theatre mission despite their basing in the United States. Unhappily, however, the Alliance will remain the prisoner of the sharp distinction that has arisen, largely out of the SALT process, between strategic and theatre forces, notwithstanding the fact that as a matter of doctrine NATO stresses the connection between the two.

A third guideline for TNF is the need to improve C3I. Moving away from short-range systems will decrease the vulnerability of command and control, but NATO leaders will still need to communicate with each other, and to do so fast, in the middle of a war raging in Europe and without the Soviet Union intercepting the communications. Again, the point is not to be able to fight limited nuclear wars. It is to make sure that NATO presents no image of recklessness in peacetime, and risks no recklessness in fact during a war. The more that political leaders, especially the American President, insist on complete control of weapons release and targeting — and they *will* so insist — the greater the need for C3I systems that provide as many choices of weapons and targets as rapidly as possible.

Given the short distances in Europe, command and control installations are likely to remain vulnerable no matter what NATO does. C3I may be made tolerably adequate for the nuclear purposes outlined here. It is not, however, easy to imagine that political leaders, in a crisis, would feel confident that they could execute and control the sophisticated, limited nuclear exchange against military targets in Europe that are conjured up by current strategic scenarios. This again argues for more thought about what nuclear weapons can and cannot do; for a doctrine which relies less heavily on nuclear threats; and for forces which combine a greater degree of survivability and flexibility with missions that make sense under realistic conditions of European warfare.

Fourth, there is no alternative to trying to invest more in conventional forces even while recognising the limitations. It will take strong efforts even to maintain the conventional balance where it is, in the face of tight budgets and declining manpower. Those efforts will be necessary just to keep the nuclear threshold from becoming lower. Yet the balance is not as bad as it has usually been thought to be, and probably never has been. The current SACEUR, General Rogers, wrote in 1982 that if NATO countries could manage military budget increases of 4 per cent yearly in real terms — most European countries have not consistently met the 3 per cent agreed to in 1977 — the alliance would not be in a position of having to contemplate using nuclear weapons early in a major war in Europe by the early 1990s.[23]

Beginning to build a tolerable consensus that the conventional situation is not hopeless is the first necessity as a public counterpart to actually trying to improve forces. A second is not to oversell any particular improvement. *Any* change NATO makes — in weaponry, technology or tactics — is bound to be at the margins. Those margins can be important. But publics will sometimes hope for more, and military analysts, especially American, like snake oil salesmen, will often advertise particular innovations as more. The result is only to set loose expectations which cannot be fulfilled, or arouse political controversy over the political implications of new measures (like deep interdiction, for example), or both. It is better to minimise the 'newness' of particular measures, even if that may appear to make it harder to elicit the necessary money from national parliaments.

A fifth guideline, also hard, is for NATO governments to make better public arguments for nuclear measures than they did in the case of the December 1979 decisions. The most straightforward rationale for the new deployments was simple modernisation — the need for new means to carry out an existing mission. While by 1979 NATO had few systems based in Europe capable of striking the Soviet Union with nuclear weapons, it did have some. However, excluding submarine-based systems, all those were nuclear-capable aircraft. Those planes, badly needed for conventional missions in any case, were more and more dubious in their ability to survive on the ground and penetrate Soviet air defence. Hence the need for modernisation.

A second line of rationale for the new systems raised nearly as many uncomfortable questions as it answered. It invoked all the esoterica of strategic analysis — escalation ladders and control, sanctuaries and thresholds — and was fundamentally inconclusive. Is an American President more likely to fire American cruise missiles based in Germany than American Poseidon submarine-launched missiles assigned to NATO and parked in mid-Atlantic? If he is not, new weaponry looks irrelevant. If he is, that raises the European nightmare of a nuclear war confined to Europe. To be sure, the new missiles in Europe would increase Soviet uncertainty by providing additional options, and thus make NATO a more difficult beast with which to deal. But that argument was hard to make, harder still to make compelling. Thus it let loose the feeling in Europe that, at best, NATO was simply piling up more nuclear weapons without reason, at worst, that the new missiles would be more endangering than protective by providing more targets for Soviet missiles.

In the circumstances, there was a temptation, understandable enough, to focus on the Soviet SS-20. Politicians and public opinion were aware of it, and concerned. Yet the focus on the SS-20 misposed the issue, since it was a small part of the military argument for new NATO deployments. It focused on what *they* had rather than what *we* needed. It handed the Soviet Union easy opportunities to make arms-control proposals intended to undermine European support for the NATO deployments. As SS-20 deployments reached what no doubt had been the original Soviet target for them, it was child's play for Soviet leaders to tempt Western public opinion with various proposals to freeze or reduce the SS-20s.

The 1982 proposal by four eminent former American officials to forswear the first use of nuclear weapons by NATO testifies to the difficulty of squaring military logic with political concerns over nuclear weapons. The arguments for making such a 'no-first-use' (NFU) pledge are substantial.[24] If changing military circumstances have made a first use incredible while retaining the doctrine makes NATO look reckless, why not change the doctrine? Renouncing first use would provide the need, and should increase the political willingness, especially in Western Europe, at last to make adequate arrangements for conventional defence. Finally, since the Soviet Union never could fully believe in a NATO NFU pledge, the effect on deterrence of making one might well be small in any event. The purpose of the change would lie more among the allies than between them and the Soviet Union; it would aim at a doctrine in which Western publics had confidence.

Substantial as those arguments are, NATO should get its force posture right first by reducing its reliance on short-range nuclear systems, and only then consider a change in declaratory policy. For the near term, NATO will remain the prisoner of the lack of public confidence in its conventional forces. In that circumstance, there is the risk that Europeans, especially Germans, would read a renunciation of first use as a sign that the United States was abandoning them. As a first reaction from governing élites that was predictable; it was the ritual – and from a European perspective, reasonable – opposition to any change in the *status quo*.[25] For its part, the peace movement in Europe initially paid little attention to the NFU idea; for it, no doubt, the change would have been pure rhetoric, scarcely worth noticing. Thus, NFU – a proposal explicitly intended to increase public support for NATO doctrine and defence arrangements – was worrisome to governing establishments in Europe and ignored by the nuclear opposition. It was a kind of political MLF: a made-in-America solution to a European political problem as misperceived by Americans.

Military Sense and Arms Control

Unhappily, recent episodes are more instructive about what *not* to do in relating arms control to military considerations than what to do. The double decision of December 1979 is a stark example. The process of consultation which preceded that decision was more painstaking than any in the history of NATO, a model blend of European involvement and American leadership. Yet the second track of the double decision – the commitment to TNF arms control negotiations with the Soviet Union – was driven entirely by calculations of European politics. Military considerations played a role only in the sense that arms-control negotiations were deemed necessary if the alliance were to have any chance of sustaining public support for actually deploying some or all of the 572 missiles.

Yet on military grounds the negotiations were unpromising in the extreme, for by-now-familiar reasons recounted in Chapter 9. Soviet longer-range TNF (now called intermediate-range nuclear forces (INF)), like the SS-20, the subject of first concern, were deployed in increasingly large numbers (350 SS-20s by the middle of 1983), while NATO was not to begin to deploy its 572 missiles until the end of 1983. NATO was thus in the position of bargaining intentions, and questionable intentions at that, against weapons in place. It was clearly too much to expect arms-control negotiations to produce a balance from such an extreme existing imbalance. NATO's position was like that with which it entered the Mutual and Balanced Force Reduction (MBFR) talks in Vienna in the early 1970s, but it was worse in two particulars: NATO reckoned the pre-existing imbalance as worse in the INF case, and, unlike MBFR, INF talks which merely dragged on with no result in sight were not likely to achieve the political objective for which they were designed. Quite the contrary, the negotiations dragging on meant continuing agony for the political leaders faced with the deployment of new systems.

In purely military terms the so-called 'zero option' — President Reagan's offer in the autumn of 1981 to forego the NATO deployments if the Soviet Union dismantled all its SS-20s, -4s, and -5s — only compounded the problems. It was good short-term politics but bad military logic. Since the reason for NATO's deployments had only partly to do with the SS-20, there would have been an argument for some deployments even if there had been no SS-20s. The zero option thus eroded whatever justification for the deployments NATO leaders were able to articulate, even as it seemed to serve their short-run political purposes.

Of course, narrow military considerations yielded to broader political concerns. Removing the political and psychological overhang on Western Europe produced by the Soviet INF no doubt would have been worth the price of not deploying the 572 missiles. NATO has other ways to modernise its own INF. However, the first guideline for arms control is that NATO must protect *some* options for modernising INF. If the 572 land-based missiles were bargained away, that would make it all the more important for NATO to retain the right to deploy sea-based cruise missiles. Given that the Soviet Union is sure to seek negotiated constraints on all types of cruise missiles, land- and sea-based, how to treat the latter will be a focus of future negotiations.

A second guideline is the need to keep the INF negotiations closely related to the Soviet-American strategic negotiations, for reasons of NATO doctrine and military logic. American strategic forces and INF are, from NATO's perspective, parts of a continuum of deterrence. The Soviet Union will always have opportunities to target arms-control proposals at points of strain between the United States and its European partners. Suppose, for instance, that the Soviet Union had accepted 'deep cuts' — sharp reductions in the strategic forces of the two sides — but only on the condition that NATO had forgone deployment of the 572 long-range theatre missiles. The Reagan administration, eager for arms control involving real reductions and preoccupied in any case with the strategic balance, might have been tempted to agree. Yet to do so would have been to sacrifice European interests to achieve American ones, in appearance if not in fact.

Approaches to the INF and strategic negotiations will have to be tightly co-ordinated. At some point, INF might be incorporated directly into the strategic negotiations, with expanded totals. For instance, aggregate limit for launchers and/or warheads on either side might be expanded to include INF, with both sides given the freedom to determine the precise mix between strategic and long-range theatre systems.[26] This approach would not solve the daunting technical problems of the INF negotiations, but it would mean that what are at present large imbalances in INF would be less dramatic, hence more manageable, in talks comprising both strategic and long-range theatre systems. More important, it would underscore the unity between NATO's INF and American strategic forces.

A third guideline is, to the extent possible, to anticipate the *next* nuclear issue. For example, neglecting shorter-range TNF was one of the dangers of NATO's preoccupation with the SS-20 after 1977-8. Just as SALT II dramatised the SS-20 by excluding it, so the risk of the INF negotiations was that they would underscore the threat posed by the shorter-range systems they left out. NATO could find that it had 'solved' its SS-20 problem only to have it replaced with an SS-21, -22, and -23 problem, especially if the Soviet Union began to deploy those systems in numbers in Eastern Europe in the wake of NATO's INF deployments. The shorter-range Soviet systems could threaten Western Europe from bases in Eastern Europe the same way as do SS-20s based in central Russia. The SS-22, for example, has a range of over 500 miles.

Anticipating the issue of shorter-range TNF will require a combination of arms control and sensible public statements. Any negotiated limits on INF should be accompanied by collateral constraints on at least those systems, like the SS-22, that could be used to circumvent limits on INF systems like the SS-20. If the Soviets responded to

NATO's Pershing and cruise deployments with increases in their battlefield and very short-range TNF forces in Eastern Europe, the allies' response should be steadiness, especially in public. After all, if NATO judges battlefield TNF to be of declining value for it, some increase in the Soviet systems of shortest range is hardly cause for alarm.

Military Solutions and Political Objectives

The history of TNF emphasises the proposition with which this chapter began: there can be no purely military solution to NATO's nuclear dilemma. Nuclear issues, sensitive by their nature, will remain barometers of Alliance cohesion and European confidence in the United States. It is worth remembering that there were European doubts over the reliability of America's nuclear deterrent even in the 1950s at a time of undisputed American strategic superiority; there would remain doubts now even if the United States were prepared to match Soviet SS-20s and Backfires system for system in Europe.

Nuclear weapons serve in part as political symbols for the alliance; they cannot by themselves provide the substance of cohesion. It clearly is important to arrange those forces — both strategic and TNF — in a way that makes sense, and moving away from such reliance on short-range TNF is the right direction. But to pretend that such measures will provide a solution is to misunderstand the problem. American support for European security is rooted in political cohesion more than military arrangements. General de Gaulle was correct in noting (although he was careful not to put it this way) that America's security commitment to Europe depends in the first instance not on military integration but on continuing political interest.

Notes

1. Richard Neustadt's conclusion about the Skybolt affair is even more apt with regard to the MLF: 'Macmillan . . . made what seems to me a classic error in high policy or politics: he pursued objectives, diplomatic and political, designed as something else, a military posture, which was suspect in its own terms, liable to attack or ridicule or both.' See *Alliance Politics* (New York: Columbia University Press, 1970), p. 147.

2. These 6,000 are itemised in Table 4.1. See Jonathan Alford, 'Tactical Nuclear Weapons in Europe', *NATO's Fifteen Nations*, Special Issue, 2 (1981), p. 80.

3. For a strong argument along these lines, see Uwe Nerlich, 'Theater Nuclear

Forces in Europe: Is NATO Running Out of Options?' *The Washington Quarterly*, vol. 3, no. 1 (Winter 1980).

4. The now classic discussion is Albert Wolhstetter, 'The Delicate Balance of Terror', *Foreign Affairs* (January 1959).

5. His speech is printed in *Survival*, 1 (January/February 1978).

6. The American Single Integrated Operational Plan (SIOP) divides Soviet nuclear targets into four categories: opposing nuclear forces and other 'hard targets'; economic and recovery targets; political control mechanisms; and other military targets (OMT). OMT is the largest of the four categories, some 20,000, comprising half the SIOP targets. See Desmond Ball, 'Soviet ICBM Deployment', *Survival*, vol. 22, no. 4 (July/August 1980), pp. 167-70. On the uses of submarine-launched missiles against OMT, see Desmond J. Ball, 'The Counterforce Potential of American SLBM Systems', *Journal of Peace Research*, 1 (1977), pp. 23-40.

7. Anthony H. Cordesman, *Deterrence in the 1980s, Part I: American Strategic Forces and Extended Deterrence*, Adelphi Paper no. 175 (London: IISS, Summer 1982), pp. 35-6.

8. Jeffrey Record, 'Theatre Nuclear Weapons:Begging the Soviet Union to Pre-empt', *Survival*, vol. 19, no. 5 (September/October 1977), pp. 208-11.

9. See Robert Kennedy, 'Soviet Theater-Nuclear Forces: Implications for NATO Defense', *Orbis* (Summer 1981).

10. US Department of the Army, *Operations: FM 100-5* (1982), pp. 7-12.

11. Alton Frye, 'Nuclear Weapons in Europe: No Exit from Ambivalence', *Survival*, vol. 22. no. 3 (May/June 1980), pp. 98-106.

12. W.S. Bennett, R.R. Sandoval and R.G. Shreffler have done the most work on such proposals. See their 'A Credible Nuclear-Emphasis Defense for NATO', *Orbis*, vol. 17, no. 2 (Summer 1973).

13. Most arguments to the contrary are, for good reason, tentative. See, for example, Pierre Lellouche's argument for a broadening of the role of British and French nuclear forces, in 'Europe and Her Defense', *Foreign Affairs*, vol. 54, no. 4 (Spring 1981), pp. 813-34; Hedly Bull's explicit call for more European cooperation, including nuclear, in 'European Self-Reliance and the Reform of NATO', *Atlantic Quarterly* vol. 1, no. 1 (Spring 1983), pp. 25-43; and a similar, though even more tentative argument from German Social Democrats, in Wilhelm Bruns and Christian Krause, 'Reflections on a European Peace Order' (Friedrich Ebert Stiftung, December 1982).

14. See his 'NATO Myths', *Foreign Policy*, 45 (Winter 1981-2), p. 55. This section owes much to Freedman.

15. This point is stressed by Horst Afheldt. See his 'Tactical Nuclear Weapons and European Security', Chapter 9 of SIPRI, *Tactical Nuclear Weapons: European Perspectives* (London, 1978). See also Robert S. McNamara, 'The Military Role of Nuclear Weapons: Perceptions and Misperceptions', *Foreign Affairs* (Autumn 1983), pp. 59-80.

16. Kent F. Wisner, 'Military Aspects of Enhanced Radiation Weapons', *Survival*, vol. 23, no. 6 (November/December 1981).

17. For a strong argument about the difficulty of controlling nuclear war, see Desmond Ball. *Can Nuclear War Be Controlled?* Adelphi Paper no. 169 (London: IISS, 1981).

18. See, for example, Senator Sam Nunn's report, *NATO: Can the Alliance Be Saved?* Report to the Senate Committee on Armed Services, 97 Cong., 2 sess. (13 May 1982); and Report of the European Security Study, Strengthening Conventional Deterrence in Europe: Proposals for the 1980s (1983).

19. For a good analysis, parallel to this one in most respects, see J. Michael Legge, *Theater Nuclear Weapons and the NATO Strategy of Flexible Response*,

R-2964-FF (Santa Monica: The Rand Corporation, April 1983).

20. See W. Kaufman, 'Nuclear Deterrence in Central Europe' in John D. Steinbruner and Leon V. Sigal (eds.), *Alliance Security: NATO and the No-First-Use Question* (Washington: The Brookings Institution, 1983), p. 41.

21. For a history of the December decision, see David C. Elliot, *Decision at Brussels: The Politics of Nuclear Forces*, California Seminar Discussion Paper no. 97 (Santa Monica, 1981).

22. See *The Modernization of NATO's Long-Range Theater Nuclear Forces*, Report of the Subcommittee on Europe and the Middle East of the House Commitee on Foreign Affairs, 96 Cong., 2 sess (1980).

23. General Bernard W. Rogers, 'The Atlantic Alliance: Prescriptions for a Difficult Decade', *Foreign Affairs,* vol. 60, no. 5 (Summer 1982), pp. 1145-56.

24. McGeorge Bundy, George F. Kennan, Robert S. McNamara and Gerard Smith, 'Nuclear Weapons and the Atlantic Alliance', *Foreign Affairs*, vol. 60, no. 4 (Spring 1982), pp. 753-68.

25. For this reaction from the German establishment, see Karl Kaiser, Georg Leber, Alois Mertes and Franz-Josef Schulze, 'Nuclear Weapons and the Preservation of Peace', *Foreign Affairs*, vol. 60, no. 5 (Summer 1982), pp. 1157-70. For background and analysis of NFU, see Steinbruner and Sigal (eds.), *Alliance Security*.

26. For an early proposal along these lines, see Lawrence Freedman, 'The Dilemma of Theatre Nuclear Arms Control', *Survival*, vol. 23, no. 1 (January/February 1981), pp. 2-10.

5 THE ROLE OF THIRD-COUNTRY NUCLEAR FORCES

Lawrence Freedman

A theatre nuclear force is an extremely ethnocentric concept. The ethnocentrism lies not so much in the designation of Europe as a 'theatre' of war, within which things might be tolerable that could never be accepted outside the theatre, but in the fact that variations in location have prompted an attempt to distinguish between weapons that have the same essential meaning for both potential users and victims. So long as the implication remains that the use of theatre (or 'tactical' or 'intermediate' or 'grey-area') weapons would somehow be less serious in its consequences than the use of 'strategic' weapons this ethnocentrism will remain.

The reliance on geography as a key criterion for differentiating weapons inevitably leads to anomalies. The 'theatre' category, for example, obscures the large differences in mode of delivery, yield and target-structure between the battlefield systems and what are now called intermediate systems while the significant similarity of these latter systems to American strategic systems is also obscured. When it comes to China, which for its nuclear history has had to rely on strategic deterrent of a purely regional force, the attempt to apply distinctions of this sort becomes even more futile.

Most Europeans have at some point grumbled about the use of 'theatre' as a sort of residual category for all those weapons that are neither based in nor targeted upon the United States. The efforts in SALT to secure agreement from the Soviet Union on a limited range for the SS-20 and Backfire bombers so that they could not threaten the continental United States were particularly irritating in this context. Germans frequently point out that if battlefield nuclear weapons were ever employed, what might appear as a 'tactical' matter to the Americans (or others outside the combat zone) would be very much strategic to them.

However, it is probably the French who have taken the most exception to the term 'theatre nuclear force', at least when applied to their own weapons. Not only have they resisted any American classifications on principle, as well as seeking to stress their separateness from other NATO forces, but they have also insisted that their *force de frappe* has exactly the same role in its deterrence posture as does the strategic triad in that of the United States. French policy-makers have therefore been anxious that their 'strategic' forces should not be confused with NATO forces, but they have also insisted that their *force de frappe* has *tous azimuths*, able to attack any part of the globe if necessary. To stress the regional constraints of the current French force, by comparison with the more grandiose plans of the mid-1960s, is only to rub salt into the wound.

British policy-makers have had a similar view though typically putting pragmatism before purity in matters of military doctrine. They have not made a fuss when in the past Britain's 'independent' strategic deterrent force warranted only a few words in American posture statements, and then in sections of theatre forces.

If we take strategic forces to refer to those able to attack the economic and political centres of the enemy (and possibly also the enemy's strategic forces), then it is clear that many nuclear weapons in the arsenals of Britain, France and China come into this category. However it is also the case that many do not, and these deserve to be classed as battlefield forces, designed to attack military targets on or around the battlefield, and yet more are in the inevitable 'grey area', geared to interdiction of supply lines or reserve forces which may well coincide with political or economic centres.

This somewhat pedantic introduction is intended to stress the importance of dividing British and French forces which happen, in American eyes, to be based in the European theatre into strategic forces and into forces which most correspond with the types that the United States places in its own 'theatre' category. For the interesting question is not what the British and French believe they are achieving by possessing their own 'independent' strategic forces, but why they need any other nuclear systems. Both have doctrines which stress the extent to which nuclear deterrence is based on threats to industry and population and are quite removed from war-fighting as traditionally conceived. The question also applies to the Chinese, although the context in this case is somewhat different.

It is arguable that if the small nuclear powers wish to avoid the expense and the bother of constructing nuclear forces of the complex structure necessary to meet the exacting standards of the superpowers then their best course is to opt for simplicity. That is if they assume, as they do, that they must plan to 'stand alone' against the Soviet Union then their best course is to threaten a virtually automatic retaliation against Soviet cities in the event of any invasion of territory. In

Role of Third-Country Nuclear Forces 115

such an approach there is little scope for messing around on a nuclear battlefield. Indeed, preparation to do such a thing might even dilute the credibility of the strategic deterrent.

There is therefore even less of an obvious role for theatre nuclear forces in the plans of smaller nuclear powers than there is in the plans of the superpowers, which must prepare for a wide range of types of nuclear exchanges. This chapter is therefore concerned with explaining why theatre forces are to be found in the inventories of the smaller powers.

Britain

The British approach to its nuclear force until the early 1960s was shaped by a sense that it was still a major power with wide-ranging responsibilities, and therefore was entitled to and needed all advanced armaments. In the first post-war decade the nuclear-weapon inventories of the major powers were determined by the size of the weapon stockpiles and by progress along the path from fission to fusion weapons. The various classifications of types of delivery vehicles by range and ostensible military purpose were far less important than now.

The initial focus of Britain's nuclear programme was to develop a force capable of attacking Soviet cities. This was in line both with the traditions of the Royal Air Force who would have operational responsibility for the new weapons, and with the perceived strategic needs of the day which was to keep the presumed expansive tendencies of the Soviet Union in check by the threat of destruction as a modern industrial society. The stress on the need to achieve massive destructive power can be seen from the decision in 1955 to push on towards thermonuclear weapons rather than remain content with the smaller fission bombs. Although there was a certain sense that national prestige required keeping up with the United States and USSR, the strategic assumption behind the decision was that the threat of large-scale destruction would, in the future, provide the main source of security. As Churchill put it at the time, 'by a process of sublime irony, we have reached a stage in this story where safety may becme the sturdy child of terror and survival the twin brother of annihilation'.[1]

The British had encouraged the move in the United States towards 'massive retaliation', taking up the main themes of basing Western strategy on its nuclear assets rather than following the communist stress on expensive conventional forces even before the advent of the

Eisenhower administration. The American 'New Look', as explained by John Foster Dulles, was thus welcomed in Britain and influenced both its doctrine and force structure.

Part of the New Look was the introduction of tactical nuclear weapons. The development of these weapons had initially been encouraged by scientists and others anxious to find a military use of atomic weapons other than mass destruction. However the breakthroughs in nuclear technology had made possible the production of large numbers of both strategic and tactical weapons.

The Eisenhower administration did not feel obliged to make a choice between them, but rather saw them as quite distinct types of weapons. The tactical weapons could be used as if they were conventional weapons and their main value would be as a relatively inexpensive form of ordnance. Atomic artillery, mines and air defence systems were introduced into Europe during the late 1950s to reinforce the NATO armies whose forces were trained to operate them, with the actual weapons themselves controlled under dual-key arrangements.

Britain did not demur from this policy. It was the British Deputy SACEUR, Field-Marshal Lord Montgomery, who heralded this development in a much-publicised speech in late 1954 on the role of atomic and thermonuclear weapons in defence plans: 'With us it is no longer: "They may possibly be used." It is very definitely: "They will be used, if we are attacked." '[2] In the 1957 Defence White Paper which provided the most dogmatic statement of the British view that there was no alternative to nuclear deterrence for NATO, the cutback in conventional forces was combined with a decision to equip British forces in Germany with nuclear artillery. It took until 1960 before Honest John and Corporal guns (which had been ordered in 1955) were brought into service by the UK, but from 1958 the defence planning and tactics of the British Army in Germany were conceived in nuclear terms.[3] The warheads were stored under American custody under dual-key arrangements. A conscious decision was taken not to develop national nuclear shells of ADMs, but to rely on the United States. However, British aircraft, such as the Valiants assigned to NATO in 1960-1, did contain nuclear weapons produced and controlled by the British.[4]

The development of a tactical capability was not particularly controversial. There were grave doubts expressed as to the wisdom of 'massive retaliation' but there was quite widespread support for tactical nuclear weapons (TNWs). The British limited-war theorists toyed with the idea that TNWs might be a sort of compromise between the need to exploit nuclear technology as the area of the West's comparative advantage, and the incredibility of threats of massive retaliation. For example, the response of Denis Healey, then making his name in the Labour Party as a defence specialist, to the launch of the USSR's Sputnik 1 in October 1957 was that the case was strengthened for 'supplementing or replacing massive retaliation by limited atomic war — and for giving tactical atomic weapons to America's allies'.[5]

By the end of the decade the problems of reconciling any use of nuclear weapons with limited war had become apparent. Led by Sir Solly (later Lord) Zuckerman, who was Chief Scientific Adviser to the Ministry of Defence from 1960 to 1966, there was a strong reaction against the whole concept of 'limited nuclear war'. Zuckerman argued that there 'is, in fact, no realistic and no theoretical justification for the belief that nuclear weapons could ever be used as a rational extension of conventional armaments'.[6] He obtained many high-level converts to his beliefs throughout NATO as well as in Britain, but, as he himself acknowledges, there was little change in weapons or plans. Certainly from this period on, however, it has been very difficult to detect much enthusiasm in the Army for battlefield nuclear weapons, which are generally considered to complicate unnecessarily the business of soldiering.

From these formative years two related observations can be made. Firstly, the debate in Britain was very similar to that in the United States. This was not only in the original adoption of TNWs by those anxious for an alternative to strategies based on terror, followed by their rejection as it was realised that the most likely consequence of their introduction would be to bring forward the start of the holocaust. The British attitude was also similar to that of the United States in the sense of distance from Germany. In the Federal Republic, reports of NATO wargames in which the use of atomic munitions by the allies decimated the country, led to public uproar and a bitter debate about whether some of the means of enhancing deterrence were just too risky. The prospect of becoming a nuclear battlefield was as unappealing in the mid-1950s as it was 25 years later. The instinct in Britain was similar to that in the United States — however unpleasant for those in the combat zone, if nuclear use served a useful military purpose and could be contained then that would be preferable.

Because it is an island, Britain has never been put as much at risk by the concept of TNWs as those closer to the border with the East. It was noticeable in the 1977-8 period that the anti-neutron-bomb campaign was not as fervent in Britain as on the continent. It was the announcement that there were to be American cruise missile bases in

Britain under American control in December 1979 that gave rise to concerns about being destroyed in exchanges that the superpowers might take to be secondary to strategic war. The character of the anti-cruise-missile campaign, and its pronounced European dimension can from one point of view even be said to be the maturing of a European consciousness in Britain.[7]

The second point is that there was little pretence that TNFs had very much to do with Britain's independent deterrent. The stress on independence, even for the strategic nuclear forces, which has largely been for domestic public consumption, always contrasted uneasily with the actual British security policy which stressed the importance of NATO and the American connection. The British aspiration was always more accurately described as interdependence than independence. The Polaris force was assigned to NATO, though with the significant qualifier 'except where Her Majesty's Government may decide that supreme national interests are at stake'.

For British theatre forces the link with NATO is even stronger. As with other European armies, the one regiment with Lance missiles and the three regiments with dual-capable artillery with the British Army of the Rhine use warheads that are controlled by the United States on a dual-key basis. The RAF still uses nationally-produced gravity bombs for its Vulcans, Buccaneers, Jaguars, and now Tornados,[8] but they are based in Germany and so more clearly assigned to NATO than the submarine-launched forces. The changes over time of the British theatre nuclear weapon inventory is shown in Table 5.1.

There has been very little discussion as to whether these TNFs could ever be used in pursuit of independent national interests (virtually none in the public literature as far as I am aware). Much discussion of Britain's nuclear forces continues without acknowledgement that the country possesses any weapons in this category. The annual Defence Estimates, at least until 1981, were hardly forthcoming on the matter. The only official references tended to come in the proud statements that Britain was the only European country fully committed to NATO that contributed to each component of the NATO triad of strategic, theatre and conventional forces.

This claim, that Britain performed some important function by offering to the alliance in parallel, if also only in miniature, the same basic types of forces as the United States, provided the context for one of the few recent policy debates on the subject. This took place in 1977-8 and the question was whether the Vulcan bombers, due to be phased out in the early 1980s, should be replaced by another system

Role of Third-Country Nuclear Forces

Table 5.1: United Kingdom Tactical Nuclear Weapons Inventory, 1960-82

	Red Beard (RAF)	Red Beard (RN)	Tactical Bomb (RAF & RN)	Total
1960	84	15	—	98
1961	141	30	—	171
1962	150	40	—	190
1963	147	38	—	185
1964	144	36	5	185
1965	141	34	10	185
1966	138	32	15	185
1967	135	30	20	185
1968	132	28	25	185
1969	110	25	30	165
1970	80	22	35	137
1971	50	10	40	100
1972	20	—	45	65
1973	—	—	75	75
1974	—	—	110	110
1975	—	—	145	145
1976	—	—	180	180
1977	—	—	215	215
1978	—	—	250	250
1979	—	—	247	247
1980	—	—	244	244
1981	—	—	241	241
1982	—	—	238	238

Taken from J. Simpson, *The Independent Nuclear State: The United States, Britain and the Military Atom* (London: Macmillan, 1983), pp. 254-5. These figures are estimates and convey a general rather than a precise picture. The Red Beard bomb first entered service in the late 1950s and had a yield of 5-20 kilotons. No figures are available for the tactical bomb. The table does not include the megaton bombs carried on the U-bomber force until it left service in 1984.

also capable of deep strikes against Soviet territory. A number of top officials argued that there was a requirement for a system with a capability to attack targets within the Soviet Union but directly relevant to the course of a land war in Europe. This would be in addition to a strategic capability for a last resort attack against Soviet cities.

The argument followed from the official rationale for the maintenance of a national nuclear force, which is that it reinforces the alliance's deterrent capability by introducing extra uncertainty into Soviet calculations. Instead of having to make a judgement solely on American intentions, the Kremlin would also have to consider the second centre of decision in London. If this doctrine is taken seriously,[9] then its logic would suggest that this particular set of uncertainties should face Soviet planners at the lower as well as the higher rungs of the escalation ladder. As at the time NATO was beginning to consider the long-range theatre nuclear force programme, and as Vulcan was a significant component of current NATO capabilities in this area but was due to be phased out, this line of argument led to the suggestion that it should be replaced by, say, a British-operated ground-launched cruise missile with British warheads.

This argument did not command general support. Others were not convinced by the strategic argument. A British role in the earlier stages of escalation could be fulfilled by the new Tornado which had been designated as a successor to Vulcan though it could not penetrate Soviet territory effectively. Moreover the resource implications of the proposal meant that it would inevitably incur disfavour when it was already likely that the successor to Polaris would require a substantial portion of the defence budget in the coming decade. Lastly there were doubts as to whether the Atomic Weapons Research Establishment (AWRE) would be able to cope with yet another warhead programme in addition to the Polaris successor.[10]

This incident illustrates the extent to which Britain lacks a well-developed doctrine for TNF. It maintains a significant capability in this area, which, largely because of Tornado and with the exception of long-range TNF, will if anything be increasing during the 1980s. As Table 5.1 demonstrates, the stockpile of weapons has also grown steadily. Britain is also improving its maritime capability.[11] To put it no higher, the use of dual-key systems at the level at which, according to NATO doctrine, nuclear war is most likely to start must qualify the concept of a second decision-centre. Britain would not be able to take the initiative at this level to 'go nuclear'. However, Britain would be able to take the initiative, with medium-range aircraft, equipped with UK-produced gravity bombs. Since these aircraft could be used for strikes in and around the battlefield, this would not necessarily involve moving to a higher level of escalation.

One of the features of the second-centre concept is that it could be used to support a policy of holding back from a nuclear conflict, by claiming 'sanctuary' status for the British Isles. Retaliation by Britain would only follow attacks on national territory. Yet if national nuclear forces were committed to combat in Germany then it might be difficult to claim this sort of sanctuary. In practice, the general integration of British territory into NATO battle-plans, including the provision of bases for the United States Air Force, would make it very difficult to keep any sort of distance from the full consequence of a war on the continent. In this sense, Britain cannot view first nuclear use in Europe by NATO with the same sense of detachment as might be possible in Washington. The only use of TNWs which might conceivably make sense, should Britain have been able to avoid implementing nuclear commitments while West Europe was being overrun, would be to thwart a cross-channel invasion by the Warsaw Pact.[12] Britain at least would have some idea of this possibility and the credibility of independent nuclear forces through observation of the fate of France!

Just as the implications of TNF for Britain's strategic nuclear deterrent have been inadequately discussed, this is also the case with the possibility of Britain getting out of the strategic nuclear business altogether. This is a very real possibility, for the Polaris successor programe, now based on the Trident D-5 SLBM, is hotly disputed. The Labour and Liberal Parties are opposed to an independent nuclear role and even supporters of such a role in the Social Democratic Party may be unwilling to pay a large price to maintain it. There has been a consistent failure to develop a compelling strategic rationale for the strategic force, with the result that it is very vulnerable to economic arguments. However, while financial pressures may push Britain out of the strategic nuclear business, they are unlikely to make much of an impact on lesser types of nuclear capabilities.[13] It is therefore possible to imagine Britain having no strategic nuclear capability yet persevering with independently developed weapons for medium-range bombers or nuclear depth charges for anti-submarine warfare. This would seem to be the worst of both worlds, as Britain would have no means of nuclear retaliation against Soviet territory yet would be preparing to engage in nuclear exchanges at a lower level. The lack of a 'last resort' capability would deprive the theatre forces of whatever credibility they might have as a source of deterrence, while the maintenance of independent medium-range forces would increase the risk of taking a prominent role in a nuclear war.

France

The capacity of TNF to confuse all attempts to develop plausible nuclear doctrine can be further illustrated with France. As expounded by General de Gaulle in the 1960s, French doctrine assumed that nuclear deterrence offered a virtually foolproof means to security, so long as it was clear that nuclear retaliation would be unleashed automatically once national territory was violated. The emphasis was on denying the enemy any hope that conflict could be contained at a conventional level that might keep risks tolerable and accentuate enemy strengths. The nuclear deterrent gained credibility because it could only be invoked by strictly national purposes. There would be no notions of extended deterrence. Lastly, France would offer no other excuses for attack by hosting provocative foreign bases. Such bases would not be accepted on French soil.

This approach was developed in opposition to the moves in NATO towards flexible response. The French critique was essentially that options diluted the credibility of the retaliatory threat, because the options were all to do less than impose on the enemy the deserved punishment. Furthermore, the American attempt to improve conventional forces was viewed as a means of reducing the risk to the United States while increasing those to Europe. A conventional bias would make war less dangerous for an aggressor (believed to be the inevitable result of stressing the nuclear threshold) even if it also made it easier for the supposed protector — the United States. The unwillingness to offer an undiluted nuclear guarantee was in itself seen as a question mark against the American commitment to the integrity of Europe.

The strategic concept was to attack the enemy's war potential and political will to persevere with an invasion rather than trying to cope directly with the invasion. As General Ailleret, one of the architects of this approach, explained, the role of conventional forces would solely be to measure the level of enemy attack to see if it warranted retaliation:

> If it were understood that breaking this line would automatically trigger a nuclear response which, by destroying the serpent's body and tail, would at the same time halt the progress of the head, then Europe, sheltered by such positions and by the nuclear arsenals of the alliance countries, would no longer fear one of the chief dangers threatening it and which is the whole object of flexible response, i.e. direct invasion by an air-land battle force.[14]

Within this concept there was little room for tactical nuclear weapons. Ailleret conceded that the 'use of nuclear fire on the battlefield and in the rear is . . . likely to block an invasion fairly quickly'. However, the cost could be too great: 'It is clear that even a purely tactical nuclear exchange would completely wipe out Europe over a depth of eighteen

Role of Third-Country Nuclear Forces

hundred miles from the Atlantic to the Soviet frontier.'[15] So blocking the invasion would not prevent destruction.

The objective was therefore to avoid battle which, conventional or nuclear, would devastate the territory in contention, and ensure that the offending superpower was clear that it was taking an enormous risk by even stepping into this territory. In 1964 Ailleret was describing how Europe would benefit from this strategy. By 1967 it was only France that would be the beneficiary. Ailleret was now explaining the need for a national 'thermonuclear force with a world-wide range'. The needs of an independent policy of dissuasion were quite different to supplementary forces of 'the main member of an a priori alliance' (i.e. the United States in NATO). After this requirement had been fulfilled, the role of TNWs remained uncertain, but some role seemed to exist: 'our existing air/ground and naval "battle forces" ' must be developed 'so as to correspond to the operational conditions of the atomic age'. These battle forces 'must necessarily be equipped with nuclear weapons and possess the required capabilities for acting offensively, even beyond our frontiers, the moment we are attacked'.[16]

There was one clear priority, which still remains part of the French consensus: France must have a strategic capability sufficient to impose costs on the USSR exceeding the possible gains that this potential enemy might envisage in occupying or destroying France (proportional deterrence). The objectives of any French strike would be unambiguous — the targets would be the civilian population concentrated in the major Soviet cities. There was no interest in selective strikes or war-fighting strategies, for such strategies are only appropriate where both belligerents have equivalent capabilities and possibly have a less-than-total interest in the dispute.

In the 1960s a 'triad' of aircraft, land-based and submarine ballistic missiles was envisaged. Some sort of triad did emerge with the Mirage IV aircraft and the intermediate-range missiles based in the Plateau d'Albion as well as a submarine-based force. The first two arms of this triad have always suffered from doubts about survivability and have not been developed to the extent originally planned. The Mirage IV bombers will be phased out by 1985. The 18 land-based missiles are to be retained, but their vulnerability is now widely acknowledged and there has been some discussion of eventual replacement with a mobile missile. Meanwhile increasing reliance has been placed on the submarine-based force. This was confirmed by the new Mitterrand government in 1981 announcing that a seventh missile-carrying submarine was to be commissioned.

Although some strategic rationales can be found for a mix of forces, including complicating any Soviet attempt at a pre-emptive strike, as important a reason is that the range of activities enhances France's reputation as nuclear power by acting as a showcase for the country's technical prowess. This desire to prove that France can do anything the superpowers can do may also explain why TNWs have been developed. At first glance the Gaullist distrust of any preparations for actual warfighting and the stress on virtually automatic retaliation against the Soviet homeland allows little scope for such weapons.

However, there is one possible rationale. If French conventional forces are not supposed to stop a Soviet invasion but to indicate that a fateful threshold is about to be crossed, then the use of TNWs would not only have the advantage of reducing the requirements of conventional forces still further, but would also provide a clear signal that any crossing of this threshold would have nuclear consequences. It was in just such terms that the Gaullists justified the development of a French short-range missile — Pluton — which became operational in 1975.

It was not until 1972, and the revelation that there was an airborne nuclear weapon, carried by Jaguar and Mirage IIIE, that there was any indication that France even had a nuclear capability below the strategic level. There was little comment at this time, possibly because the range of the aircraft took them beyond NATO soil into Warsaw Pact territory. Pluton caused more of a stir because with a range of 120 km it had one highly embarrassing property: it was most likely to explode on German soil.

It is difficult enough for Germans to accept that in order to deter an invasion they must accept nuclear weapons that would destroy Germany in the process of defending it. To be in range of French weapons that were not even deployed for the sake of German interests was intolerable, especially when there were signs that many Frenchmen seemed to think that the targeting policy so implied was perfectly proper for their country.

It is not altogether clear why Pluton was ever developed. It was conceived in November 1966 and approved by de Gaulle. It has been suggested that it was a concession to the Army, still bruised after Indo-China and Algeria and feeling left out of the nuclear business. It was only when the Pluton was close to deployment that anxiety began to develop over the implications for relations with West Germany and over how it fitted in with Gaullist doctrine.[17]

It was possible to smooth over the differences with West Germany by pointing to the mobility of Pluton. It moves in the field on trucks supported by armoured cars and can be transported considerable distances by helicopter. The firing mechanism need not be loaded until the last moment. Thus Pluton could be moved forward in support of France's allies, and it was possible to reach agreement with West Germany on the mechanism by which this could be achieved.

However, to do this would challenge Gaullist tenets, and in particular the doctrine of the 'two battles'. By this doctrine, there was a distinction between the 'first' battle to be fought by NATO in West Germany and a 'second' battle for France, which would be fought on French frontiers or even French territory and for which the core of the French forces would have to be held back. Taken to its logical conclusion this would have the rest of NATO taking the brunt of a Warsaw Pact attack, diminishing its impact for France but without France's assistance. Under this concept, Pluton should be held back for the decisive 'battle of France', so as to be available to signal the consequences of invading the country. This is precisely what West Germany feared. If Pluton was to be committed to the first battle then French nuclear capabilities could get involved before there was any direct threat to French territory. This is what the Gaullists feared.

In a remarkable speech for a Gaullist Prime Minister, Jacques Chirac indicated that the government had opted to blur the distinction between these two battles. This speech, of February 1975, is worth quoting at length because of the general light it throws on official thinking at this time. Chirac offered three reasons for TNWs: not 'to let anyone have a monopoly of any particular category of weapons'; to 'extend our deterrent capability to meet those forms of aggression to which the threat of a strategic strike would not constitute an immediately credible reply, and which are therefore the most likely'; and to 'make a contribution to the defense of Europe which is as yet immeasurable to our allies and ourselves alike'. He then went on to identify two essential qualities of Pluton. Firstly, by limiting the nuclear risk to a clearly defined geographical area it would make it possible to establish a 'zone of nuclear interdiction'. The adversary would know this zone could not be penetrated without risking a nuclear confrontation. Secondly, 'since Pluton is an organic part of the First Army, its deployment implies the commitment of tens of thousands of Frenchmen who thus take all the risks'. Chirac took care to stress that 'the function of TNW is not to "win the war" '.[18]

Despite the distinctive Gallic flavour all this was not far removed from flexible response. At one point Chirac even spoke of the need 'for a strategy which is more subtly graduated — and hence more effective

— than a deterrent which depends solely on strategic weapons'. To the traditional Gaullist there was no need to worry about lesser threats needing lesser responses because all that mattered was an attack on France itself, and once that had happened, however limited the incursion, then the adversary must expect the full weight of strategic retaliation.

Official thinking had never been quite so divorced from the rest of NATO. Not even de Gaulle had ever envisaged quite so selfish a strategy. Even when the General was at his most detached from NATO he did no more than say that French participation in a European war could not be taken for granted. So long as it was clear that the USSR was the aggressor then France would fight with its allies.

To avoid being drawn into a war provoked by, say, the United States, France would not integrate its forces with those of the rest of NATO let alone accept American bases. Thus, while France might well join in on the side of the West, its forces were not organised to maximise the effectiveness of their contribution. The heresy revealed by Chirac's speech was that this might well now be the objective of Giscard d'Estaing. Over the next year, the President, with his Chief of Staff General Guy Méry, began to explore this issue. The 1976 military *loi de programmation* acknowledged the futility of attempting to keep France separate from a land war in Europe:

> It would indeed be illusory to hope that France could maintain more than a reduced sovereignty, if her neighbours had been occupied by a hostile power or were simply under its control. The security of Western Europe as a whole is therefore essential for France.[19]

General Méry developed the concept of *sanctuarisation élargie* (enlarged sanctuarisation) suggesting that the benefits of France's deterrent could extend beyond its own frontiers to embrace its neighbours. Under this concept France might well contribute to the 'forward battle' in Germany.

French strategic thought began to move in the same direction as had that of the Americans in the aftermath of the doctrine of 'massive retaliation'. There was the same concern with being left only with the options of 'suicide or surrender' leading to a renewed stress on improving conventional forces. This improvement would allow for greater flexibility in all diplomacy. There were the same doubts about the credibility of retaliatory threats.

The initial inclination was to redress the balance between conventional and nuclear forces. Indeed, budgets for TNWs suffered in the 1976 *loi de programmation* along with strategic forces. Pluton production was cut and decisions were deferred on the new 'tactical' air weapon, the *air-sol moyenne portée* (ASMP) air-to-surface missile. Nevertheless, in the debate that had now been opened up TNWs were to play a central role.

It is important to remember that the key issue was not whether or not TNWs have a function to 'test' adversary intentions, but whether or not any of France's nuclear forces should be of benefit to its neighbours. Thus General Lucien Poirier, who helped formulate the concepts behind the 1972 white paper, criticised a 1977 comment by Prime Minister Raymond Barre that France's deterrent could apply to 'neighbouring and allied territories'. According to Poirier: 'That is to ruin, with a single phrase, the coherence of a strategic discourse that is otherwise of exemplary rigour.'[20]

However, because 'tactical' (the French never call them 'theatre') forces are so ambiguous in the role in which they can be used it follows that they fudge strategic issues. Because Giscard was unable to sustain the 'Europeanist' heresy sufficiently to extend to conventional forces, TNWs offered a means of compromise. In a speech by General Méry in 1977, the concept of 'a gradual escalation of conflict from conventional to tactical nuclear to controlled strategic weapons' was renounced. There might be use of TNWs, but Méry explained that 'the brutal use of our TNW in large numbers . . . must have a political significance . . . The military effectiveness remains secondary by comparison with the demonstration of our political will.'[21]

This seemed to offer a return to Gaullist purity but the clarification was insufficient. Military effectiveness would only be a 'secondary' criterion, but a criterion none the less. If only a few weapons were used against targets devoid of military relevance what sort of signal would that provide? Alternatively, if a substantial number were used against military targets was that not engaging in a land battle? In practice was the French force posture going to look much different than that of the rest of NATO, except with a more truncated conventional phase? The fact was that the very existence of TNWs created an ambiguity over French doctrine, and that this ambiguity could only be resolved by a clear statement of French intent towards the rest of NATO. Such clarity the government could not provide because it could bring itself neither to deny that nuclear deterrence was only credible if used solely to protect France nor that France's security was bound up with that of its neighbours.

It is in this context that one must view the debate about enhanced radiation weapons (ERW). In December 1976, prior to the great fuss in NATO on the matter, Giscard ordered feasibility studies of ERW. In 1978 Méry commended the neutron bomb 'insofar as it gives greater military effectiveness by enabling one to fire closer to one's own troops, and enlarging the zone within which the weapon can be used without too many risks for the population'. He still discounted the idea of a 'nuclear battle'.[22] Méry was describing such a move in such a way as to make it seem no more than perfecting the means of sending a nuclear signal, but it was still difficult to avoid the fact that ERW had been promoted elsewhere in the West because of their capacity to attack large tank formations. Moreover, ERW were praised by Colonel Marc Geneste, the most prominent French advocate of a TNW-based defence, in a book he wrote with Sam Cohen, the so-called 'father of the neutron bomb'.[23]

In June 1980 President Giscard revealed that development work had begun, but that the production need not begin until 1982-3 and possibly later if a different design were needed. This announcement set off an argument within the ruling majority, but only as part of the persistent dispute over how European the defence policy should be and whether a battle for France could be separated from a battle for Western Europe as a whole. The Giscardian UDF (Union pour la Démocratie Française) took the more European road and in doing so argued for the French Army to be equipped with numerous enhanced radiation warheads. By contrast Michel Aurillac put together a report for the Gaullists in which he was scathing about the notion of a tactical nuclear war with ERW. To Aurillac such a notion was another step on the road to diluting the credibility of the strategic nuclear deterrent (by raising doubts about French determination to engage in all-out anti-city attacks) and to co-operation with NATO. While not ruling out some production of these weapons Aurillac put them as a lower priority than the Hades successor to Pluton, which is acceptable to Gaullists as being inappropriate for nuclear war-fighting.[24] Suggestions from the Defence Ministry that no more than 300-400 ERW were ever likely to be deployed indicated that the compromise was again to be found in production of a weapon suitable for war-fighting but deployment only to a level that would restrict use to signalling.[25]

After the spring 1981 presidential election it had been suspected that the Mitterrand government might abandon the neutron bomb project. Charles Hernu, the Defence Minister, had previously been lukewarm to ERW development. Like many, but by no means all, socialists, he did not differ markedly from many Gaullists in his distrust of entanglement in a forward battle in Germany and the stress on the independent strategic deterrent as the centerpiece of French policy. The communists had consistently opposed the neutron bomb.

However, the government did not abandon the project. In September 1981 Prime Minister Pierre Mauroy, addressing the Institute of Higher National Defence Studies, noted that the United States (in August) had decided to produce ERW and that the Soviet Union had declared its ability to produce them if necessary. 'We must bear these facts in mind,' said Mauroy, providing some evidence for those who believe that the desire to demonstrate that France can do anything the superpowers can do is always a powerful influence on its policy. Mauroy continued, 'it would not be rational to give up the acquisition of an armament which could increase our deterrent force'. He added that the policy remained one of massive retaliation, not of flexible response, while acknowledging that they could not think only about an attack on France. 'We must draw our own conclusions when we examine our border defences and their approaches.'[26] So 1981 ended with a new government but still no final decision on ERW, nor any new reconciliation of the tension between a defence policy which stresses independence and an interest in the fate of close neighbours and allies.

In 1982 there were signs of a move towards a positive decision on production. By the autumn Defence Minister Hernu was saying that such a decision was 'conceivable' while Prime Minister Mauroy described the neutron weapons as 'the atomic weapon *par excellence*'. However, when a newspaper reported to this effect in October, President Mitterrand said only that 'I have given the order to continue studies so as to place us in a situation to immediately build a neutron bomb, if I make the decision. But the moment has not come. We have other priorities in armaments.'[27] A year later the President declared France ready 'to mass produce the neutron bomb. We must be ready to have the technical means to do so. But the decision to do so has not yet been taken. . . .'[28]

What was clear was that the other priorities were in nuclear rather than conventional armaments. French philosophy, as expressed in 1981, was that co-ordination with NATO 'only concerns our classical forces, and excludes, consequently, all planning in the use of nuclear forces; the classical forces were now to be cut, possibly including those based just over the border in Germany.' Nevertheless, at the end of

October, President Mitterand was in Bonn, meeting with the new German Chancellor Helmut Kohl, and talking about co-ordination of defence policy. The April 1983 *loi de programmation* demonstrated an increased emphasis on the nuclear forces. Funds are required for the new M-4 submarine-launched missile and the seventh submarine due to be introduced in 1994. In addition the old Mirage IV and new Mirage 2000 and Super Etendand fighter bombers are to be armed with the ASMP short-range nuclear missiles. The S-X mobile missile is to be developed for introduction starting in 1996. The first regiment of Hades should be ready for 1992. To make way for these programmes, conventional forces have to be cut. The Army has been reduced by 32,000. However, to soften the blow to allies, a new Rapid Deployment Force has been created. On the face of it this seems to be a typical piece of French audacity. The force is to be lightly armoured and more suited to external intervention than the Central Front.

In the Franco-German dialogue the French were interested in the concept of a European defence force, more independent of the United States, but the Germans squashed any such suggestions — including that they might be willing to fund this sort of departure. Chancellor Kohl and President Mitterrand did not ever really consider the neutron bomb, possibly because of the question this raises for French participants in a forward battle. The main thing appeared to be the increased range of Hades as against Pluton which Mitterrand was pleased to point out meant that the initial French nuclear shots would not inevitably land on West German soil.[29] Contrary to this expectation, the West Germans do not seem to view nuclear attacks on their fellow Germans of the East with indifference. Bonn was asking for a voice in the use of nuclear weapons against either Germany. A top official was reported as saying: 'We want some sort of nuclear guarantee whereby France regards German territory, East and West, as its [Bonn's] own security area.' There was little evidence that such a guarantee was forthcoming.[30] The extra range may alleviate some of the more visible problems created by French nuclear policy, but hardly resolves the doctrinal problem concerning the circumstances in which France would begin to release its nuclear arsenal. As *The Economist* pointed out: 'Why build missiles that can reach the East if you are going to use them only when Russian tanks are in range of Strasbourg?'[31] If its tactical nuclear forces could only be used while Warsaw Pact forces were still at the East-West border would that mean initiating nuclear hostilities while the rest of NATO was still hoping to deal with any invasion by conventional means? If nuclear release were held up until enemy forces had broken through and were *en route* to France then the weapons would still be landing in West German territory.

To recapitulate, this section has concentrated on exploring the contradiction between French doctrine, as articulated in its purest form in the mid-1960s, and the development of TNWs. It has described the reluctance to accept any responsibility for the defence of allies and to move towards a strategy approaching that of flexible response, and the difficulty of avoiding either of these tendencies in practice. The pattern of limited TNW development exemplifies the resultant tension. Their limited range means that any use would inflict enormous damage on the territory of West Germany, even if also on the forces of an adversary. Their existence offers an alternative to automatic strategic retaliation on attack and so tacitly concedes doubts about the willingness of France to fulfill the threat upon which the deterrent is based.

The European element of this problem remains the most difficult and a succession of French politicians and Generals have failed to come to terms with this issue. It is arguable that the point in flexible response was conceded as soon as a TNW project was approved. This has been difficult to criticise because initial approval came from General de Gaulle himself. It is also the case that strategic doctrine normally allows great flexibility in interpretation. The French approach to TNWs is differentiated from that of NATO by the stress on a purely signalling function and the rejection of the concept of a nuclear battle. To underline this self-limitation, numbers of TNWs to be deployed are to be kept down to the level unsuitable for anything other than signalling. There nevertheless remains an impulse to improve the military effectiveness of TNWs, for example through enhanced radiation. Apart from anything else the message conveyed by a nuclear signal is likely to be confused unless significant damage is inflicted upon adversary forces, especially if the explosions are not taking place on adversary territory.

However, the main point is that this is all comparable with debates within NATO where there is now a consensus that also favours 'signalling' rather than 'war-fighting'. This has, in fact, been the basis of NATO guidelines for initial nuclear use since 1969. The main divergence between France and the rest of NATO in doctrine comes with the role of conventional forces, although even here the actual French position is far from clear. The real question remains whether or not France's conventional forces or TNWs would be used to dissuade Warsaw Pact forces solely from turning left into France or else to help its allies.

The relevance of this inconclusive French debate for NATO has been rather unexplored. It is one of its curious features that the

'Europeanists' in France are associated with strategies based on deployments, possibly large-scale, of TNWs. The European orientation comes from proposing weapons and strategies that have an unavoidable 'European' logic, but not those that are most congruent with NATO strategy. Such 'integration' would be just too much of a heresy.

It is not clear, however, how French TNWs could actually be used in an alliance-minded way without such integration. For example, NATO has clear rules for the use of TNWs which recognise their effects on the territory upon which they are to be used. Would France follow these rules? France tends to play down the conventional phase so it might be more impatient to get into nuclear signalling, but that would require forward basing otherwise it could only unleash its signal *behind* allied lines. In any case, would it be tolerable for France to start the nuclear phase quite independently of the wishes of the rest of NATO? If French nuclear use is to be synchronised with the rest of NATO, perhaps to symbolise solidarity, then that would require established communication lines and a willingness to use TNWs before there is a direct threat to France.

For all these reasons, as well as the evidence that opinion within Europe is moving against reliance on battlefield nuclear weapons, TNWs seem an unlikely vehicle for an attempt to bring France closer to its allies in the defence area. None of the problems described above arise with conventional forces.

China

The Sino-Soviet nuclear relationship is largely made up of weapons that the West would describe as 'theatre nuclear forces'. The prime Soviet threat to China is the SS-20, while China's response is still largely based on medium- and intermediate-range weapons derived from an early Soviet SS-4. It was only in 1980 that China first tested an ICBM, which has yet to be deployed, and its longest-range rockets can barely reach Moscow. However, while essentially regional in nature, to a country operating the most minimum of deterrents, this is very much a strategic capability.

In addition, China does appear to have some nuclear weapons intended for use on the battlefield. Little publicity has been accorded these weapons and their existence has not been officially confirmed. There is evidence that they are caught up in some doctrinal controversy. This controversy is just one part of a fundamental and long-standing dispute over the role of conventional forces in China's defence. In the 1960s Maoist doctrine in China stressed a combination of two forms of unconventional warfare — people's war to swamp an invader and nuclear war to deter nuclear attack. There was little tolerance of traditional military formations, and contempt for the notion that advanced technology could give one side a decisive edge. This contempt was only partly based on the political distance that China had placed between itself and the international sources of advanced technology. It also reflected a revolutionary confidence in what a suitably motivated population could achieve against an aggressor, especially with a population as numerous as that of China.

One can set a number of dates for when this approach began to be qualified, but 1969 is as good a year as any. This was long before the underlying ideological conflict was sorted out. That needed the disgrace of the 'Gang of Four', but 1969 was the year that the military began to assert itself as it restored order after the excesses of the Cultural Revolution and the year that the leadership discovered that the 'Soviet threat' was for real.

Up to that point the Chinese nuclear force had developed according to political as much as military goals. The actual achievement of a nuclear capability was taken to be an important demonstration of the potential of the Chinese revolution, of a capacity for independent action even against the wishes and pressures of the superpowers, and of the impermanence of the superpowers' nuclear monopoly. The weapon was directed against both the United States, the established enemy, still fighting close by in Indo-China against a fellow-communist state, and the Soviet Union, the former friend now seen as another imperialist power anxious to establish hegemony over China. In the political circumstances, with a full-scale deterrent out of reach for many years, the optimum force structure was one which could pose a tangible if largely symbolic threat to *both* superpowers simultaneously. Over time this could be expanded into a more impressive deterrent.

The assumptions were of a long-term threat from both superpowers but not necessarily of any immediate danger. To the extent that attacks were threatened there was great confidence in the capacity of local militias, trained in guerrilla tactics according to the tenets of 'people's war', to frustrate an occupying force. There was very little room in this scheme of things for a concept of 'battlefield' never mind of 'battlefield nuclear weapons'. Indeed those professional military men who still worried about conventional military engagements and hankered after advanced military technology and orderly battle formations were castigated for their bourgeois cast of mind and indifference to the wisdom of Chairman Mao.

What changed in 1969 was the perception of the Soviet threat. It was no longer an ideological and political assault without a serious physical form — only bullying and posturing. The clashes on the Amur and Ussuri Rivers of March 1969 and a considerable amount of Soviet sabre-rattling turned war with the powerful neighbour into a real possibility. The Chinese concern is evidenced by a spate of precautionary measures that were set in motion in mid-1969 — the dispersal of key facilities and the digging of an elaborate system of air raid shelters and tunnels. It is also evidenced by a sharp shift in nuclear-weapon development.

It became necessary to consider how best to deter a Soviet nuclear attack with only limited resources. The stress had to be on extending the number of Soviet targets in range and decreasing the vulnerability of the few Chinese nuclear systems to pre-emptive attack, possibly by developing a token launch-on-warning capability. Token forces of purely symbolic value became a luxury. The ICBM programme, which had already run into technical difficulties, was assigned a much lower priority. Up to that point this programme had been taken seriously enough by the United States to justify a limited ABM system (announced by Secretary of Defense McNamara in September 1967) to protect US cities against a Chinese attack. Possibly this development also encouraged the Chinese not to bother to push extra resources into an ICBM. Over the next few years Chinese priorities became clear with first a medium-range ballistic missile and then intermediate-range ballistic missiles extending the deterrent threat to the USSR.

Less clear was whether any priority had been attached to tactical nuclear weapons. The Chinese military were certainly well aware of the possible role of tactical nuclear weapons. Prior to the Cultural Revolution, during which any alternative to people's war for conflict on land was taken to be heretical, there had been informed discussions of these weapons. Chinese military material made available in 1961 had discussed the need for training to defend against TNWs and also in the principles of using them effectively. In discussing possible American escalation of the Vietnam War in the mid-1960s there was mention of the possibility that 'tactical nuclear warfare [on the part of the United States] will be put into practice, that is, the use of small nuclear weapons in war zones'.[32]

By the late 1960s China had to contemplate the use of TNWs not only by the United States but also by the Soviet Union. The first move of battlefield nuclear weapons to the Sino-Soviet border probably took place during 1966-7. In October 1966 China tested a 20-30-kiloton nuclear warhead. The most impressive feature of the test was that the warhead was carried 400 miles on a medium-range missile. This seems to have alerted Soviet planners to the near-term risks of the Chinese nuclear programme. Already by then a conventional military build-up had begun, prompted by the border provocations, anti-Soviet rhetoric and general disturbance which characterised the Cultural Revolution. Highly trained units with advanced weaponry were moved from Eastern Europe to the Soviet Far East, these may well have included batallions equipped with short-range Frog nuclear-capable missiles. In 1968-9 about a third of the Soviet medium- and intermediate-range missiles and bombers facing Europe were moved to sites facing China. In July 1970 it was reported that the USSR had deployed 'many hundreds' of TNWs along the border including the new 500-mile-range Scaleboard. Furthermore, the battalions armed with the Frog missiles had been strengthened by the addition of a fourth company.[33] When compared with the three companies per battalion common in Europe this indicated a greater expectation that TNWs would be needed on the Soviet side, possibly to compensate for the sheer quantity of manpower available to China. By 1980 it was estimated that the USSR had 2,500 nuclear warheads under its Far East command.[34]

So China was aware of the potential of TNWs and had to consider the possibility of their use by its enemies. There were no explicit statements on Chinese TNW development, but some indications that the relevant technology was being explored. In September 1969, when concern about a Sino-Soviet war was at its peak, China conducted its first underground nuclear test, detonating a device of some 20-25 kilotons. The three previous tests had been of thermonuclear weapons of the order of three megatons, presumed suitable for either an ICBM or the TU-16 aircraft. This new test could be seen as an attempt to perfect a fission trigger for this weapon.

However, there was an alternative explanation. Underground testing made possible controlled experiments, allowing for effective analysis of nuclear-design information and the physical effects of a detonation, as well as limiting the collection of intelligence by the West and the Soviet Union. The underground test might therefore have been about more than just a fission trigger. Alice Langley Hsieh argued that China might well be developing a TNW:

[The] Chinese may be experimenting not only with the size of the device but also with the fissionable material it contains, in order to develop a tactical nuclear weapons capability; that is, weapons which could initially be carried by a fighter or fighter-bomber. This theory can be supported on several grounds. The first is that of timing. Timing plays no important role in so far as a test is tied to R&D in the reduction of the size of the warhead. On the other hand, timing would play an important political role were the test designed to develop tactical nuclear weapons. In such a case, the objective would be not only to reduce the size of the device but also to minimize the fissionable material, with plutonium as the key element. The Chinese may well have considered it imperative to deny debris or technical intelligence to western and Soviet observers at this time. They may believe that positive indications that they were experimenting with fission (plutonium) weapons would be regarded as provocative by the United States in light of the Vietnam situation and more so by the Soviet Union in view of the border issue.[35]

Mrs Hsieh described the above thesis as 'controversial', yet she was soon caught up by other analysts.

There were further small-yield nuclear tests in 1971 and 1972 using plutonium. In 1972 it was reported that the American intelligence community was now convinced of a Chinese TNW programme. The testing programme was believed to be linked to the mass production of the F-9 fighter-bomber (a modification of the Soviet MiG-19) presumed capable of carrying a 20-kiloton warhead. By 1972 some 200 F-9s had already been deployed (although by 1974, with evidence of technical problems, IISS had reduced its estimate in *The Military Balance* from 300 to 'some'). Estimates of the numbers of TNWs available ranged from 50 to 100 bombs. It was suggested that Chinese military concepts were changing from a dependence on people's war, by which it was envisaged that Soviet troops would be drawn into the country, to the view that any invading troops should be held as forward as possible by regular troops. According to the revised strategy it would be advisable to meet Soviet forces in the border areas, for if there were small-scale nuclear exchanges collateral damage would then be kept away from the major cities.[36]

In 1973 the Chinese leadership made a strategic judgement that an attack by the USSR was not imminent and defence was reduced as a national priority. The new ties with the West took some of the pressure off China. Meanwhile the dust had still not finally settled after the turbulence of the Cultural Revolution. A bitter political struggle was under way for the ideological soul of the nation and the succession to Mao Zedong (who died in 1976). A degree of stability was not achieved until the defeat of the 'Gang of Four'. Then there was the adoption of the ambitious modernisation programme of 1978 in which, again, defence took on a low priority. The emphasis again was on the symbolic political aspects of military force. One example of this was the decision, probably taken around 1976, to complete the development of an ICBM. This would remind the United States that China did not take the current cordial relations for granted.

In this context of the 1970s, with defence a reduced national priority, doctrine still under dispute as part of a wider political struggle and the stress on the most visible features of military strength, the TNW programme appears to have been demoted. Certainly there was no evidence of activity in this area with virtually no small-yield nuclear tests. It is however likely that the role of TNWs was actively discussed as part of the continuing debate over the relevance of people's war to contemporary conditions. Unlike Britain and France, the issue of battlefield nuclear weapons was more a part of a debate about concepts of conventional operations than of those of nuclear deterrence.

It was the war with Vietnam in early 1979 that gave an added twist to the debate on military doctrine. Although China achieved its strategic objectives in this war, there was reason for some alarm at the inadequacies in conventional capabilities illuminated in the conflict. Moreover, this was a reminder that it was possible to get into limited wars in which national survival was not at stake but with national interests still depending on the outcome of engagements between regular forces. In the post-mortem following the war the proponents of high-quality and professional conventional forces were on the ascendant. As part of this debate, TNWs appear to have come back to the fore.

The most dramatic evidence of this was an outspoken article by Xu Baoxi, who appeared to have some connection with the modernising 'school' of the People's Liberation Army, and wrote under the heading, 'Research into the Initial Stage of Future War': 'The enemy's use of nuclear weapons against us is not frightening. What is frightening is our lack of preparation.' Xu's argument was that the small size and mobility of TNWs made them valuable for offensive purposes — to blast open enemy lines. If the aggressor could achieve such a breakthrough without resistance then Beijing would be faced with the awful dilemma of escalating to the strategic level or accepting defeat. The answer, he suggests, lies in a Chinese TNW capability. 'For instance, in a future conflict, if the enemy uses tactical nuclear weapons to bombard our main defense lines, and we also use tactical nuclear weapons in retaliation, the enemy would then hesitate to resort to strategic weapons.' He derides hope that it would be possible to cope with a Soviet nuclear attack from fortified positions in the mountains.[37]

For other evidence of interest, Gerald Segal notes a favourable Chinese analysis[38] of the French decision to develop its own theatre nuclear forces as a medium power facing the USSR. Segal suggests that the major problem facing China in TNW development might have been not so much the weapon itself but command and control. For the central authorities in Beijing there must be some concern over the loss of control involved in dispensing these weapons to battlefield-level commanders, especially given the problems of distance and regionalism in China. However, he sees evidence of a reassertion of central control, for example by regular moves sideways of regional commanders, and a greater attention to the problems of command and control as indicating that this may be becoming less of a constraint.[39]

In July 1982 a simulated nuclear explosion was reported in a military exercise in the Ningxia region. A local newspaper published a photograph of a mushroom cloud with a caption: 'An "atomic bomb" exploding deep in the ranks of the "enemy" '. The bomb had apparently been dropped from an aircraft.[40]

Chinese concepts of nuclear deterrence have always been straightforward. There has never been any suggestion that nuclear deterrence can compensate for weaknesses in conventional forces. Right from its first atomic test it pledged itself to a 'no-first-use' policy. Notions of using nuclear weapons as a substitute for conventional weakness, either as a form of super-efficient fire-power or through threats of destructive escalation, have never had prominence in Chinese thought. The logic of second-strike deterrence nevertheless has still pushed China towards active consideration of a TNW capability to counter that of the USSR.

Notes

1. Hansard, 537 HC Official Report (5th series), col. 1899 (1 March 1955).
2. Field-Marshal, The Viscount Montgomery of Alamein, 'A Look Through a Window at World War III', *Journal of the Royal United Services Institute*, vol. XCIX, no. 596 (November 1954).
3. Andrew Pierre, *Nuclear Politics: The British Experience with an Independent Strategic Force, 1939-1970* (London: Oxford University Press, 1972), p.167.
4. John Simpson, *The Independent Nuclear State: The United States, Britain*

and the Atom (London: Macmillan, 1983), p. 156.

5. Denis Healey, 'The Sputnik and Western Defence', *International Affairs*, vol. 34, no. 2 (April 1958), p. 147.

6. Solly Zuckerman, *Nuclear Illusion and Reality* (London: Collins, 1982), p. x. Zuckerman's views were first presented publicly in his 'Judgement and Control in Modern Warfare', *Foreign Affairs*, vol. 40, no. 2 (1961), pp. 196-212. In a recent article he has recalled: 'I forget how many sales talks I had to listen to from a Pentagon scientist as he tried to persuade me when I was Chief Scientific Adviser to the Ministry of Defence in the United Kingdom that a small nuclear weapon called Davy Crockett, which could be carried by an infantryman, was a war-winner. I was not the only one who failed to see the strategic merit in distributing nuclear weapons so widely that control over their use became impossible.' ('Nuclear Fantasies', *New York Review of Books*, 14 June 1984).

7. The bible of the current anti-nuclear campaign is E.P. Thompson and Dan Smith, *Protest and Survive* (London: Penguin Books, 1980). This book has a distinct Pan-European flavour, e.g., Thompson: 'The movement will encourage a European consciousness, in common combat for survival, fostering informal communication at every level, and disregarding national considerations of interest or "security." ' (p. 58).

8. At one point in the early 1970s, British Phantoms were equipped with American nuclear bombs as they had not been modified to take the British versions. However as new bombs were developed and Jaguars and Buccaneers in the 1970s the Phantoms were able to revert to a conventional role. See Simpson, *The Independent Nuclear State*, p. 170.

9. See Lawrence Freedman, *Britain and Nuclear Weapons* (London: Macmillan, 1980), Chapter 12 for a discussion of rationales.

10. Ibid., pp. 123-5.

11. Britain operates, afloat and ashore, various maritime helicopters capable of delivering British nuclear depth bombs. The first two embarked Sea Harrier squadrons (on Invincible-class carriers) will also be capable of delivering free-fall nuclear bombs. In addition four squadrons of Nimrod maritime patrol aircraft are based in the United Kingdom equipped with American nuclear depth bombs. See *Statement on the Defence Estimates 1981*, Cmnd 8212-1, p. 16.

12. Michael Legge notes that in NPG studies of the early 1970s one of the few exceptions to the proposition that became retaliation 'neither side could gain a significant military advantage as a direct consequence of using nuclear weapons' was halting an amphibious landing. See Michael Legge, *Theater Nuclear Weapons and the NATO Strategy of Flexible Response*, R-2964-FF (Santa Monica: Rand Corporation, April 1983), p. 26.

13. Lawrence Freedman, 'Britain: The First Ex-Nuclear Power?' *International Security*, vol. 6, no. 2 (Autumn 1981), pp. 80-104.

14. General Ailleret, 'Flexible Response: A French View', *Survival*, vol. 6, no. 6 (November-December 1964), p. 264.

15. Ibid., p. 262.

16. General Ailleret, 'Directed Defence', *Survival*, vol. 10, no. 2 (February 1968), p. 42.

17. Jacques Isnard, 'Pluton's Ambiguous Virtues', *Guardian*, 2 August 1975.

18. Jacques Chirac, 'The Purpose of Pluton', *Survival* (September-October 1975), pp. 241-3.

19. Quoted in David S. Yost, 'The French Defence Debate', *Survival* (January-February 1981), p. 20. For a discussion of the 1975-6 debate see 'French Defence Policy', *Strategic Survey 1976* (London: IISS, 1977).

20. Quoted in Yost, 'The French Defence Debate', p. 23.

21. Quoted by Bruce Marshall, 'The Evolving French Strategic Debate', *Strategic Review* (Spring 1980).

22. Quoted in ibid., p. 70.
23. Marc Geneste and Samuel Cohen, *Echec à la guerre: la bombe à neutrons* (Paris: Editions Copernic, 1980). See also Marc Geneste, 'The City Walls: A Credible Defense Doctrine for the West', *Orbis* (Summer 1975), pp. 477-96.
24. *Une Doctrine de défense pour la France* (Paris: Union pour la démocratie française, 1980). Michel Aurillac, *Reflexions sur la défense* (Paris: Rassemblement pour la République, 1980).
25. Yost, 'The French Defence Debate'., p. 25. Yost points out that there might be practical limits on the number that could be produced, including availability of special materials (plutonium and tritium) as well as cost.
26. *International Herald Tribune*, 15 September 1981.
27. *International Herald Tribune*, 15, 16 and 17 October 1982.
28. *The Times*, 19 June 1983.
29. *The Times*, 23 October 1982; *International Herald Tribune*, 23 October 1982.
30. *Washington Post*, 20 April 1984.
31. *The Economist*, 30 April 1984. For an interesting argument about French strategy, see *Armed Forces Journal International* (June 1983).
32. Quoted in Alice Langley Hsieh, 'China's Nuclear-Missile Programme: Regional or Intercontinental?, *The China Quarterly*, no. 45 (1971), pp. 89-90.
33. *International Herald Tribune*, 22 July 1970.
34. Gregory Treverton, 'China's Nuclear Forces and the Stability of Soviet-American Deterrence', in *The Future of Strategic Deterrence*, Part 1, Adelphi Paper no. 160 (London: IISS, 1980), p. 41.
35. Alice Langley Hsieh, 'China's Nuclear-Missile Programme'.
36. *New York Times*, 25 July 1972.
37. *Far Eastern Economic Review*, 25 April 1980.
38. See *Beijing Review*, 33 (1980).
39. Gerald Segal, 'China's Nuclear Posture for the 1980s', *Survival* (January-February 1981), pp. 14-15, 18.
40. *Washington Times*, 14 July 1982.

6 NUCLEAR WEAPONS AND NATO POLITICS

Jeffrey H. Boutwell

As much as anything, the NATO alliance has been defined by its ability, or inability, to forge a consensus on nuclear-weapons issues. From the moment that nuclear weapons were first deployed on the continent, in the early 1950s, to the recent issue of intermediate-range nuclear forces (INF), NATO has been faced with the seemingly insurmountable task of implementing nuclear-weapons policies that could satisfy the disparate political and security needs of its 15 members. More often than not, the alliance has solved its 'nuclear dilemma' by agreeing to disagree. At worst, a particular nuclear-weapons plan, such as the Multilateral Force (MLF), dies at birth. At best, as with INF, different countries offer up different rationales for either supporting, or disagreeing with, a particular policy.

The difficulties faced by NATO in developing and implementing nuclear-weapons policies stem from both the multi-faceted nature of the 'problem' itself (i.e. how best to integrate nuclear weapons into the alliance's defence and détente policies), and from the various national prisms through which that 'problem' is viewed. To use a clinical analogy, the capabilities represented by nuclear weapons can be said to form a split persona, with as many as a half a dozen different 'personalities'. Depending on the political or military utility that is being sought, nuclear weapons are proclaimed as being important for coupling the security of the United States and Western Europe, deterring Soviet nuclear and/or conventional forces, providing limited nuclear options, compensating for shortfalls in conventional forces, as arms-control bargaining chips, or, in the case of Britain and France, as symbols of national prestige and independence.

To push the analogy further, this nuclear persona is then analysed by a team of 15 psychiatrists each of whom approaches the case from a different vantage point. Because of the wide variety of national interests within NATO, different countries will attach differing importances to one or more of the capabilities represented by nuclear weapons. In addition, changes in political leadership within each country mean that these national perspectives themselves will change over time.

Further complicating the situation is the fact that the chief psychiatrist, the United States, is privy to more information about the patient than his colleagues, yet it is among these colleagues that the patient lives. Little wonder, then, that the patient has such trouble finding a comfortable identity, or that the psychiatrists find it so difficult agreeing on a cure.

The differences here between NATO and the Warsaw Pact could not be more striking. In much the same way that the Soviet Union forces psychiatric 'cures' on its political dissidents, so it also rules by fiat when it comes to formulating Warsaw Pact nuclear-weapons policies. Moscow's Eastern European colleagues may disagree with and even slightly criticise their chief's diagnosis and treatment (as happened during the INF affair), yet they are powerless to change that treatment.[1]

NATO, on the other hand, is comprised of 15 sovereign nations (16, if one includes France),[2] each of whom must take national concerns and domestic pressures into account when bargaining within the alliance. To be sure, some members of NATO are more equal than others, with the United States the most equal of all. None the less, even the smaller partners have some leverage over NATO nuclear policies, especially when the alliance is looking for consensus so as to demonstrate resolve and political unity, which is exactly what happened in the INF episode.

Previous chapters in this book have highlighted the difficulties of NATO's nuclear dilemma. This chapter will survey the structural reasons for these difficulties, given the multi-tiered composition of the alliance and the different political considerations that the European NATO members must take into account. In doing so through the INF experience, this chapter will concentrate especially on the interplay of domestic and foreign policy concerns within the non-nuclear European NATO members. (For more on Britain and France, see Chapter 5.)

Composition of the NATO Alliance

There is a tendency when dealing with the West European politics of nuclear weapons, found especially in the United States, to look for a common West European position or policy. What has often happened in the past is that American governments have expected the European NATO members to fall into line with American strategic and defence thinking. Given the disparate geostrategic and domestic political concerns of these European states, of course, there can never be a unified position, especially on such a sensitive issue as nuclear-weapons policy.

For one thing, there is the fundamental division within the alliance between the nuclear 'haves' (the United States, Britain and France) and the nuclear 'have-nots'. Complicating this division is the fact that the fourth major Western power, West Germany, is prohibited by treaty from acquiring its own nuclear weapons, yet it is on West German soil that the majority of the more than 5,000 NATO nuclear warheads are deployed.

Concerning the rest of the NATO nuclear 'have-nots', two countries, Denmark and Norway, refuse to station nuclear weapons on their territory in peacetime, while a third, Canada, refuses to deploy nuclear weapons with its forces stationed in Europe. Three additional countries, Portugal, Iceland and Luxembourg, have chosen not to participate in alliance nuclear decisions at all.

Of the four Mediterranean NATO members, Greece and Turkey are politically at odds with each other, making their participation in NATO deployment schemes difficult. A third, Spain, has only recently joined the alliance, and is still in the process of defining its NATO role. Only the fourth, Italy, has consistently been an active participant in deciding on, and deploying, NATO nuclear weapons, in part because of an Italian desire to be considered a 'major' NATO partner. The two remaining alliance countries, Belgium and the Netherlands, are both active participants in the nuclear decision-making process, but have been often constrained by governmental instability in putting their full weight into the process.

Given this multi-tiered structure of the alliance, and the fact that European national positions will be shaped by existing domestic and foreign policy concerns, it is not surprising that NATO has found it easier to agree on the process by which nuclear decisions are made, rather than the substance of those decisions themselves.[3] The classic example of this was the Multilateral Force issue, out of the ruins of which emerged the Nuclear Planning Group (NPG) and various Programmes of Co-operation (POCs) on nuclear weapons between the United States and its European allies. Yet even the recognition in the late 1960s of a need for increased consultation and information-sharing on nuclear-weapons developments and technologies, which led to the creation of the NPG, can never fully overcome the most fundamental division of all: that between the United States as a global nuclear superpower and the rest of NATO. The fact that European NATO has lagged behind the US in developing national elites familiar with nuclear-weapons issues, to say nothing of European dependence on the United States for classified intelligence relating to both American and Soviet nuclear-weapons developments, constantly puts the Europeans at a disadvantage when it comes to evaluating the Soviet threat, and devising NATO policy to meet that threat.[4]

In the past, this transatlantic disparity has also put European governments at a disadvantage in building domestic political support for NATO decisions. Although this is due in part to the contentious nature of such issues for European publics, given that they are the ones asked to deploy nuclear weapons, there is also the problem of a disjuncture in expertise on nuclear-weapons issues between the governments and the wider publics.[5]

Although this problem has diminished in recent years, given the rise of defence experts both within and without the various European governments who are knowledgeable about nuclear-weapons issues, it will never disappear entirely. Countries like France and Britain, with their own nuclear forces, and the United States, with both nuclear forces and an extensive intelligence-gathering apparatus, will continue to be faced with the problem of sharing sensitive technologies and assessments of the Soviet threat. During the INF episode, for example, the United States reportedly went to greater lengths than previously in sharing intelligence data with the European members of NATO to convince them of the threat posed by the SS-20. On the other hand, problems arose when the Carter adminstration was perceived as downplaying the SS-20 threat at home, at the same time as it was accenting that threat in Brussels.[6]

Finally, there is the fundamental problem associated with the leadership role played by the United States on nuclear-weapons issues. Admittedly, Washington often finds itself in a double-bind, where it is looked to by the Europeans for strong leadership, but then criticised when such leadership is perceived as neglecting European interests. The neutron-bomb experience of 1977-8 is instructive here, given the cat-and-mouse game that went on between the Carter administration and the European NATO allies. In the case of West Germany especially, the fact that President Carter wanted the FRG to agree to deployment of enhanced radiation weapons (ERW) before the United States had made a production decision, while Chancellor Schmidt wanted an American production decision before he would agree to deployment, made it difficult to know which element of the ERW fiasco was more poignant: 'the German desire to avoid making a decision, or the German disappointment when the Americans seemed to make the decision for them'.[7]

Not surprisingly, one of the results of the ERW episode was that the alliance again tried to improve the nuclear decision-making process.

Nuclear Weapons and NATO Politics

Largely at the instigation of the Dutch and West Germans, the NPG in 1979 was enlarged from its then composition of four permanent members (United States, United Kingdom, West Germany and Italy) and four rotating members to eleven full-time members (all but Iceland, Luxemburg, Portugal, France and of course, Spain, which did not join NATO until 1982).[8] Yet, given the nature of extended deterrence, where European NATO relies on the nuclear weapons of a superpower that is geographically separated by the Atlantic Ocean, no amount of consultation can reconcile the differing political needs of the NATO partners. Looking back over 35 years of NATO nuclear decision-making, one is left with the feeling that there indeed may be no ultimate cure for the nuclear 'patient'.

INF and West European Politics

In spite of the above difficulties, the NATO decision of December 1979 to proceed with INF modernisation and arms control initially appeared to be heading for a more successful resolution than previous NATO nuclear-weapons deployment decisions. Although Norway and Denmark rejected any stationing of INF systems on their soil, and the Netherlands and Belgium took a wait-and-see attitude on deployment, there was none the less broad consensus within the alliance in support of the INF double-track approach. Despite the breakdown of INF negotiations in the fall of 1983, which occurred when the Soviets walked out of the talks as the first Pershing and cruise missiles were deployed, that consensus continued to hold up, albeit a bit precariously. As time went by, however, a combination of distrust over the Reagan administration's arms-control and defence policies, the rise of peace movements across northern, Protestant Europe and constant Soviet political pressure induced the most severe case of self-doubt within the alliance in its history.

With hindsight, what made the 1979 INF decision comparatively easy was the four-year time-lag before the INF systems would even be ready for deployment. Sceptics of the military rationale for INF could hope that an arms-control solution to INF would be found before the systems themselves were actually deployed. Indeed, the NATO communiqué following the Brussels conference of December 1979 explicitly called for folding INF into the SALT process, which at the time remained a viable proposition.[9] Few could have foreseen that only a few weeks later, the Soviet invasion of Afghanistan would not only stop the SALT process cold, but lead essentially to the death of superpower (as compared with European) détente.

In addition, the INF decision was facilitated because it came so soon after the divisive neutron-bomb episode. Given the political mistrust engendered by the ERW issue, especially between the Schmidt and Carter governments, there was broad agreement that NATO could not afford to stumble so badly a second time. Thus the INF issue took on a symbolic importance as a test of alliance decisiveness and cohesion, over and above its relative military merits. As one senior US official noted at the time, the INF issue at times seemed to revolve around the question 'can and will the [Carter] Administration lead the Alliance, and can and will the Alliance follow'.[10]

In the event, the Carter administration did show that it could patiently lead the alliance to a successful decision on INF. The work of the High-Level Group and the Special Group within NATO, and bilateral consultations between Washington and the European NATO capitals, were a model of alliance decision-making.[11]

Yet the question remains, what purpose did the various European members of NATO see the INF decision as serving? Over and above the limited value of demonstrating alliance cohesion, what was the Soviet politico-military threat that made INF double-track decision necessary? Just as importantly, what were the domestic and intra-alliance concerns that motivated European acceptance of the INF consensus? In short, what did the West Europeans want these nuclear weaons, the first land-based missile systems capable of striking the Soviet Union that NATO had deployed since the 1960s, to do for them?

West Germany

Without a doubt, West Germany played the most prominent role of the European NATO members throughout the INF affair. In the mid-1970s, it was the government of Helmut Schmidt that emphasised the problem of 'grey-area' weapons not being included in the SALT process. Indeed, Schmidt himself has come to be seen as the originator of the INF decision because of his now famous speech at the International Institute for Strategic Studies in London in October 1977, where he stressed the danger that superpower strategic parity would magnify NATO's disadvantage in conventional and theatre nuclear forces in Europe.[12] Although at the time Schmidt himself was less concerned with Soviet SS-20s than with the Soviet advantage in conventional forces, it is true that the members of the Schmidt government were instrumental in 1977 and 1978 in convincing the Carter administration of the need for establishing parity in European theatre nuclear forces.[13]

There were a number of reasons for this West German interest in establishing parity in so-called Euro-strategic systems, especially as the Soviets steadily deployed the SS-20 throughout 1978 and 1979. Politically, Schmidt was concerned that there be an overall parity in the East-West military balance (*Gleichgewicht*) so that West German Ostpolitik would not become subject to Soviet political pressure.[14] When coupled with the vacillations and indecisiveness of American foreign policy under the Carter administration, Schmidt was all the more anxious that NATO redress its conventional-force and theatre-nuclear-force deficiencies, through both arms control and modernisation. Thus Schmidt was a strong supporter of the alliance's conventional modernisation plan (the Long-Term Defence Programme) and of new initiatives in the MBFR talks, as well as a double-track approach to the issue of European theatre nuclear forces.

Militarily, the Schmidt government was concerned with the ramifications of US-Soviet strategic parity for extended deterrence and the American nuclear guarantee to Western Europe. As both de Gaulle and Adenauer had foreseen as early as the 1950s, the ability of the Soviet Union to deter American strategic forces by its ability to inflict massive damage on the United States would increasingly call into question the viability of the American security guarantee to Europe. When the SALT process codified superpower strategic parity in the 1970s, the West German government began to look for ways to recouple the security of Western Europe with that of the US. One such means was the possible deployment of cruise missiles in Europe, which officials in the Schmidt government became increasingly interested in by the mid-1970s. Indeed, it was the disturbing prospect of the United States' agreeing to cruise-missile limitations during the SALT II negotiations (with no comparable limits on the SS-20)[15] that prompted Schmidt to criticise the SALT process for neglecting European security concerns in his IISS speech, which in turn provided a marked stimulus to NATO interest in INF.

Since joining the NATO alliance in 1955, it has been the West German position that deterrence against a possible Soviet attack ultimately must rest on Soviet uncertainty over the possible use of American strategic systems. With the attainment of Soviet strategic parity in the 1970s, West German defence officials argued that NATO must acquire a long-range theatre-nuclear-force capability (i.e. systems capable of striking the Soviet Union) so as to maintain the credibility of the NATO continuum of deterrence, up to and including American strategic forces. Long-range INF systems were not seen as providing an in-theatre military capability that by itself could deter Soviet aggression or the use of Soviet SS-20s; their importance lay in acting as a trigger for the possible use of American strategic systems. As was stressed in the 1979 West German Defence White Paper, these intermediate-range nuclear forces were 'closely interlinked with the strategic long-range potential of the United States in terms of concept and structure'.[16] INF systems were seen by the Schmidt government primarily as a means of holding American strategic forces 'hostage' to the defence of Europe:

> The idea is certainly not to win a war . . . deploying a limited number of these systems . . . would not enable us to fight a nuclear war in Europe, but would enable us to escalate a conflict that we couldn't dominate otherwise.[17]

For all their interest in plugging the gap in the continuum of deterrence, however, Schmidt government officials by no means thought purely in terms of weapons deployments. Given the special West German interest in and need for détente and Ostpolitik, its preferred strategy for dealing with Soviet theatre-nuclear and conventional-force superiority was to combine arms control and NATO force modernisation. Yet deliberations within NATO in 1978 over INF modernisation and deployment quickly began to run ahead of arms-control considerations. The fact that NATO might begin to deploy such systems without having offered to negotiate over them with the Soviets could undermine the FRG's relations with East Germany as well as the USSR.[18] In addition, Schmidt began to face mounting criticism from within his Social Democratic Party over what SPD leaders Willy Brandt, Herbert Wehner and Egon Bahr saw as an upward spiral in the European arms race that could threaten European détente. At the SPD party congress in Hamburg in November 1977, and even more so at the West Berlin party congress in December 1979, a significant bloc of the SPD voiced its displeasure with what it termed the danger of 'automaticity', the fact that NATO would deploy its Pershing and cruise missiles regardless of the state of INF arms-control negotiations.

Thus, even though Schmidt himself had been instrumental in ensuring that the NATO decision on INF would be a double-track approach, the Chancellor faced considerable opposition within his own party in supporting the alliance's INF policy. Coming as it did just a week before the NATO INF meeting in Brussels, the SPD party congress in West Berlin was of crucial importance in signalling West German support for INF. In the end, Schmidt had to use all the political pressure he could muster, including the threat of resigning as the party's Chancellor candidate for the 1980 national elections, to swing his party behind him. Yet Social Democratic support for the NATO position remained ambivalent, and very much predicated on the priority of arms control and continuation of the SALT process.[19] With the Soviet invasion of Afghanistan at the end of December 1979, and the resulting breakdown of both superpower détente and the SALT process, the split within the SPD between the Schmidt 'government' faction and the Brandt-Wehner-Bahr 'party' faction increasingly widened, and in part was responsible for the fall of the Schmidt government in September 1982.

At the same time, East-West tensions over Afghanistan and then the Polish crisis helped spark the emergence of the largest West German peace movement since the late 1950s. Aided as well by the anti-détente, anti-arms-control tenor of the newly elected Reagan administration, the West German peace movement was able to mobilise hundreds of thousands of West Germans against the NATO INF policy.

Although outwardly similar in composition to the peace movement of the late 1950s (the Campaign Against Atomic Death — *Kampf dem Atomtod*), the 1980s *Friedensbewegung* represented a marked change in the fabric of West German domestic politics.[20] Beginning with the student protests of the late 1960s, and continuing in the 1970s with the rise of single-issue politics as represented by the *Bürgerinitiativen*, West Germany experienced a notable increase in the number of political groups outside the established political parties. In the mid-1970s, many of these political groups coalesced to form the Green Party, which began in the late 1970s to contest elections at the state level. Although the Greens were initially unsuccessful in gaining representation in the state parliaments, the electoral threat that they posed to the SPD in such places as Hamburg, Bremen and West Berlin, and the public support they received for their environmental and anti-civilian nuclear power positions began to worry not only the Social Democrats, but Schmidt's coalition partner, the FDP, as well. Most importantly, by the time the peace movement began to emerge in 1980, there was already in place a well-established political structure that could give direction to and articulate the concerns of those West Germans who were anxious about deteriorating East-West relations, symbolised more than anything by the INF issue. Indeed, the increasing domestic debate over INF provided the Green movement with a needed shot of momentum, and leaders of the Green Party made clear their intention of becoming the foreign-policy spokesmen of the peace movement. Not only did this momentum propel Green candidates into an increasing number of state legislatures in the early 1980s and the Federal Parliament in 1983; it also served to increase the divisions within the SPD, as many left-wing SPD members argued the need for moving their party to the left so as to co-opt the environmental and peace issues being championed by the Greens.[21]

Although the Greens and the peace activists (the so-called Eco-peace movement) were ultimately unsuccessful in their attempts to block deployment of the first Pershing missiles in November 1983, they none the less had had a substantial impact on the West German domestic debate over security issues in general and INF in particular. For one thing, the peace movement was helped substantially by the emergence of a new defence elite, the *Gegenexperten* (counter-experts), centred in German universities, peace-research institutes and the media, which helped spread the nuclear-weapons debate by both criticising the government and publicising alternative security policies. Unlike the situation during the 1950s, there existed in the early 1980s a network of German and West European elites outside the national bureaucracies who were conversant with the more arcane aspects of nuclear-weapons strategies. When coupled with a large number of younger journalists and editors from the so-called successor generation who were highly critical of American and NATO policies, these defence experts were able to provide the peace movement with a steady stream of ammunition against the policies of the Schmidt government and its successor, the Christian Democratic coalition led by Helmut Kohl.

At the same time, the entry of 27 Green deputies into the West German Bundestag following the March 1983 elections ensured that the peace movement would have a continuing national forum in which to air their criticisms of INF and NATO nuclear-weapons policies. Despite the philosophical and organisational divisions which increasingly plagued the Greens following their electoral success, the Eco-peace movement as a whole was given the opportunity of protesting against the INF deployment both in the streets and in the corridors of power.

Most importantly, however, the electoral impact of the Greens served to hasten the already noticeable leftward drift of the Social Democratic Party, and thus undermine the security consensus that had existed between the major West German political parties since the early 1970s. With Helmut Schmidt's having been replaced by Hans-Jochen

Vogel as the SPD Chancellor-candidate in late 1982, the SPD moved steadily to a position of outright opposition to the NATO INF decision. At the party's special congress in Munich in September 1983, Schmidt was one of only 14 SPD delegates (out of 397) who voted against the party platform denouncing the deployment of INF in the FRG.[22] Where the SPD-led government in the late 1970s had been one of the prime initiators of the NATO INF policy, it was now the SPD that was one of the severest critics of that policy in all of Western Europe.

Ironically, one of the main criticisms against INF deployment put forth by the Greens and many in the SPD, that such deployment would endanger relations between the two Germanies, failed to materialise. Although East Germany as early as the summer of 1979 was warning the FRG of the consequences of deploying INF, and although East German leader Erich Honecker as late as 1983 warned that a 'political ice age' would freeze inner-German relations once the first Pershings arrived, relations between the FRG and GDR remained remarkably steady. To the surprise of many, it was business as usual between the two Germanies. West Germany continued to grant large credit guarantees to East Berlin, while the GDR allowed a greater number of its citizens to emigrate to the Federal Republic.

By the summer of 1984, the inner-German relationship was becoming so well insulated from the tensions of overall East-West relations that the Soviet Union felt obliged to mount a vociferous propaganda campaign against the FRG directly, and East Germany by implication. Ultimately, this Soviet pressure was successful in forcing Honecker to postpone his planned state visit to the FRG in September 1984, which would have been the first ever by an East German head of state.[23] None the less, Honecker continued to speak of a special 'community of responsibility' between the two German states, and the dependence of East Germany on the FRG for economic growth and internal stability suggested that inner-German relations would not be seriously impaired.[24]

More than anything else, continued improvements in inner-German relations vindicated the Kohl government's support of NATO INF policy. By the same token, it vindicated Helmut Schmidt's concept of *Gleichgewicht* as the only sound basis on which to base West German Ostpolitik. In terms of domestic politics, the Social Democrats discovered, to their political cost in the 1983 election, that a majority of West Germans continue to favour a double-track policy of détente with the East and solidarity within the Western alliance. Yet the internal contradictions of such a policy will continue to complicate West Germany's relations with its neighbours and NATO partners, especially when nuclear-weapons issues are pushed to the fore.

The Netherlands and Belgium

One of the most interesting aspects of the NATO INF decision-making process was the concerted effort of the Schmidt government to secure the assent of the other non-nuclear alliance partners to the INF double-track decision. Given the West German insistence on 'no singularity' (that the FRG not be the only non-nuclear state to deploy INF), this should not be so surprising. Yet the range and depth of governmental and political party contacts between West Germany and the smaller NATO members, the Netherlands and Belgium especially, was somewhat unprecedented.[25] In part it was an attempt to avoid a repetition of the neutron-bomb fiasco, in part a desire of the Schmidt government that the INF decision not be perceived as a bilateral US-West German affair. In addition, however, it represented a desire of all the West European members of NATO for a greater role in the NATO nuclear decision-making process.

Despite this increased intra-European consultation, however, a number of the West European members of NATO were unable fully to accept the 1979 Brussels decision. Both the Netherlands and Belgium made their acceptance of cruise-missile deployment contingent on arms-control progress, with the Dutch postponing any deployment decision for two years while the Belgians initially postponed their decision for six months.

In the Netherlands, the government of Prime Minister Ruud Lubbers announced in June 1984 that it was once again deferring a deployment decision, this time until 1 November 1985.[26] In part the Dutch justified their decision on the need to get the Soviet Union back to the bargaining table in Geneva, stressing that the Netherlands would accept the full complement of 48 cruise missiles by the end of 1988 if no arms-control agreement was reached. The Dutch cabinet communiqué announcing the decision also noted that, if the Americans and Soviets did agree to reduce the number of INF, then the Netherlands would agree to deploy a smaller number of cruise missiles, proportional to the overall total agreed on in Geneva.[27]

The Dutch failure to take a firm deployment decision has been the result of strong domestic opposition to INF and the possibility that such a decision would bring down the Lubbers government. In particular, Dutch Defence Minister Jacob de Ruiter was a strong opponent of accepting the cruise missiles, and the fact that de Ruiter agreed to the Cabinet decision was taken by many as a partial victory for continued Dutch involvement in NATO INF policy.[28] Given that the first cruise missiles were not scheduled for deployment in the Netherlands until late 1986 anyway, officials in other NATO countries took some comfort in the fact that the Dutch had not dropped out of the INF process entirely.

However, as was the case during the ERW episode in 1977-8, when 1.2 million Dutch signatures denouncing the neutron bomb were collected in the space of six weeks, anti-nuclear opposition in the Netherlands continued to run high. The coalition of Dutch religious and civic groups that mobilised against the neutron bomb in the late 1970s reappeared in the early 1980s to oppose INF, and was supported by as much as 70 per cent of the population.

Widespread anti-nuclear sentiments among the Dutch people have been reflected as well in the Dutch Parliament, where many Dutch parliamentarians are more radical on nuclear-weapons issues than the leaders of the government. In 1979, for example, the Christian Democratic government of Andreas van Agt thought it had found a compromise formula that would allow it to accept INF deployment, yet was frustrated just two weeks before the NATO meeting in Brussels when several parliamentarians from the government coalition defected and voted against the proposal.[29] Similarly, Prime Minister Lubbers in 1984 was concerned that an attempt to force the deployment issue would bring down his government and pave the way for the entry into power of the staunchly anti-nuclear Dutch Labour Party.

The Dutch dilemma of trying to reconcile strong support for NATO with widespread anti-nuclearism was noted by van Agt when he took office in 1978 promising to 'give high priority to preventing the proliferation of nuclear weapons', while at the same time increasing the Dutch contribution to NATO.[30] Even at the height of the protest marches against INF in 1981-2, 75 per cent of the Dutch people preferred to remain in NATO, while 60 per cent of those polled thought that the alliance was 'still essential' to Dutch security. Thus, despite the passionate opposition to INF found in the Netherlands, the Dutch generally remain firm supporters of the alliance. As Richard Eichenberg has noted, if there is anything unique about the Dutch case, it is not the level of anti-nuclear feelings, 'but the comparatively strong impact [such] opinions have had on Dutch governments'.[31] The existence in the Netherlands of thin parliamentary majorities, shifting political coalitions, and intra-party disagreements over security policy has resulted in successive Dutch governments' being unwilling to go against the strong anti-nuclear sentiments found in the Dutch populace at large.

In much the same way, problems of governmental stability made it difficult for successive Belgian governments to take a firm decision to deploy NATO INF. The Belgian decision in 1979 to postpone deployment for six months was extended a number of times, and it wasn't until March 1985 that the Wilfred Martens government approved the arrival of 16 cruise missiles at the Florennes air base south of Brussels. Unlike the Netherlands, the inability of Belgian governments to take a stand on INF deployment had less to do with widespread domestic opposition to nuclear weapons than it did with the Walloon-Flemish split that divided the country. The difficulties of the Belgian governmental devolution process and the setting up of regional assemblies for Flanders, Wallonia and Brussels, coupled with the political opposition aroused by the government's economic austerity programme, made it difficult for the Martens government to expend political capital by deploying cruise missiles.[32] Even after the cruise missiles arrived, there was a week of uncertainty as the Belgian Parliament debated the issue finally approving deployment by a vote of 116 to 93 when dissidents in Martens' Christian Democratic Party put aside their opposition to the cruise missiles and voted with the government.[32a]

While the Dutch INF debate has influenced the Belgian situation to some extent, given the linguistic ties between the Flemish and the Dutch, the more important link for Belgium is to the south, with France. Strong French support of NATO INF policy[33] has had a considerable impact on the thinking of both Belgian élites and the public at large. In particular, the Belgians have echoed French concerns that the NATO consensus on INF be maintained so as to not politically isolate West Germany. In addition the Martens government has stressed the importance of strengthening the consultation procedures within NATO's Special Consultative Group, which is responsible for formulating INF arms-control and defence policies, so that the smaller NATO countries retain their influence in NATO nuclear decision-making.

Whether the Netherlands ultimately follows Belgium's lead in deploying NATO cruise missiles will depend both on the Dutch domestic political situation and the progress, or lack of it, in US-Soviet arms-control negotiations. Whatever the situation in 1986-8, however, the two countries can be counted on to follow two quite different styles of foreign policy-making. As the Belgian diplomat Etienne Davignon once remarked: 'Our Dutch friends and ourselves just do not have the same temperament . . . Of a tiny step forward we make an enormous success, whereas it is a defeat to the Dutch ... because they have not got more.' In short, the Dutch approach to the INF dilemma will continue to be tinged with moralism, while that of the Belgians will reflect what one Dutch observer once characterised as the 'typically Belgian *maladie de compromis*'.[34]

Italy

Of the five NATO countries scheduled to receive INF systems, Italy has experienced the least amount of public debate and domestic opposition over the issue. Especially prior to the NATO decision of December 1979, public awareness of the INF issue was minimal, and the government of Francesco Cossiga was able to win parliamentary approval for Italian participation in the deployment plans by a margin of 328-230. Although large public demonstrations occurred in Italy as elsewhere in Europe in the early 1980s, especially in Rome and at the NATO cruise missile base at Comiso, Sicily, Italy has experienced no anti-nuclear movement comparable to its Protestant neighbours to the north.

The lack of serious domestic opposition to INF in Italy is due in part to the relative low importance of foreign issues for the Italian public, at least compared to other Western European countries. Particularly important in this regard is the nature of governmental policymaking in Italy, especially on issues of defence and national security. To a great extent, the Italian governmental bureaucracy is insulated from the manoeuvring and factionalism that characterises the country's party politics. Despite, or perhaps because of, the frequent changes in the make-up of Italian governments in the post-war period (there have been more than 40), the career bureaucrats in the various ministries have been able to implement policies with a fair degree of independence from political party positions and public opinion.

Just as important, however, have been the roles played by the Italian communist (PCI) and socialist (PSI) parties. Regarding the PCI, the importance of remaining independent of Moscow has meant that the party has been equally critical of both NATO INF and the Soviet SS-20s. As PCI foreign section chief Antonio Rubbi declared in 1979:

> the path we must follow is certainly not that of establishing parity at higher levels, but quite the opposite; that is, eliminating the cause which presumably led to the alleged [NATO] unilateral alteration. And if this cause is called SS-20, we have no hesitation in demanding that the cause be eliminated.[35]

Mindful of the need to attract moderate voters if it was to have any chance of joining a coalition government with the Christian Democrats, the PCI continued to assert its independence of the Soviet Union, especially after the latter's invasion of Afghanistan. The PCI also criticised Moscow's role during the Polish crisis and refused to attend a meeting of European communist parties that was called by the Soviets to denounce the NATO INF decision.

Prior to 1983, the PCI was actually more even-handed in its criticism of both superpowers than many in the peace movements and socialist and social democratic parties elsewhere in Western Europe. For example, a party proposal issued in 1979, aimed at avoiding an escalation of European theatre nuclear systems, called for: (i) NATO suspension of any decision on INF production and deployment for six months or more; (ii) Soviet suspension of the manufacture and deployment of the SS-20; and (iii) the start of negotiations that would fix a lower ceiling on the military balance so as to guarantee mutual security.[36]

As the date for NATO INF deployment neared, the PCI position did become more critical of NATO. Shortly before the first cruise missiles arrived in Sicily, the PCI came out in favour of a moratorium on NATO deployments. Yet the PCI position was no harsher than that already taken by other left-wing parties in Europe, and was a good deal more moderate than some.

The position of the Italian Socialist Party (PSI), under Bettino Craxi, was also quite moderate compared to other European socialist parties. In part, the PSI stance was influenced by the moderation of the PCI, as Craxi was determined to swing his party toward the centre of Italian politics and present himself as a viable power-broker. Taking his cue from François Mitterand and the French Socialists, Craxi strongly supported the NATO INF decision as the only means by which to get the Soviets to negotiate seriously over European theatre nuclear deployments. In criticising the anti-NATO tenor of many in the peace movements, Craxi approvingly quoted Mitterand to the effect that 'France does not confuse pacifism as a principle with peace as a result'.[37] Upon becoming Prime Minister in 1983, Craxi continued to stress the overriding importance of maintaining alliance cohesion, while also calling on both the United States and the Soviet Union to reduce their nuclear-weapons deployments.

The position of the Craxi government, then, despite some pressure from a growing Italian peace movement composed of environmentalists, feminists, the radical fringe, and a portion of the Catholic hierarchy, has been but a continuation of the previous Christian Democratic-led governments.

Italy's continued support of the alliance's INF policy has gone well beyond the deployment of Italy's allotted 112 cruise missiles, the first 16 of which were deployed at Comiso in late 1983. Throughout the INF episode, Italian governments have been strong supporters of the political and economic burden-sharing aspects of the NATO double-track decision. In part this was due to Italian resentment at being left out of the Guadeloupe four-power summit in January 1979, when President Carter met Prime Minister Callaghan, Chancellor Schmidt and President Giscard d'Estaing to discuss Western security, SALT and INF. Having felt slighted at being left out of the inner council of alliance decision-making, Italian governments since then have sought to use their unqualified support for INF as a means of re-establishing their influence. About the only issue on which Italy has differed from the NATO INF policy is that of expressing its preference for a double-key arrangement. Yet, while the Socialist-Christian Democratic coalition government has sought to assure the Italian Parliament that Italy will have some control over the decision to launch cruise missiles stationed in Sicily,[38] the country may go along with the NATO consensus for single-key American control.

Other NATO States

None of the remaining NATO countries has expressed any desire to participate in the deployment of Pershing and cruise missiles. Indeed, some NATO members are content not to be involved in the alliance decision-making process at all. Yet because of the importance attached to reaching as broad-based a consensus on INF as possible, many of these countries will continue to play significant roles in NATO nuclear-weapons policies generally.

Of these, Norway is one of the most important, given the country's strategic location on the NATO northern flank and its proximity to Soviet naval and air bases in Murmansk and on the Kola peninsula. Although there has been widespread anti-nuclear opposition in Norway, Norwegian governments have traditionally been strong supporters of strengthening NATO conventional capabilities. In January 1981, for example, the Norwegian Parliament approved a proposal to allow the United States to stockpile conventional armaments some 600 miles from the Soviet border, despite continuing Soviet threats that such a move would heighten tensions between the two countries.[39]

Indeed, while both Labour and Conservative governments in Norway in recent years have opposed participating in INF deployment, both parties have demonstrated an increased willingness to stand up to Soviet political pressure concerning Norwegian contributions to alliance defences.[40] In the early 1980s, the Labour government of Odvar Nordli vigorously protested against Soviet encroachments in the Norwegian Sea around the island of Svalbard, and also took a tougher line on the issue of a Nordic nuclear-free zone. In comparison with previous Norwegian (and Danish) responses to the proposal of former Finnish President Urho Kekkonen for the establishment of such a zone, Nordli and his Defence Minister Thorvald Stoltenberg argued that any Nordic nuclear-free zone should include the Soviet Kola peninsula as well. When a Soviet submarine, reportedly armed with nuclear-tipped torpedos, ran aground near the Swedish naval base at Karlskrona in 1982, the Norwegians again objected to any proposal for a Nordic nuclear-free zone that did not include Soviet territory or the presence of Soviet nuclear weapons in the Baltic. Since then, numerous reports of Soviet submarines violating Norwegian territorial waters have only worsened relations between the two countries.

Although Denmark, like Norway, does not allow the stationing of NATO nuclear weapons in peacetime, the Danes have generally been less supportive of the alliance's INF policy and more critical of the Reagan administration. Denmark has a widespread peace movement that maintains strong links with peace movements in West Germany and the Netherlands, and even the replacement of the Social Democratic government by a centre-right coalition in 1982 did not greatly alter Danish policy on nuclear weapons.[41] While there is some support in Denmark for increasing the country's contribution to alliance conventional forces, especially in the Baltic, a lingering economic recession has ruled out consideration of any large increases in defence spending.

Among the remaining NATO members, there have been two important developments since the Brussels decision on INF in 1979. The first was the election of a socialist government in Greece in 1981 under Andreas Papandreou, who prior to his election called for the removal of American military bases and nuclear weapons from Greece. Although there were never any plans for stationing INF systems in Greece, the hard line taken by Papandreou on denuclearising Greece, and his support for a Balkan nuclear-free zone, promised to introduce new tensions into the alliance. Since his election, however, Papandreou has moderated his demands, in part to gain greater leverage for Greece within NATO in her dispute with Turkey over the Cyprus issue and territorial rights in the Aegean Sea.[42] None the less, Papandreou has continued to irritate his NATO partners, and especially France, by endorsing the Soviet position which called for including British and French nuclear forces in the Geneva INF talks.

The other major development, that of Spanish entry into NATO in June 1982, has largely offset the critical stand of the Greek government. Even when the Spanish Socialist Party (PSOE) under Felipe González took power in October 1982, having promised to hold a referendum on Spanish membership of NATO, Spanish policy continued to be broadly supportive of alliance defence efforts. Anti-Soviet attitudes in the PSOE, coupled with González's desire to use a Spanish contribution to NATO as leverage in his dealings with the British over the status of Gibraltar, has meant a less critical attitude towards INF deployment than might have been expected of the PSOE prior to its entry into power.[43]

The remaining NATO members have played fairly secondary roles during the INF affair. As has been noted, Portugal, Iceland and Luxemburg are not members of the NPG; domestic political instability in Turkey has reduced that country's role in alliance decision-making; and Canada, with a policy of not deploying nuclear weapons with its forces in Europe, has limited itself to general support for the NATO double-track approach on INF.

Summary

In evaluating the long-term implications of the intense European political debate over NATO nuclear-weapons policy, the question arises whether European dissatisfaction with NATO nuclear strategy is merely a chronic ailment of the alliance, or a terminal one. On both sides of the alliance, it is said that NATO can no longer live with the ambiguities inherent in the flexible-response doctrine, or depend on the uncertainty of the American strategic nuclear guarantee. Henry Kissinger for one has characterised the problems facing the alliance as 'unprecedented', resulting in an 'exceedingly dangerous situation'. For Kissinger, the conflicting political aims within the alliance need to be resolved by 'fundamental, even radical' measures, including, but not limited to, a much greater role for Eruopean members of NATO in providing for their own defence and in negotiating with the Soviet Union over European-based nuclear and conventional weapons. To ensure greater European participation in formulating and in articulating NATO strategy, Kissinger has also advocated appointing a European as Supreme Allied Commander, a post heretofore always filled by an

American.[44]

In Western Europe, many of the prescriptions for what ails NATO have gone much further. Leading figures of the anti-nuclear peace movements have called for the dissolution of NATO and the Warsaw Pact, while many British Labourites and West German Social Democrats have advocated unilateral nuclear disarmament and the creation of a European nuclear-free zone.

To be sure, the transatlantic debate over the future of NATO has extended well beyond the role of nuclear weapons in the alliance's deterrent and defence stategies. Broader issues of East-West relations, the search for peace in the Middle East, political stability in Latin America, and even economic policy have all surfaced to complicate relations within the alliance. Ultimately, however, nuclear weapons issues have remained the primary symbol of NATO divisiveness and discord.[45] In no other policy area are the European members of NATO, and this includes the British and French as well, so dependent on American decisions. More important, no other issue is seen as touching so directly the fundamental issue of European security. Despite the increase in intra-alliance consultation on nuclear-weapons issues over the past three decades, the fact remains that the security and survival of Western Europe still remains largely in American hands.

On the other hand, it isn't necessarily the case that this situation will drastically change in the years ahead. Public concern with nuclear-weapons issues, in both Western Europe and the United States, has ebbed and flowed since the 1950s. By the time the first Pershing and cruise missiles were being deployed in late 1983, the European peace movements were already beginning to lose some of their momentum. The anti-nuclear-weapons policies of the British Labour Party and the West German SPD had generated limited electoral appeal, and there is reason to doubt that these policies would be put into practice even if the two parties returned to power. Finally, the discontent with the alliance voiced by large segments of Western European youth (the successor generation) could be a more transitory than enduring phenomenon.

Most important, however, are the seeming lack of viable alternatives to the continued dependence of Western Europe on the American nuclear guarantee. The tremendous political difficulties inherent in attempting to fashion a European nuclear force that could replace the American guarantee seem to rule out such a possibility.While there have been numerous proposals for strengthening NATO conventional forces so as to reduce the alliance's dependence on nuclear weapons, it is unlikely that such improvements can ever substitute for the deterrent value of American strategic forces. Short of a dismantling of the two opposing blocs in Europe, or the implementation of a European nuclear-free zone, the security of Western Europe will continue to rest on the NATO triad of conventional forces, theatre nuclear forces and American strategic forces.

None the less, the internal alliance debate over nuclear weapons will not return to the quiescence of the previous decades very soon. Even in the absence of massive demonstrations, the publics, political parties and governments of Western Europe will continue to explore alternatives to current NATO nuclear-weapons strategy. The potential outcomes of this debate are discussed more fully in the concluding chapter of this volume. Suffice to say here that, whatever the outcome, the debate will be a complex and drawn-out affair, as NATO seeks to reconcile the differing political and security requirements of its individual members.

Notes

1. See the analysis by Condoleeza Rice in Chapter 8.
2. Although France withdrew from the NATO military command structure in 1966, this analysis will treat France as a member of the alliance.
3. See, especially, David N. Schwartz, *NATO's Nuclear Dilemmas* (Washington, DC: Brookings Institution, 1983).
4. For a detailed treatment of the Nuclear Planning Group, see Paul Buteux, *The Politics of Nuclear Consultation in NATO, 1965-1980* (New York: Cambridge University Press, 1983).
5. See Catherine McArdle Kelleher, 'The Political Context of Cruise Missiles', in Richard K. Betts (ed.), *Cruise Missiles: Technology, Strategy, Politics* (Washington, DC: Brookings Institution, 1981).
6. In July 1980, the *Frankfurter Rundschau* ran a story saying that Secretary of Defence Harold Brown had confirmed the claim by Leonid Brezhnev that the Soviets had not increased their total number of theatre nuclear weapons aimed at Western Europe. This claim, which Brezhnev made in a speech in East Berlin in October 1979, had been dismissed by several Carter administration spokesmen at the time, including National Security Adviser Brzezinski. Several members of the West German Social Democratic Party, including Erwin Horn and Karsten Voigt, immediately criticised the United States for seeming to withhold information so as to magnify the SS-20 threat. American officials denied that Brown had made any such statement, and the issue soon disappeared. Yet this minor flap was symptomatic of the disadvantage that European officials feel concerning access to intelligence data about Soviet forces. See *Frankfurter Rundschau* 31 July and 1 August 1980.
7. Stanley Hoffmann, 'NATO: New Variations on Old Themes', *International Security* (Summer 1979), p. 92.
8. See Richard Shearer, 'Consulting in NATO on Nuclear Policy', *NATO Review* (October 1979).
9. In that communiqué, the alliance listed five principles which should govern

INF arms-control negotiations, one of which called for bilateral US-Soviet talks in the framework of SALT III: see *New York Times*, 13 December 1979, p. 3.

10. A West German defence official expressed the same sentiment when he noted that the INF issue 'should not be seen in terms of what Europe wants; rather the question is what the US needs to keep the nuclear umbrella intact and how Europe is prepared to support that US decision, both politically and financially'. See Klaas de Vries, 'General Report on the Security of the Alliance – The Role of Nuclear Weapons', prepared for the North Atlantic Assembly (Brussels: November 1979), pp. 14-15.

11. See, especially, Stephen Hanmer, Jr., 'NATO's Long-Range Theater Nuclear Forces: Modernization in Parallel with Arms Control', *NATO Review* (February 1980).

12. For the text of the Schmidt speech, see *Survival* (January/February 1980).

13. For more on the INF policy of the Schmidt government, see Jeffrey Boutwell, 'External and Domestic Determinants of West German Security Policy: Adenauer, Schmidt and Nuclear Weapons' (PhD dissertation, Massachusetts Institute of Technology, 1984), to be published by Cornell University Press.

14. Schmidt's concern with the necessity for maintaining a military balance of power in Europe on which to base East-West détente is elaborated at length in his *Strategie des Gleichgewichts* (Stuttgart: Seewald Verlag, 1969).

15. As Gregory Treverton has noted: 'Throughout discussion of SALT II within the Alliance, West Germany was the ally most skeptical about American assurances on non-circumvention provisions, most concerned about cruise missile restrictions, and most eager that the United States commit itself . . . to some negotiations of gray area weapons in SALT III.' See Treverton 'Nuclear Weapons and the "Gray Area" ', *Foreign Affairs* (Summer 1979), p. 1080.

16. *Defence White Paper of the Federal Republic of Germany* (Bonn: The Federal Ministry of Defence, 1979), p. 107.

17. Interview with Peter Corterier, foreign policy spokesman for the Social Democratic Party in 1979, in *New York Times*, 9 December 1979, p. E3.

18. See the article by Kurt Becker in *Die Zeit*, 14 December 1979.

19. See especially, Alfons Pawelczyk, 'Sicherheitspolitik im Rahmen der Friedenspolitik', *Die Neue Gesellschaft* (January 1980).

20. See Jeffrey Boutwell, 'Politics and the Peace Movement in West Germany', *International Security* (Spring 1983).

21. For an analysis of these internal party divisions, see Claus Genrich, 'Die Linken in Zuchtmeister Wehners neuer Fraktion', *Frankfurter Allgemeine Zeitung*, 29 September 1980.

22. For more on the SPD special party congress in Cologne, see *Die Zeit*, 2 December 1983.

23. See 'German Detente: Soviet Quandary?' by James M. Markham, in *New York Times*, 6 September 1984.

24. For more on the developing security relationship of the two Germanies see Jeffrey Boutwell, 'Inner-German Relations and gesamtdeutsche Security', *International Journal* (Summer 1984).

25. For accounts of these contacts, see *Süddeutsche Zeitung*, 14 August 1979; *Financial Times*, 15 August 1979, and *Neue Zürcher Zeitung*, 12 December 1979.

26. See 'Dutch Cabinet Decides to Delay A Decision on Deploying Missiles', *New York Times*, 2 June 1984, p. 1.

27. For the text of the statement issued by the Dutch Cabinet, see ibid., p. 5.

28. According to a US State Department official, '[No] one expected a decision [by the Dutch] to deploy now; we were more afraid that the Government might collapse'. See 'US Takes Optimistic View of Dutch Missile Decision', *New*

York Times, 2 June 1984, p. 5.

29. See, especially, *Der Spiegel*, 10 December 1979.

30. *The Economist*, 15 December 1979, p. 40.

31. Richard Eichenberg, 'The Myth of Hollanditis', *International Security* (Autumn 1983), p. 145. Public opinion data cited can be found on p. 156.

32. For more on the Walloon-Flemish split, see the article by Heinz Stadlmann, 'Politik in Belgien findet immermehr ohne Teilnahme der Bürger statt', *Frankfurter Allgemeine Zeitung*, 31 October 1980, and *The Economist*, 28 January 1984, p. 47.

32a. 'Belgian Parliament Backs Deployment of Missiles', *New York Times*, 21 March 1985.

33. At the opening of the 35th annual spring meeting of NATO Foreign Ministers, for example, French Foreign Minister Claude Cheysson strongly defended NATO INF policy and criticised the Soviets for having 'destroyed the balance of forces' so as to 'place the alliance under psychological and political pressure'. See *New York Times*, 30 May 1984, p. A7.

34. Quotes taken from Jan Deboutte and Alfred van Staden, 'High Politics in the Low Countries', in William Wallace and W.E. Paterson (eds.), *Foreign Policy Making in Western Europe* (Westmead: Saxon House, 1978), pp. 56-7.

35. Foreign Broadcast Information Service (Springfield, Va.), *Western Europe Daily Report*, 29 November 1979.

36. *Western Europe Daily Report*, 29 November 1979.

37. See the Craxi interview in *Corriere della Sera*, 25 October 1981 and *Western Europe Daily Report*, 6 October 1981, pp. L2-L5.

38. *Washington Post*, 16 November 1981, p. 11.

39. *New York Times*, 31 January 1981, p. 3.

40. For more on Soviet efforts to coerce Norway away from NATO, see Robert K.German, 'Norway and the Bear: Soviet Coercive Diplomacy and Norwegian Security Policy', *International Security* (Fall 1982).

41. *The Economist*, 17 September 1983, pp. 61-2.

42. *The Economist*, 4 September 1982, pp. 46-7.

43. *Western Europe Daily Report*, 15 June 1982, pp. N1-N3.

44. Henry Kissinger, 'A Plan to Reshape NATO', *Time*, 5 March 1984, pp. 20-4.

45. See, especially, Leon V. Sigal, *Nuclear Forces in Europe: Enduring Dilemmas, Present Prospects* (Washington, D.C.: The Brookings Institution, 1984).

7 THE SOVIET THEATRE NUCLEAR FORCE POSTURE: DOCTRINE, STRATEGY AND CAPABILITIES

Stephen M. Meyer

Much has been said and written during the past five years about Soviet theatre nuclear forces (TNF). Unfortunately, in most instances these discussions were intended largely to establish a context for examining American or European defence policy problems. As a result, the general view of the Soviet TNF posture in Western writing and discussion is incomplete. It is the purpose of this paper to summarise the main conclusions of a study that focused on Soviet TNF planning and force structuring in a more comprehensive manner and to provide some updating.[1] Soviet professional military journals, books, force planning exercises, and analytic modelling efforts were examined systematically. Successive generations of Soviet TNF weapons systems were analysed in terms of both performance capabilities and operational (mission) capabilities.[2] The objective was to understand changes that had occurred in Soviet TNF planning, procurement, and capabilities and to describe and analyse those changes and the relationships among them.

Of particular interest here are two generic questions: How do contemporary Soviet military planners expect to employ available TNF assets? What capabilities have they acquired to carry out those plans? The first generic question is tied specifically to Soviet nuclear-employment policy, military strategy, and the operational art of the individual service branches: How do Soviet military planners view the nuclear escalation ladder? Against what will Soviet TNF systems be targeted, and in what manner will they be used? How are different weapons systems distributed across the TNF missions? Answers to these questions not only provide insights into Soviet planning concepts, but also provide a useful yardstick against which the 'opportunity costs' of employing Soviet TNF assets in alternative ways can be measured.

The examination of Soviet TNF capabilities is important not only for the purpose of threat assessment but also because we would like to be able to evaluate the extent to which the Soviet Ministry of Defence has been buying the kind of weaponry implied by Soviet military strategy. Trends in weapons procurement — analysed both in

Soviet TNF Employment Concepts

In order to understand fully Soviet TNF employment concepts it is necessary to examine a number of aspects of Soviet military doctrine, military strategy, and the operational art of the armed forces branches. Briefly, military doctrine refers to the officially sanctioned views of the Soviet political leadership on the nature of future war, likely adversaries, the putative goals of war, the required levels of military and economic mobilisation of the nation, and the technical aspects of equipping the Soviet armed forces. It is a collection of premises and assumptions upon which the Soviet professional miltary is supposed to base its military planning. Soviet writers note that military doctrine can be divided into political-social components and military technical components; the former referring to issues of party concern exclusively, and the latter involving legitimate professional military consultation.

Military strategy, then, lays out the broad principles and concepts of force employment that are to guide the use of the Soviet armed forces in accomplishing the goals set out by military doctrine. The fundamentals of Soviet military strategy are the same for all service branches and combat arms of the Soviet armed forces: there is no separate 'nuclear strategy', 'naval strategy', or 'land-battle strategy'.

Lastly, there is operational art and tactics. Operational art encompasses both the concepts of combined arms operations in a theatre (e.g. front activities) and the specialised concepts of operations by particular service branches and combat arms. There is, for example, a Navy operational art, which takes into account the peculiar characteristics of naval armament and operations. The limits on 'innovation' in operational art are set by military strategy; the former must be consistent with the latter. Tactics emphasise subunit activities (e.g., fighter-interceptor manoeuvres) and is, likewise, constrained by operational art.[3]

A number of significant changes have occurred in Soviet military doctrine, strategy, and operational art since nuclear weapons were first introduced into the Soviet armed forces in 1954.[4] Contemporary Soviet military views on theatre nuclear warfare evolved from a rather tumultuous history. That process saw several fundamental themes surface repeatedly in policy debates. Concepts of TNF targeting, problems of escalation, views on limited nuclear warfare, and their special fears and concerns regarding theatre nuclear warfare in Europe have been particularly important themes. An understanding of Soviet military views on these issues over time is essential to an analysis of past and current Soviet TNF capabilities. Not only do they provide windows into Soviet weapons programmes and force structuring, but they also offer clues to possible Soviet actions and reactions in the face of NATO's evolving military posture.

In the discussion which follows, the 'views' described refer to the Soviet professional military — in most instances, officers on the General Staff or the service planning staffs — based on writings appearing in the professional military literature; primarily service journals, the restricted General Staff journal *Voyennaya Mysl'*, studies published by the various Soviet military academies and Soviet analyses of their own exercises.

How do Soviet Military Planners View the Concept of Limited Nuclear War?

It is often observed that the Soviet military rejects the notion of 'limited nuclear war', suggesting that any conflict in Europe involving nuclear strikes must instantly escalate to intercontinental nuclear strikes. The use of even a few nuclear weapons would seem to lead directly to global nuclear war.

The rather loose use of the term 'limited nuclear war' by Western defence specialists has resulted, unfortunately, in considerable confusion regarding their Soviet counterparts' views. At one time or another, limited nuclear war has been invoked by Western writers to characterise:

(i) a US-Soviet intercontinental nuclear exchange in which only military forces are targeted — i.e. cities are 'avoided' in initial nuclear strikes;

(ii) a NATO-Warsaw Pact war in which only nuclear weapons based in the theatre are used — including strikes against the European USSR;

(iii) a NATO-Warsaw Pact war in which nuclear weapons are used on the battlefield but in which the American and Soviet homelands are sanctuaries from nuclear strikes;

(iv) a NATO-Warsaw Pact war involving nuclear strikes where the American and Soviet homelands are sanctuaries, but in which relatively few nuclear weapons are used (say, several dozen).[5]

Soviet political and military leaders clearly reject the notions that variants (i) or (ii) represent limited nuclear wars. First of all, a US-Soviet intercontinental nuclear exchange that is 'limited' to military-force targeting is a main element in the Soviet notion of central strategic war. Since the Soviets use the term strategic to connote any event that has a decisive effect on the course and outcome of a war, the destruction of Soviet intercontinental nuclear forces is, by definition, a strategic strike. Moreover, the tight co-location of major Soviet cities and industries with likely military targets implies that intended limitations may be more imaginary than real in impact.

The use of American nuclear weapons based in other theatres of military operations (i.e. outside the United States) to strike the Soviet homeland in no way lessens their strategic effects, or masks the true source of the attack. In much the same way that President Kennedy declared that a strike by Soviet missiles based in Cuba would be considered a strike from the Soviet homeland, so, too, would Soviet military leaders look upon an American TNF strike on the USSR as a nuclear strike originating from the continental United States.

In particular, American Pershing II and GLCM strikes against targets in the USSR would not be distinguished from Minuteman or Poseidon strikes. Since the late 1960s Soviet military planners have conjectured that the first wave of an intercontinental nuclear strike would be led by an initial attack on major command, control and communication (C3) installations, which would be followed by attacks on strategic nuclear force installations, military bases, airfields, air defence sites, military industries, etc.[6] Pershing II missiles might play an important role in timely NATO strikes against Soviet C3 facilities, while the GLCM could be used to follow up against less time-urgent targets. It is not that Pershing II or GLCM would be better than existing American strategic nuclear forces at carrying out these missions, but simply that the combination of range and performance capabilities of these two TNF systems strongly suggest military missions that make them strategic weapons as well.

However, I would argue that limited-war variants (iii) and (iv) are considered as possible by the Soviet military leadership. Irrespective of Soviet 'declaratory' policy regarding the inevitability of nuclear use in the theatre escalating to intercontinental nuclear strikes, Soviet action policy during the 1960s must have been sensitive to the fact that if nuclear weapons were used in a theatre conflict (but not on Soviet territory) it would have been the height of folly for Soviet leaders to react by launching nuclear attacks on the American homeland. The strategic nuclear balance clearly militated against such a policy. Indeed, it is more likely that professed Soviet pessimism on the topic of limited nuclear conflicts is, in part, an effort at deterrence. Soviet military planners also seem to hold the belief that the United States would be unlikely to subject its NATO allies to theatre nuclear warfare unless the Americans were prepared to destroy the Soviet Union once and for all: the historical conflict of opposing social systems.

In particular, the adoption of flexible response by NATO in 1967 gave considerable impetus to Soviet military planners to take seriously the possibilities of waging limited nuclear wars variants (iii) and (iv). Soviet military writings throughout the late 1960s and early 1970s reflected a concentrated Soviet effort to come to grips with the various implications of flexible response for Soviet military doctrine, strategy, operational art, and tactics. As early as 1968, Marshall Sokolovskiy noted that 'the possibility is not excluded of war occurring with the use of conventional weapons, as well as the limited use of nuclear means in one or several theaters of military operations'.[7] Two obvious theatres would be the European theatre and the Far East theatre (i.e. mainland China). Moreover, the advent of strategic nuclear parity between the United States and the Soviet Union in the early 1970s served to reduce the likelihood that either side might perceive advantages in a nuclear action policy that revolved around pushing a theatre nuclear conflict to global nuclear exchanges. Some interesting evidence in this regard is provided by Kissinger.[8] He recounts that in the early 1970s Soviet General Secretary Brezhnev proposed a treaty in which the two countries would pledge not to strike each other's homelands should they become engaged in a conflict somewhere in the world. This sanctuary concept was to apply, in the Soviet view, even if allied territories were hit with nuclear weapons. (The United States rejected the proposal but it eventually evolved into the US-Soviet treaty to prevent nuclear war.)

It would be misleading not to acknowledge that most Soviet military writers remain fairly pessimistic that extensive theatre nuclear warfare in Europe (variant (iii)) could be kept from spiralling up ultimately to variant (ii). This is especially true as the independent French and British nuclear forces, and planned dual-key long-range nuclear systems in German hands, were brought into play. Variant (ii), in turn, would almost certainly escalate to variant (i) — a central nuclear war between the United States and the USSR. Consequently, by the late 1960s Soviet military planners began to acknowledge a number of incentives to keep any European war down at the conventional level. As a result Soviet military doctrine and military strategy experienced some fundamental revisions.

Theatre Warfare: the Conventional Phase

During the late 1950s and early 1960s, a standard assumption of Soviet military planning was that any major war in Europe would begin with massive nuclear strikes — in both the theatre and against the United States and Soviet homelands. Indeed, Soviet military forces were structured in a fashion that seemed to offer few alternatives. Whether this was primarily a case of military capabilities constraining military doctrine and strategy, or military doctrine and strategy dictating military capabilities, is not clear. However, over the last decade there has been a clear move away from this formulation in the Soviet military literature and this has been accompanied by substantial changes in the structure, organisation, and equipping of the Soviet armed forces.

In order best to understand the current Soviet military view of theatre nuclear operations, it is necessary to place the nuclear escalation issue in the larger context of the theatre conflict. Contemporary Soviet military doctrine holds that a war in Europe may begin with a conventional phase that might persist for a long period. Indeed, Soviet military writings and exercises in the past decade strongly hint that the military leadership would *prefer* that a European conflict, should one occur, remain in the conventional phase.[9] Several reasons exist. Firstly, for all their studies and analyses, Soviet military planners have yet to figure out how to manage a full-scale theatre nuclear war. While, in this author's view, the Soviet military appreciates the possibilities and problems of military operations in a nuclear environment better than do their Western counterparts, the prevailing Soviet military view seems to hold that as the contemplated number of nuclear strikes within the theatre increases, irresolvable uncertainties come to frustrate military planning. The historical database upon which Soviet military science is grounded becomes less and less relevant, as theoretical analyses and analogies predominate. The efficacy of conducting large-scale ground-force operations declines as C3 breaks down, entire units and subunits are destroyed by enemy single nuclear strikes, rear echelon forces and reserves are decimated, rear area logistics collapse and broad zones of radioactive contamination are created. In contrast to the uncertainties and imponderables inherent in a large-scale theatre nuclear conflict, Soviet military planners apparently find comfort in the relative orderliness and predictability that a conventional theatre war holds.

Of course, a somewhat different situation would exist if *only* Soviet TNF were employed — that is if an effective Soviet nuclear pre-emptive strike against NATO TNF were possible. A nuclear pre-emptive strike would require prompt nuclear release by the Soviet political leadership at the earliest stages of a crisis — i.e. perhaps even before any direct hostilities had taken place. The reason is that as the crisis evolves, it is likely that NATO nuclear forces will be dispersed, thereby sharply reducing the effectiveness of any forthcoming Soviet pre-emptive effort. In this regard, some Soviet military writers hint at a healthy scepticism regarding the willingness and ability of the Soviet political leadership to permit the timely release of nuclear weapons to the military command.[10]

The enormous Soviet investment in tactical strike aircraft and ground-force fire-power beginning in the late 1960s, and helicopter assault forces in the 1970s, reflects conventional (and perhaps, chemical) alternatives to what were formerly nuclear missions. Under contemporary Soviet military planning Soviet TNF would still play an important role: deterring NATO use of its TNF assets. While NATO withheld its TNF — deterred by massive Soviet TNF capabilities — Soviet conventional forces would attempt to destroy NATO TNF in preventive strikes.[11] In fact, discussions of the operational art and tactics of the ground forces, the air forces, and the Navy emphasise that their first and foremost task is to use their conventional fire-power capabilities to seek out and destroy enemy nuclear assets in the theatre, to the exclusion of other, more traditional, missions. In other words, the first missions to be executed in the opening stages of a conflict are the preventive destruction of enemy TNF by Soviet conventional forces.

This emphasis on destroying NATO TNF follows from the Soviet assessment that nuclear weapons are capable of executing independent strategic missions in the theatre. The vast destructiveness of nuclear weapons enables them, within very short periods of time, to produce strategic defeats of opposing forces. Where, in the past, strategic defeat occurred as a result of an accumulation of tactical defeats incurred over a lengthy period of time, nuclear weapons can produce strategic defeats by direct strikes. Consequently, the enemy's use of nuclear weapons could radically alter the tempo, course, and outcome of a conflict. No other class of weaponry has so great a potential to inflict damage on Soviet troops, reserves, air forces, and command, control, and communications.

In this respect one of the key principles of Soviet military art since the late 1950s has been 'preserving the combat effectiveness of friendly troops' in the theatre. The most important component of this principle is destroying the enemy's nuclear means of attack before they can be used against Soviet forces. The special emphasis given to these missions against NATO TNF suggests that if Soviet military planners have any intentions of employing chemical weapons, they would do so during this conventional phase. As a result, as conflict evolved, the theatre nuclear balance would continue to shift towards greater Soviet dominance – its TNF safely husbanded in the Soviet homeland while Soviet conventional forces destroy NATO TNF assets. Ideally, the end of these missions would see a Soviet nuclear monopoly in the theatre while nuclear parity at the central nuclear forces level deters the United States from resorting to its central systems.[12]

The critical fire-break would occur if and when Soviet political leaders determined that NATO was about to employ its TNF.[13] At this point it would be up to the political leadership to authorise nuclear strikes.

Theatre Warfare: The Nuclear Phase

With nuclear-release authorisation from the political leadership, how would Soviet military planners prefer to employ their TNF assets? In fact, Soviet nuclear-targeting priorities in the theatre are easily gleaned from military writings: enemy nuclear forces and associated bases (especially nuclear-command and control facilities), enemy general purpose forces, and enemy military-industry. By far the most important targets for attack are enemy nuclear forces not destroyed during the conventional phase. That is to say, upon entering the nuclear phase Soviet TNF will take over the task of destroying NATO TNF from Soviet conventional forces. The main TNF missions will be borne by Soviet strategic TNF systems: the IRBMs of the Strategic Rocket Forces (SRF), long-range aviation (LRA) aircraft, and the SLBMs of the Soviet Navy. These systems will be used in the first wave of Soviet TNF strikes against NATO targets.

Nuclear missiles of the SRF (these include the SS-4 and SS-20 IRBMs, and peripherally targeted SS-11 and SS-19 ICBMs) are assigned to destroy NATO air bases, naval facilities, and other military bases where tactical nuclear delivery vehicles (TNDVs) are stationed and nuclear warheads are stored. NATO C3 facilities, likely to be part of the nuclear release and employment network, are also targeted. The latter are deemed particularly important in maximising the effects of pre-emptive strikes against the TNDVs, by slowing dispersion, release and employment of NATO nuclear weapons. In general, the SRF have been assigned the large and fixed targets of NATO's nuclear forces. Long-range aviation (this includes, for example, the Tu-22 (Blinder) and Tu-26 (Backfire) intermediate-range bombers) has been assigned to real-time reconnaissance and strike missions against mobile and point targets associated with NATO's TNF assets. These would include NATO's land-mobile missile launchers and associated C3 centres. Nuclear-storage sites would also be included. LRA may also be assigned to support Navy operations against NATO ships carrying nuclear weaponry (e.g., American aircraft carriers) and submarine port facilities. Navy SLBMs — specifically, the SS-N-5 and SS-N-6 — may be employed against air bases and other military bases where TNDVs are housed.

The operational/tactical and tactical TNF systems of the Soviet ground forces and frontal aviation will be used almost simultaneously in the second wave in order to (i) finish off targets that survived the first wave and (ii) destroy lower priority targets not included in the target list of the first-wave strikes by the strategic TNF. Specifically, the missile troops of the ground forces will concentrate on destroying residual fixed targets, while frontal aviation concentrated on nuclear strikes against mobile and hard-point targets.

Important militarily, but of lesser urgency in terms of the timeliness of their destruction, are major groupings of enemy conventional forces, mobilisation and staging areas, logistics nodes, and port facilities. Also, recent Soviet works on tank and anti-tank warfare devote considerable amounts of space to the use of battlefield nuclear systems against dispersed anti-tank forces. Since the destruction of the group of targets holds little significance unless NATO TNF systems have for the most part been eliminated, and since non-TNF targets are not time-urgent (the utility of their destruction is fairly constant over several days), it can be expected that extensive TNF strikes against them would not be initiated until the destruction of NATO TNF systems had largely been accomplished. While the Strategic Rocket Forces and the Navy are likely to be assigned some conventional-force targets (e.g., logistics nodes and ports) much of the targeting burden here is likely to be borne by LRA, the ground forces, and frontal aviation.

Nuclear strikes also might be ordered against key military industries in Europe. However, since the late 1960s, nuclear strikes on European military-industrial facilities have not figured prominently in Soviet military writings and in fact the notion has been repeatedly criticised. Instead, conventional ground-forces operations are expected to take these facilities out of action, while preserving valuable industrial equipment for eventual use in rebuilding the socialist economies.[14]

It is in this context that an important misperception must be addressed. It is widely believed in the West that prior to the 1970s, Soviet TNF — especially MRBMs and IRBMs — were targeted primarily on European cities. This, simply, is not the case. From the early 1950s, Soviet military planning — as reflected in Soviet military writings, force modelling, and weapons procurement — has revolved around targeting NATO military assets, especially NATO nuclear forces. In works of the 1950s and 1960s, Soviet military writers frequently acknowledged that European urban areas would suffer severe damage, but this would result from collateral effects, not explicit targeting policy. Targeting of European cities was viewed as neither interesting nor consistent with Soviet military doctrine or strategy. Success in war is determined primarily by the defeat of enemy military forces. In attempting to optimise the military effectiveness of TNF strikes during the 1950s and 1960s, Soviet military planners apparently gave little attention to (or were unable to do much to limit) the likely effects of collateral damage to Europe's urban areas.[15]

The Soviet design or direct escalation to extensive deep nuclear strikes by strategic TNF to NATO rear areas, followed by battlefield nuclear engagements near the forward edge of the battle area (FEBA), stands in contrast to NATO planning which, historically, has envisioned gradual theatre escalation from conventional, to limited battlefield nuclear strikes aganst Soviet ground forces (most likely on NATO territory) to extended battlefield strikes, to the second echelon forces, and then finally to deep rear areas. In this respect, the Soviets appear to be jumping the intermediate rungs of the escalation ladder. What must be emphasised is that Soviet military strategy and operational art, exercises, force posture, and C3 principles are all structured in such a way that any NATO nuclear use will be met by extensive concentrated nuclear strikes across NATO territory.

If things actually got this far, the ICBMs and the SLBMs of the Strategic Rocket Forces and the Navy would play a deterrent role, inhibiting further escalation — hence the importance of achieving central nuclear parity with the United States during the 1970s.[16] Indeed, I would argue that the re-equipping and modernisation of Soviet conventional forces, the peripheral nuclear attack forces, and the central nuclear forces carried out in the 1970s were all part of a basic force-structure plan aimed at bounding the escalation ladder between the nuclear deterrent and conventional war-fighting rungs.

Soviet TNF Capabilities

The pace and momentum of Soviet weapons-development programmes tied to TNF missions have been remarkably strong and consistent over the past 15 to 20 years. In particular, the direction of Soviet TNF procurement has systematically followed the path set down by Soviet military writings. In this respect, the scale of Soviet TNF modernisation efforts is especially noteworthy given the fact that NATO has done little in this area since the late 1960s.

Contemporary Soviet TNF systems are the outgrowth of design concepts developed during the early to mid-1960s. The mobile SS-20 IRBM, for example, is the direct descendant of an experimental mobile IRBM programme that produced the SSX-14 and SSX-15. (And as the SSX-14 and SSX-15 were derived from the SS-13 ICBM, so the SS-20 was derived from the SS-16 ICBM). Marshal Krylov, among others, noted that mobile strategic missile programmes were well under way by 1961 — specifically linked with efforts to develop solid-fuelled missiles.

The Tu-26 Backfire bomber is an outgrowth of the Tupolev design bureau's long-standing efforts to produce a regional bomber with very high dash and deep-strike capabilities. (The hiatus between the Tu-22 design and the follow-on Tu-26 was largely a product of doctrinal debates over the future utility of aircraft, not technology.) The Soviet SLCM/SLBM programmes date back to the early 1950s. As originally conceived, these weapons were valued for their contribution to strategic reach and strategic manoeuvre — not survivability. The SS-N-3 cruise missile, first deployed in the late 1950s, was later modified, and has recently been followed by the SS-N-21. Beginning in the late 1950s, there has also been a progression of SLBMs: the SS-N-4, the SS-N-5, and the SS-N-6.

Soviet SRBMs are also being replaced; most interesting is the replacement of the SS-12 by the SS-22. The 900-km reach of these missiles has puzzled many defence specialists, given that these missiles are organic to the front level formations. The significance of their range may not lie so much in their forward reach, but rather in their contribution to strategic manoeuvre. From the rear-most position of a front, the SS-12/SS-22s can strike targets in the forward-most operations area of other non-adjacent fronts within a given strategic direction. This permits flexiblity in the concentration of independent nuclear fire-power in the theatre.

Also relevant to Soviet TNF missions is the introduction of high-performance strike aircraft attached to frontal aviation. The MiG-23,

MiG-27, Su-17, and Su-24 are all potentially capable of delivering nuclear ordnance, though it is likely that only select groups of Su-24s based in the USSR will be used in this role. Retaining a force of Su-24s in the USSR ensures that there will be comparatively rapid access to nuclear munitions, that these will be under tight command and control, and that these systems will be relatively safe from enemy conventional strikes (i.e. compared to frontal-aviation assets in Eastern Europe). As such, the Su-24 force represents a strategic reserve force. The other aircraft will carry out pre-emption missions against NATO TNF using conventional (and chemical) ordnance. In either case, these tactical aircraft systems — and their likely follow-ons —are among the most important additions to the Soviet TNF posture because they make the conventional pre-emption option viable.

Though the range of technical improvements and investments in Soviet TNF systems have been great, what we are really interested in are changes in the operational capabilities of Soviet TNF: that is to say, relative improvements in Soviet capabilities to carry out key TNF missions. Space limitation does not permit a complete and systematic analysis of the whole spectrum of Soviet TNF operational capabilities. However, because of the special role they have played in Western defence debates, it is important to discuss the operational implications of two principle weapons: the SS-20 and the Tu-26.

SS-20

Much has been made over the introduction of the SS-20 IRBM. To be sure, its performance characteristics are vastly superior to those of the missiles it is replacing (i.e. the SS-4s and SS-5s). Where the older missiles are believed to have a circular error probable (CEP) of the order of 1.5 km, the SS-20 may have a CEP around 0.2 km. It has more than three times the range of the SS-4 — 50 per cent greater than that of the SS-5. Its MIRVed payload allows Soviet military planners to target three 150-kiloton warheads independently. This, coupled to the SS-20's mobility, gives Soviet military planners increased flexibility in reconfiguring long-range TNF during peacetime and increased confidence in survivability during war. With a set-up time of an hour or so, the SS-20 represents a vast improvement of the one-day-plus preparations required by the SS-4 and SS-5 force. Perhaps the most important enhancement is the SS-20's greater overall reliablity, which serves to reduce operational uncertainties considerably for Soviet military planners.

The SS-20 does enhance the deterrent quality of the Soviet TNF posture by increasing its survivability. Simply stated, the lower NATO's confidence in being able to destroy Soviet TNF, the less likely is NATO to escalate to nuclear use. Moreover, the high force loading (i.e. deliverable warheads) of the SS-20 force implies a greater deterrent value from the perspective of the Soviet military's conception of deterrence.[17]

To the Soviet military planner, the SS-20 is a very important development because it reduces significantly operational uncertainties. That is to say, the SS-20 allows Soviet military planners to use one weapons system where four were formerly required (each with very different operating characteristics). Moreover, the combined high reliability and MIRV design of the SS-20 means that a smaller quantity of weapons needs to be ready for launch than was previously the case. Thus, if there is a reason for NATO military planners to be concerned about the SS-20 it is because of the increased confidence and operational flexibility that it gives to their Soviet counterparts. All in all, from the perspective of the Soviet military planners, the SS-20 represents a very important development in the Soviet TNF posture.

Yet, in terms of net effects, for all its performance improvements, it can be argued that the SS-20 poses little in the way of new qualitative or quantitative military threats to NATO forces. Primary targets for the SS-20 are NATO air bases, nuclear-storage sites, and other military facilities where nuclear weaponry are based as well as other fixed military installations. Depending on predetermined damage criteria, a 3 pounds per square inch (psi) envelope (for destruction of aircraft) to 10 psi envelope (for destruction of buildings and POL storage tanks) spread over 22 km^2 would be required to kill an air base, a port, or an army base.

Here, contrary to popular impressions, it can be shown that the SS-4 and SS-5 force was more than capable of striking the full complement of these fixed soft military targets. Their combinations of nuclear yields and delivery accuracies offered greater than 95 per cent probability of complete target destruction — given a reliable launch and detonation. The number of these early missiles procured was sufficient to compensate for their relatively poor performance reliabilities. Thus, in terms of posing a threat to primary NATO targets, the SS-20 merely replicates the mission capabilities of the SS-4 and SS-5 force, albeit with a more refined mix of performance characteristics. The only notable improvement in operational capabilities produced by the SS-20 pertains to options for strategic manoeuvre available to the Soviet High Command. From the NATO military planners' perspective, however, the

Soviet TNF Posture

SS-20 poses no greater qualitative threat to most primary targets — specifically, NATO air and military bases — than existed previously. (However, one thing that the substitution of SS-20s for SS-4s and SS-5s does accomplish is to reduce expected collateral damage in Europe significantly. Theoretically, this will reduce complications in Soviet battle management of their ground forces in the theatre and reduce destruction of European industrial facilities deemed useful to Soviet economic recovery.)

One apparent difference that does emerge between the old SS-4 and SS-5 force and the new SS-20 force is the latter's ability to kill hardened C3 facilities and nuclear-storage sites. In all cases, these are likely to be no more than 300 psi — probably around 100 psi for major C3 centres and about 250 psi for nuclear-storage sites. (In the 1960s, even the nuclear-storage sites were likely to have been under 100 psi.) Where the SS-4 and SS-5 missiles could not be expected to dig out these hardened targets (even with multiple-warhead strikes), the SS-20 has a single-shot kill probability over 95 per cent. However, before one makes too much of this observation, three points must be noted. Firstly, during the 1960s these hardened targets were well covered by long-range aviation using gravity bombs and air-to-surface (ASM) cruise missiles. These aircraft systems did possess the nuclear yields and CEPs needed to ensure high kill probabilities, along with times-to-targets under two hours. By the early 1970s, these targets were 'picked up' by peripherally targeted Soviet SS-11 ICBMs, and later by similarly targeted SS-19s. Secondly, NATO did much to increase the vulnerability of its own nuclear-storage sites by reducing their number from over 110 in the 1960s to about 40 in the 1970s. Thirdly, the prior destruction of NATO TNDV assets makes the timely destruction of the nuclear-storage sites less urgent. Nuclear warheads — secure in hardened shelters — are not much good without surviving delivery vehicles. Consequently, while this subset of hardened targets may not have been vulnerable to attack by the old SS-4 and SS-5 force they were highly vulnerable to other Soviet nuclear forces assigned to theatre missions (including ICBMs).

Tu-26

The importance of the Backfire bomber to the theatre nuclear strike capabilities of the Soviet armed forces has been obscured by the efforts of some analysts to attribute an intercontinental-strike role to it. One thing is clear: the diversion of the Tu-26 to an intercontinental mission would seriously undermine Soviet TNF operations.

There are two tasks to which this aircraft represents an important addition to Soviet TNF operational capabilities: follow-up nuclear strikes against hard-point targets, and strikes against enemy sea-based TNF. It is highly likely that many Backfire aircraft would be used in carrying out conventional pre-emptive strikes against primary targets. Indeed, the magnitude of the task may *require* the majority of Backfires to be used in this way. The performance characteristics that are most noteworthy are its combination of enhanced reliability, payload, dash-speed, and range over its predecessors. Reliability is particularly important because it reduces operational uncertainties — i.e. the number of reserve planes required per target. The combination of increased payload and range is significant not as is often remarked because of the implicit combat reach, but rather because it allows for greater flexibility for strategic manoeuvre against close-in targets, it permits basing Tu-26s deeper inside the Soviet Union to improve survivability, and it gives the aircraft a significant loiter and delivery capability against sea-based targets. Finally, its high dash-speed increases penetration potential beyond that already provided by its ASM armament, as well as permitting time-urgent strikes. These are important improvements from the perspective of the Soviet military.

The Tu-26 also affords the Soviet military leadership the potential option to flush its bomber force to alert during theatre crises (though they have never done this in the past), much as the United States military command has with respect to its B-52 force. As a recallable TNF strike system, the Tu-26 adds flexibility to Soviet military options. It would seem, then, from the Soviet military planners' perspective, that the Tu-26 is an important addition to the Soviet TNF posture.

However, from a NATO perspective, it is not clear that the operational capabilities of LRA have changed much. In large measure, the older Tu-16/Tu-22 force was capable of fulfilling the same hard-target strikes. It should also be kept in mind that, during the 1960s, these targets were softer than they are now. Of course, the reliability/penetration rates of these aircraft were lower than the Tu-26, but this shortcoming was easily remedied by assigning several systems per target. Then, too, many Tu-95 long-range bombers would also have participated in theatre strikes, having been reassigned to missions in the continental theatres in the mid-1960s. It is doubtful that NATO military leaders would notice the difference between the 1965 Soviet bomber strike and the 1980 Soviet bomber strike (aside from the reduced collateral damage in the latter instance).

Soviet SLBM Capabilities

Often ignored in analyses of Soviet TNF are the strike capabilities in Soviet SLCMs/SLBMs. Perhaps, because the number of Soviet SLBMs in the 1960s was relatively small, they seemed insignificant. However it should be kept in mind that the overall European target array was relatively small as well.

From a qualitative perspective, even the early SS-N-4 seemed to have a capability to fulfil the basic mission of strikes against soft-area targets close to Europe's shores — i.e. air bases, ports, etc. However, the short range of SS-N-4s required that Soviet submarines practically come on shore in order to reach many of the most interesting prospective targets. Of course, this requirement greatly multiplied the anti-submarine warfare (ASW) barriers and hazards that Soviet submarines had to run. The SS-N-5 brought significant range and reliability improvements, and still came well within the target kill boundaries. When reliability rates and station considerations are taken into account about one to two dozen European targets were likely to have come under Soviet SLBM attack during the 1960s.

The SS-N-6 with its 3,000-km range is becoming increasingly relevant to TNF analyses as it is replaced by more advanced SLBMs in the Soviet strategic arsenal. It is capable of firing from near home waters and still reaching most primary targets. Its performance characteristics are clearly better than those of its predecessors. There can be no doubt that the SS-N-6 is capable of covering a substantial fraction of the primary target array, and if NATO naval forces succeed in bottling up most of the SS-N-6 carrying SSBNs behind the Greenland-Iceland-UK gap, it is most likely that — for lack of other alternatives — the SS-N-6s would be targeted on Europe.

Command and Control of Soviet TNF

The command and control of nuclear weapons has always been a high-priority item for the Soviet political leadership. The seriousness with which they viewed the problem of command and control is reflected by the fact that up until the mid-1960s all nuclear warheads were kept apart from the nuclear delivery vehicles. In the case of MRBMs, IRBMs and ICBMs, warheads were stored 50 to 75 km away from launcher sites, and held under KGB guard. Nuclear warheads were finally emplaced on USSR-based missiles only in the aftermath of the Cuban missile crisis. No Soviet nuclear delivery aircraft have ever been placed on air or standby ground alert. This remains true today, with aircraft nuclear payloads held separately in special storage sites guarded by KGB troops. There are reports that KGB officers serve on all Soviet nuclear-weapons-carrying submarines as part of the command and control system.

While recent press reports point to the existence of numerous Soviet nuclear storage sites in the GDR, as well as elsewhere in Eastern Europe, there continues to be some uncertainty of the extent of actual Soviet warhead deployment in Eastern Europe; Soviet strategy for employing these weapons (i.e. the role that they are assigned) ensures that the warheads will be available in the theatre when needed. This is true even if the warheads need to be transported in from the USSR.

The Soviet political leadership has always demonstrated a strong interest in maintaining firm control of TNF warheads because — like the Western political leadership — they are concerned about escalation control.[18] The extent to which Soviet political leaders do worry about escalation control can only be discerned from the manner in which military doctrine, weapons-procurement programmes, deployment of nuclear warheads, and C3 arrangements are defined. In July 1982, Minister of Defence Ustinov revealed high-level concern over this issue when he noted that one of the major tasks confronting Soviet military work in the coming years would be to enhance efforts to prevent the unauthorised use of Soviet nuclear weapons — from tactical to strategic.[19]

Tactical Nuclear Missiles in Eastern Europe

Soviet TNF modernisation continues. As already noted, they are currently in the process of replacing 1960s vintage tactical and operational-tactical missiles with the SS-21, SS-22, and SS-23 systems. The complete re-equipping of Soviet field units with these new missiles is likely to take quite a few years. The only significant change in Soviet deployment policy has been the movement of SS-22 operational-tactical missiles of increased range into Eastern Europe — specifically, East Germany and Czechoslovakia. It is likely that no more than several dozen SS-22 launchers will complete the Eastern European deployment. While this change offers some marginal military utility, it does not add up to anything of significance in the larger scheme of the Soviet theatre nuclear missions.

At the end of the summer of 1984 the Soviet Union announced the successful testing of its version of the ground-launched cruise missile. This was no surprise, except perhaps to Soviet readers of *Pravda*. What is truly fascinating about this weapon, if it indeed is deployed, is that it will not offer the Soviet military any new or enhanced capabilities in the theatre. Even under the most conservative estimates of reliability, survivability, and performance capability the number of deliverable SS-20 warheads already is in excess of the number of independent targets. Therefore I would hazard a guess that the Soviet GLCM is largely a political development that is intended to re-establish their nuclear dominance in the theatre. From the perspective of the Soviet leadership, re-establishing the pre-1983 correlation has politico-diplomatic value, deterrent value, and potential negotiation value should some form of TNF negotiations resume. Why not simply deploy more SS-20s? Offsetting deployments of Soviet GLCMs will be far less costly than an equivalent number of new SS-20 sites with the added plus of appearing to match American nuclear delivery technology.

Summary

The basic-argument presented here is that most of the improvements noted in Soviet TNF weaponry during the past decade have been improvements in performance characteristics which have affected operational reliability and flexibility but have not altered the overall damage capability of the Soviet TNF against NATO assets. These changes are significant from the perspective of the Soviet military planners because of the efficiencies, flexibility, versatility, and C3 qualities they imply. Greater operational certainty leads to higher confidence in military planning and more efficient execution. However, from the NATO military planners' perspective there are no NATO assets vulnerable to a high confidence Soviet nuclear strike today, that were not vulnerable in the 1960s. Indeed, the Soviet nuclear superiority in the theatre that many note today has existed for well over a decade.

If anything has changed, it is the growing capability of Soviet conventional forces to destroy NATO TNF in pre-emptive strikes. To be sure, this is a complex and difficult task, and one that Soviet military planners still believe requires much additional investment and effort. Yet this is one area in which Soviet operational capabilities to destroy NATO TNF are remarkably better than they were a decade-and-a-half ago.

Stepping back and looking at Soviet military activity in the aggregate suggests a fairly continuous effort over the past decade-and-a-half to constrain NATO options in conflict and war. There is more to the Soviet military concept of deterrence through superior force posture than the passive notion of deterrence widely held in the West. While in peacetime this form of deterrence presents objective reasons for potential aggressors to avoid a clash with the USSR, for the Soviet military restraining the aggressor is also an active military function. That is to say, the Soviet military incorporates deterrence missions into their combined arms approach to strategic operations in the theatre. In the context of a NATO-Warsaw Pact confrontation, the objective is so to constrain the most obvious NATO military options as to paralyse NATO decision-making. Such paralysis buys the Soviet military much coveted time to carry out a number of important missions. For example, as was described earlier a superior Soviet strategic theatre nuclear posture greatly enhances the possibilities for the successful preventive destruction of NATO TNF by Soviet conventional forces.

Ironically, the net result of Soviet theatre-nuclear-force developments in the 1980s may be the realisation by NATO that it will have to prepare for a much more demanding conventional conflict in Europe, if its conventional-force posture is to serve as a decisive deterrent.

Notes

1. See Stephen M.Meyer, 'Soviet Theater Nuclear Forces: Parts I and II', Adelphi Paper nos. 187 and 188 (London: International Institute for Strategic Studies, 1984). Many supporting references for statements made in this chapter will be found here.

2. Perfomance capabilities refer to the technical characteristics of a weapon system — e.g., range, accuracy, and yield. Operational capabilities refer to the ability to fulfil an assigned mission — e.g., destroy a given array of targets in a single salvo, prevent aircraft penetration to a defence point, etc. One can vastly improve performance capabilities while only marginally affecting operational capabilities.

3. For an excellent article that explains clearly the distinctions between these three terms and the importance of those distinctions, see C.N. Donnelly, 'The Development of Soviet Military Doctrine', *International Defense Review*, vol. 14, no. 12 (December 1981), pp. 1589-1608.

4. These changes are described especially well in Thomas Wolfe, *Soviet Strategy at the Cross Roads* (Cambridge, Mass.: Harvard University Press, 1965); Raymond Garthoff, *Soviet Strategy in the Nuclear Age* (New York, NY: Praeger Press, 1958); and Herbert Dinerstein, *War and the Soviet Union: Nuclear Weapons and the Revolution in Soviet Military and Political Thinking* (New York, NY: Praeger Press, 1962).

5. That is to say, few in comparison to overall TNF stockpiles.

6. See K.V. Tarakanov, *Mathematics and Armed Combat* (Moscow: Military Publishing House, 1974); I. Anureyev, 'Determining the Correlation of Forces in Terms of Nuclear Weapons', *Military Thought*, 6 (1967), pp. 33-45.

7. V.D. Sokolovskiy, and M. Cherednichenko, 'Military Strategy and Its Problems', *Voyennaya Mysl'*, no. 10 (October 1968), pp. 32-43.

8. Henry Kissinger, *The Years of Upheaval* (Boston, Mass.: Little Brown, 1982), p. 277.

9. What Soviet military leaders would prefer, should not be confused with what they feel compelled to practise for. Specifically, some have argued that the large percentage of soviet military exercises involving theatre nuclear warfare reflects a

preference for this kind of conflict. However, Soviet military writings suggest that this nuclear emphasis may not be so much a preference as a forced requirement stemming from their reading of NATO's military doctrine. Soviet analyses of flexible response tend to emphasise its aspects involving TNF, while Western discussions of flexible response concentrate on the conventional defence aspects.

10. Release would flow from the political leadership to the Headquarters of the Supreme High Command, then to the General Staff for execution. While General Staff controls directly the Strategic Rocket Forces and the long-range aviation (LRA), release authority would have to cascade down to the front commanders for the employment of frontal-aviation assets and ground-force missiles.

11. It should be pointed out that NATO's own TNF strategy suggests withholding TNF to deter Soviet use of nuclear weaponry. This would seem to be exactly what Soviet military planners would like.

12. This approach is not, in any way, inconsistent with Soviet combined-arms concepts. Soviet notions of combined-arms operations have frequently been misconstrued as advocating a simultaneous orgy involving all possible weapons in combat. In essence, combined-arms combat (or, the interworking of combat arms) connotes 'the coordinated actions of all combat arms and means of destruction by mission, axis, position, and time'. (See V. Savkin, *Operational Art and Tactics* (Moscow: Military Publishing House, 1972), p. 260.) The specification of 'by mission' and 'by time' clearly supports a broader interpretation of combined-arms warfare. The phasing of missions in time — and the phasing in of specific weapons systems in time — is an inherent part of the Soviet combined arms concept.

13. M.D. Skirdo, *Narod, Armiya, Polkovodets* (Moscow: Military Publishing House of the Ministry of Defence, 1970), pp. 96-150.

14. Since the late 1960s, the Soviets seem to have adopted a two-level strategy towards NATO. In essence, should global nuclear war erupt, the United States should be removed as a viable economic-industrial-military power, while European economic-industrial resources should be spared as much as possible in order to aid in rebuilding the Soviet economy.

15. Similarly, the notion that Soviet nuclear targeting of European cities during this period was essentially a surrogate hostage to deter the United States is incorrect. The same argument as in note 16 applies. The priorities of Soviet nuclear targeting have, since the mid-1950s, always been tied to the location of opposing nuclear forces. Through the late 1950s, the principal nuclear threats confronting the Soviets were based in Europe, North Africa, the Middle East, and Asia. The bulk of the threat, however, was based in and around Europe. The surrogate role of Europe is belied by the fact that the Soviet military leadership saw fit to target, eventually, over 100 of its SS-11 ICBMs on Europe, during a period in which it was still noticeably inferior to the United States in intercontinental attack capability. Europe continues to be the most strategically important theatre of military operations in Soviet military planning. Thus, the Soviet emphasis on peripheral nuclear-attack forces is a continuation of long-standing policy, and the surrogate hostage role played by Europe during the 1950s and 1960s was a by-product of more purposeful Soviet nuclear force planning.

16. I would just note that, contrary to impressions conveyed by many students of Soviet military affairs, Soviet military planners recognise that escalation to central nuclear warfare ends the game. Political rhetoric and morale-building efforts aside, Soviet military writers have been quite frank in admitting that they have no plan for managing an all-out US-Soviet nuclear exchange.

17. Simply stated, the Soviet military's conception of deterrence is that the greater the asymmetry of force favouring the USSR, the less likely is an enemy's

attack.

18. Many Western analysts are baffled by the contrast between Western and Soviet discussions of theatre nuclear warfare, where the former concentrates on limited use, escalation control, fire-breaks, and 'signalling', while the latter completely ignores these issues and instead talks in terms of 'massed nuclear strikes across the full depth of enemy territory', 'multiple nuclear salvos', etc. What must be kept in mind, however, is that Western writings on TNF are mostly authored by civilian defence specialists, while Soviet writings are authored by professional military officers. In the latter case, it is not the Soviet military's job to worry about escalation control; they are supposed to be concerned with the most militarily effective use of nuclear weapons in the theatre — i.e. nuclear war-fighting.

19. D. Ustinov, 'Otvesi ugrozu yedernoy voyni', *Pravda*, 12 July 1982, p. 4.

8 NUCLEAR WEAPONS AND THE WARSAW PACT

Condolezza Rice

The NATO deployment of intermediate nuclear forces (INF), the breakdown of the arms-control talks at Geneva in late 1983 and the Soviet decision to take counter-measures closed, at least temporarily, a very turbulent chapter in European security affairs. The outcome can only be seen as a mixed one for NATO. On the one hand, the successful deployment clearly signals to the Soviet Union that NATO is capable of decisive action in spite of the uncertainties of domestic politics. On the other, the causes of the tensions in Europe have been exacerbated by the failure of the talks and a round of theatre arms competition has begun.

The outcome is, however, an unambiguous defeat bordering on disaster for the small Warsaw Pact states. Characteristically, the Eastern Europeans fell into line, supporting the Soviet walk-out and lending their territory to Soviet counter-deployment. Nevertheless, scarcely beneath the surface there are rumblings, as there were throughout the INF debate, which suggest that a number of Eastern European leaders understand that on this issue, their interests have not been well served by the Soviet Union.

It should be expected that Soviet and Eastern European interests might diverge. However, it would be surprising if any signs of disagreement came to the surface. Certainly nothing approaching the policy debate within NATO has been apparent. Western analysts have, however, tended to overlook the rather muted signs of divergence. The Warsaw Pact's façade is monolithic. But to take the façade as the state of affairs is to miss very interesting developments in the Pact over the last two years. Historical perspective is important too, because this is not the first time that tensions have surfaced in the Warsaw Pact over European nuclear weapons, limited nuclear war and Soviet security guarantees. This paper explores some aspects of the evolution of the Warsaw Pact's nuclear arrangement and with that historical background in place, examines Eastern European attitudes during the INF debate. Only Romania dared to advocate mutual reductions of nuclear weapons in Europe, but the Eastern Europeans have their own agenda in supporting arms-control initiatives in Europe and their failure to reach any of their goals in this case was a severe blow to Eastern European interests. In the final section, the paper explores the Eastern European response to the new situation in Europe and its potential impact on politics in the Warsaw Pact.

Eastern European Security Before the Warsaw Pact

The Warsaw Treaty Organisation, formed in May 1955, rationalised and justified a number of post-World War II security arrangements between the Soviet Union and the small Eastern European states. The Soviets insisted on post-war dominance of Eastern Europe in pursuit of a security buffer for the Soviet homeland. The presence of the Red Army in Eastern Europe was the first guarantee of this important policy aim; the second was the gradual development of military institutions within the small communist states which formed that buffer.

The decision to recreate individual armed forces within national boundaries was taken in conjunction with the development of the entire range of governmental institutions − police, economic, educational, etc. − which provided a semblance of legtimacy and independence for the new satellite regimes. None the less, there was never any question that the institutions were to be dominated by Moscow and in the case of the instruments of military power, Soviet control was overt and total.

Still, the creation of 'national' armed forces was risky. They had to be formed in states filled with anti-communist and often blatantly anti-Soviet sentiment. In several, like Romania, the armed forces had been allied with the Axis powers and had fought viciously against the Soviet Union. The Soviet leadership was keenly aware of the dilemma of reconstructing these new armed forces with enough strength to form an extended line of socialist defence but lacking the strength to threaten Soviet and communist hegemony. Consequently, the armed forces were kept small, dispersed and ill-equipped shells of the modern armies which they would become. Clearly, in the early days, the immediate concerns were more important than the military potential of the Eastern European armed forces.

It was not until 1949, when the consolidation of communist rule in Eastern Europe was more or less complete, that the Soviets transformed them into forces capable of playing a role in the defence of the extended socialist buffer. In keeping with Soviet strategic reliance upon large, standing conventional forces, the emphasis in Eastern Europe was upon numbers. Universal conscription was initiated and the forces grew rapidly from 1949 until the death of Stalin. Equipment was upgraded and defence spending sky-rocketed, but the missions of the forces were simple.[1] They provided a large trip-wire, which could delay the advance of Western forces and give Moscow warning and time for preparation. These were factors that had been very important in the last war. They were soon transformed, however, into a militarily significant appendage of the Soviet army. Headed largely by Soviet commanders and advisers, the officer ranks underwent extensive purges, which eventually made them both loyal and militarily efficient. By 1953, the groundwork was in place for the extended line of socialist defence and for the formation of a socialist military alliance.

The Formation of the Warsaw Pact

In May 1955, Eastern European security entered a new stage with the formation of the Warsaw Treaty Organisation. It was a hastily conceived effort to create pressure on the Western alliance against the rearming of the Federal Republic of Germany and was a direct counter to the decision (in 1954) to include West Germany in NATO. Since then the Soviets consistently have used the Pact to counter every troublesome NATO move. The early anti-NATO nature of the Warsaw Treaty is evident both in the charter and in the underdeveloped character of the original organisation. The charter, emphasising the peaceful nature of the Pact, stated:

> The Warsaw Treaty is open to all states of any social system. It is not a closed grouping, but an organisation of peace-loving countries ... participants have agreed to end the operation of the treaty as soon as a system of collective security is formed in Europe and a corresponding all-European treaty is concluded.[2]

The organisation was so hastily constructed that the charter created only two organisations in 1955; the Political Consultative Committee and the Joint Command. The latter was intended to command forces earmarked for extra-national duty, but little was accomplished during the first five years of the Pact's existence. One year later, in 1956, the Joint Secretariat and a Permanent Committee for Recommendations of Foreign-Political Questions were established. But all the organs met irregularly and Eastern European military affairs were changed very little by the treaty.

The Pact was, however, the logical means by which further to legitimise and rationalise the military relationship between the Soviet Union and Eastern Europe. It bolstered bilateral arrangements and replaced status-of-forces agreements of the post-war period, strengthened the justification for stationing of Soviet troops and encouraged the development of the Eastern European armed forces. Secondly, the Warsaw Pact eventually emerged as a convenient tool for 'internationalising' the military assets of member states. Stalin's imperial use of Eastern European wealth for Soviet purposes was replaced by a multilateral 'sharing' agreement. Krushchev gambled that because of Soviet wealth and power, Soviet hegemony would actually be enhanced. In this regard, the Warsaw Pact, like the rejuvenated COMECON, allowed the exploitation of the diversity of the alliance. Since there was, in the Soviet mind, no divorce between the goals of socialism and those of the Soviet Union, the Warsaw Pact and other multilateral trappings of the new inter-state system combined the assets of the members in support of Soviet policy.

The Warsaw Pact in the Nuclear Age

The evolution of the nuclear component of the Warsaw Pact's security arrangement is difficult to discern. The contribution of the Eastern European conventional forces to coalition doctrine has been examined in depth. But the importance of the Eastern European armed forces and their territory to Warsaw Pact nuclear strategy has been all but overlooked. This oversight in part reflects our ignorance of the facts but also derives from the fact that the Warsaw Pact's nuclear arms defence is based primarily in the Soviet Union. But it should not be forgotten that until the early 1960s, the long-range capability of Soviet nuclear forces was minimal. During that period the Soviet Union was faced with the difficult task of quickly tapping the potential of nuclear weapons and using Eastern European territory for this goal.

The evolution of the Warsaw Pact's nuclear arrangement took place in the context of an internal Soviet debate on the 'decisiveness' of nuclear weapons. The debate raged — with varying intensity — from the immediate post-war period until the beginning of the 1960s. It was not until 1963 that the decisiveness of nuclear weapons was elevated to a 'general law of warfare', the highest designation for a principle of military doctrine.[3] This debate did not prevent the Soviets from vigorously pursuing nuclear technologies, even during Stalin's reign. They did, however, encounter technical difficulties in delivery. These technical problems persisted during a period in which Krushchev sought to tap the political potential of nuclear weapons. Not only did he bluster publicly about Soviet advances, he proclaimed — quite prematurely — Soviet readiness to 'defend the socialist alliance' by nuclear means. In short, the ability of the Soviet Union to 'match' the nuclear capability of the United States was a guarantee for all socialist states. As early as 1957, Krushchev proclaimed a kind of security umbrella when he promised that the Soviets would defend the territory of Eastern Europe as its own. Finally, this pressure to gain political currency from nuclear weapons was increased by the installation of American nuclear weapons in Western Europe. It is not surprising that one of the first concrete actions of the fledgling socialist alliance was a threat that missiles in Western Europe would 'oblige the Warsaw Pact states to consider the question of deploying missiles in Czechoslovakia, Poland, and the GDR in the interest of defending peace and their own security'.[4]

The strategy was to hold Western Europe 'hostage', threatening it with destruction, should the United States threaten the socialist alliance. The nuclear delivery vehicles (NDVs) installed in Eastern Europe in 1957, were the first step in the strategy. Frogs arrived, making good Krushchev's threat to counter NATO deployments with similar ones on Warsaw Pact territory. At about the same time, Eastern European officers began to assume that they would play a role in a nuclearised theatre and the first training missions in the nuclear environment began. In May 1957, Poland's high command authorised the Training Inspectorate to organise instruction for small-unit operations under nuclear conditions.[5]

This initial decision to forward base NDVs was followed by Soviet attempts to make more extensive use of Eastern European territory for their nuclear strategy. Again, the historical circumstances are very important. By 1960, Krushchev was firmly in control of Soviet policy, and at the turn of the decade he had begun the shift toward greater reliance upon nuclear forces. The period was also one of great tension between East and West, especially the crises over Berlin. Consequently, there was new pressure on the Soviets to back the aggressive nuclear posturing in which Krushchev was engaged. As a part of a strategy to meet the Western challenge, Krushchev apparently decided that a more efficient use of the socialist alliance was warranted. Thus, the Warsaw Pact began to wrestle with the problems of coalition doctrine in the nuclear age.

Coalition doctrine, which is still official Warsaw Pact doctrine, presumed that all socialist forces would be used as one. Theoretically, the territory of the Warsaw Pact is indivisible, extending from western GDR to the European territory of the USSR.[6] Warsaw Pact forces are thus committed to external defence as well as defence of national territory. This is a concept which dates to the earliest days of the alliance. As Soviet strategists became preoccupied with nuclear options, however, the Eastern Europeans became increasingly concerned with the vulnerability of their territory to nuclear attack.

Polish strategists were particularly concerned about the vulnerability of their homeland. They developed the concept of the defence of the national territory (*Obrona terytorium krajni* —OTK). General Boleslaw Chocha, who authored the formulation, eventually became Chief of Staff. OTK emphasises the need for civil and air defence and actually predates most Soviet civil defence efforts.[7] The complete formulation of the doctrine was set out in Choca's book, *The Defense of National Territory*, first issued in 1956.

The Poles argued, in line with the principle of the offensive, that the war would be fought on NATO territory. There would be rapid escalation to nuclear war and it was thus necessary to prepare the homeland fully, using sophisticated air- and civil-defence measures. The Poles were not apparently worried about the credibility of Soviet guarantees, however, and, at least publicly, accepted the indivisibility of the interests of socialist states. There is also no evidence that the Poles objected to the installation of Frogs in 1957 or to the deployment of Scuds in 1965.

The sense of vulnerability in the nuclear age led Czechoslovak military strategists to quite different conclusions about nuclear guarantees and NDVs on Czechoslovak territory. Reportedly, sometime around 1960, the Soviets approached the Czechoslovak leadership about 'upgrading' the nuclear forces on Czechoslovak territory.[8] The nature of the 'upgrading' is not known, but the Czechoslovak leadership was apparently sensitive to three concerns: the danger of NDVs as provocation to NATO, the issue of allowing Soviet troops to accompany the upgrading, and the problem of warhead storage. One interesting question is, of course, whether the Soviets requested permission to store warheads in Czechoslovakia, a central issue in forward basing.

The evidence from this early period, though sketchy and inconclusive, suggests that — under pressure to lend credibility to Krushchev's nuclear posturing — the Soviets actually did raise the idea of warhead storage in Eastern Europe. Whatever the exact nature of the request, there was a wide rift between the military leadership of Czechoslovakia and the USSR which became evident during the Prague spring, though there were indications of it earlier. There were many disagreements at that time but the nuclear issue played a major role, and it is still the only evidence of open disagreement between the Soviets and their allies on nuclear issues that we have, save that of Romania.

In retrospect, it appears that the Czechoslovaks objected to warhead storage largely because of the stationing of Soviet troops which would have followed to safeguard the nuclear ammunition dumps. Unarmed NDVs were already on Czechoslovak territory and the Soviets had not seen fit to transfer Soviet troops to man the early FROG missiles.

Initially, the Czechoslovaks offered to accept the upgrading if it was in the 'custody' of the Czechoslovak People's Army.[9] The leadership must have been aware that this would be unacceptable to the Soviet leadership. Soviet forces were already stationed in the GDR and Poland, and warheads (if they were involved) could have been transferred to those forces. Czechoslovakia, however, had been free of Soviet forces since 1945, and the Soviets needed to gain permission for stationing troops. There was no status-of-forces agreement in place.

Whatever the case, the argument continued for several years. The Soviets argued that tactical nuclear forces in Western Europe necessitated similar deployments along the Warsaw Pact's northern tier. The Czechoslovak refusal to agree to the deployment of 'appropriate Soviet troops' at missile installations angered the Poles and the East Germans. Both argued that the Czechoslovaks were endangering not only their own western border, but also the entire southern flank of the central front and compromising the territories of the GDR and Poland.[10]

The Soviets objected to Czechoslovak control of the tactical forces but argued that an upgrading had to take place because 'transportation of warheads on such a scale could not be concealed from the enemy and could challenge him to strike before the Czechoslovak tactical missiles could be armed'.[11] The Czechoslovak forces were not at 'full readiness'. Reputedly, the Czechoslovaks agreed to a limited compromise solution, by which installations were to belong not to the Czechoslovak People's Army but directly to the Soviet Army and were to be operated by small Soviet units. This was designed to solve the otherwise virtually insoluble problem of putting the Czechoslovak Army into full combat readiness, in other words, the transportation of tactical nuclear warheads to their carriers in the equipment of the Czechoslovak People's Army.

During this time, Soviet attitudes toward warhead storage were apparently being reassessed. In the early 1960s the warheads were transferred from the KGB to the armed forces, though release authority remained with the political leadership. Moreover, it was about this time that nuclear ammunition dumps were discovered in Cuba, suggesting that attitudes toward warhead storage outside the USSR had changed.[12]

By 1965, when the actual deployments were to be made, the time had passed when Eastern European territory was critical for forward basing. The SS-4 and SS-5 were deployed in significant numbers, lessening the need for the FROGs and SCUDs in Eastern Europe. It is still not known whether the warheads were transferred at the time or whether they are presently deployed in Eastern Europe.[13]

The settlement of the question of upgrading did not alleviate tension within the alliance, however. The problem of Soviet nuclear guarantees soon overshadowed any concerns about NDVs on Eastern European territory. The problem of coupling the security guarantee of a superpower to the defence of small states is a problem familiar to NATO. It should not be surprising to find that the Eastern Europeans expressed worry about the reliability of Moscow's nuclear umbrella as well. The problem of coupling is really a psychological one; the guarantees are either believed or not, and it is all but impossible to remove all doubt that the umbrella is intact. The Soviets continued to declare the indivisibility of socialist territory. 'If a war against the Soviet Union or any other socialist state is unleashed by the imperialist bloc . . . it will become a world war,' stated V.D. Sokolovsky.[14] But in the mid-1960s, it was the Czechoslovaks who were most troubled by the question of the reliability of the guarantee. At least one Czechoslovak account identifies the Cuban missile crisis as a major source of concern.[15] Until the crisis, the Soviets had claimed equality and in some instances superiority to the United States in nuclear arms. The exposure of the fraudulent claims and the realisation that the Soviets had to back down is said to have unsettled the Czechoslovaks. How could the Soviet nuclear guarantee extend to Prague if it could not even protect Moscow? The Czechoslovaks later suggested that 'in the new age' small states should consider their own security, based upon geopolitical and historical factors.[16]

This blatant departure from Warsaw Pact coalition doctrine was buttressed by a rather startling attack on the Soviet nuclear guarantee. During the mid-1960s crisis, wide-ranging debates on Sokolovsky's *Military Strategy* took place. It appears that some Czechoslovak strategists saw remarks in the volume which left open the issue of the defence of socialist states by nuclear attacks launched from East Germany. Were the Soviets contemplating limited responses which left

Eastern Europe exposed? In fact, Sokolovsky's volume leaves few doubts about the location of a theatre war that may quickly become a nuclear war. But Soviet strategists were beginning to examine options short of Krushchev's 'one-variant war'. Any limited war, whether there was a conventional phase or not, was sure to damage heavily Eastern European territory.

As one Czechoslovak commentator dared state in 1968, 'if the creators of Soviet strategic concepts today no longer consider it necessary to reply to an attack on one of the Socialist countries with a nuclear strike causing wholesale destruction [of the NATO force], the Warsaw Pact member countries might ask questions similar to those which some time ago caused de Gaulle to quit NATO'.[17]

The radicalising military intelligentsia took the question of limited war as a point of departure and explained that Czechoslovakia's very existence depended upon rational evaluation of the value of the alliance. Clearly dissatisfaction with the alliance was brewing within Czechoslovakia and given the recalcitrance of the leadership on some issues, those attitudes were not confined to the intelligentsia. The signs of divergence on issues of doctrine and strategy were thus quite clear. All evidence suggests that the Czechoslovaks intended to solve those problems within the confines of the Warsaw Pact. Nevertheless, the warning of Kopecky could not have gone unnoticed in Moscow:

> When there exist basic differences and disagreements between individual states with regard to understanding the cardinal problems of revolutional political strategy and tactics . . . when there is no unity of views with regard to the political part of socialist military doctrine . . . if certain key problems of national defense are not solved . . . an objective base for the appearance of certain trends toward disintegration would be apparent.[18]

The invasion of Czechoslovakia silenced the most outspoken critics of Soviet nuclear strategy. Acceptance of coalition doctrine was assured by removal of the officers who had been responsible for the divergence. Throughout the 1970s, all was quiet within the military alliance, though Romania's isolation continued to grow.

But the lessons of the 1960s should not be forgotten in assessing the current situation. Eastern European concerns about the special vulnerability of small states in Europe did surface and the tension which they produced drove the members of the normally monolithic Warsaw Pact to disagree and to do so publicly.

Eastern Europe in the Current Theatre Force Posture of the Warsaw Pact

The precise outcome of the debates on the alliance's nuclear strategy which the invasion of Czechoslovakia so effectively silenced is not known. In general, a very strict division of labour between the Eastern European forces and the Soviet forces eventually emerged with the former given primarily conventional roles. Although short-range dual-capable systems have been deployed with non-Soviet Warsaw Pact forces, intermediate-range weapons were, until recently, based on Soviet soil.

The non-Soviet Warsaw Pact's primary contribution on the central front is the augmentation of Soviet ground and air forces. The forces on the northern tier provide about 450,000 ground forces and 179,000 airmen. Because coalition doctrine presumes a lightening offensive action on the territory of NATO by ground forces with air support, these 'forces in being' constitute a sizable contribution if their reliability can be assumed.

Eastern European strategists remain wedded to the assumption that European war will quickly escalate to nuclear. There is little evidence that the actual role of the Eastern European armed forces includes nuclear missions, however. Rather, it would seem that any nuclear missions from forward bases would be carried out by the 27 forward-based Soviet divisions, especially the elite Group of Soviet Forces in East Germany.

The Eastern Europeans discuss the role of nuclear missions in combined-arms doctrine, but there is little evidence that they would participate. Polish strategists have noted that it is very important to destroy the enemy's primary line of defence — considered to be nuclear weapons — before they can be armed and used.[19] This restatement of Soviet pre-emptive strategy suggests only that the offensive push would be accompanied by an attempt to disarm NATO's nuclear forces so that the conventional phase of the war could be prolonged. Polish frontal aviation could be used, for example, in conventional attack against NATO's nuclear forces. Whether the Polish air force would actually fly nuclear missions is quite another question. Clearly, in comparing the Warsaw Pact armies along the northern tier, the superiority of the Polish air force is quite clear. It should be noted, for example, that the Polish forces were, in 1974, supplied with the export version of the Su-17 Fitter C (a ground-attack aircraft) and that the craft is capable of nuclear delivery. The air forces of both Czechoslovakia and Poland have in their inventories the much older predecessor to Fitter C, the nuclear-delivery capable Su-7 Fitter A (1959). Nevertheless, recent events in Poland call into question the real value of these well-equipped forces.

Additionally, there are reports that the Soviets have ordered the hardening of the silos for the new missiles in East Germany. This is said to be the first time that silos outside the USSR have been hardened.[20]

Until 1978, the Soviets had not modernised the short-range ballistic missile forces deployed in Eastern Europe. The SCUD (SS-IC), SCUD B and SCUD C of the FROGs were of 1960s vintage. But new follow-ons have finally been developed. The SS-21 which is of slightly longer range than the FROG and the SS-23 which will replace the SCUD have been seen in the inventory of Soviet forward-based troops. Whether they will also be delivered to the Eastern Europeans is a matter of some speculation. The newer missiles have a number of advantages, including longer range, greater accuracy and significantly higher yield. These missiles, like their predecessors, are dual capable, leaving the issue of their actual mission in some doubt. Dual use gives the Soviets great flexibility including use with chemical warheads or (though the efficiency of such could be questioned) with high explosives.

The Soviet forward-deployment strategy is further clouded by the question of warhead storage. It has been argued that while NDVs are forward deployed, the warheads have been stored on Soviet territory. Recently, Secretary of Defense Caspar Weinberger stated categorically that the Soviets have long kept nuclear weapons in Eastern Europe. Asked to clarify, an aide stated that the Secretary was referring to warheads, not just delivery vehicle. But in his remarks Secretary Weinberger said only that the deployments 'started to occur since about 1979 ... many of them mobile and can go in and out'.[21] This would seem to be a reference to the delivery vehicles and would coincide with known Soviet deliveries of the new SRBMs to their forces in Eastern Europe.

If the Soviets have deployed warheads in Eastern Europe it should be noted that their numbers are still an issue. One good reason for restricting the deployment to a few warheads is their vulnerability in forward bases. While 'permissive action links' (PALs) could be employed to prevent unauthorised release, the warheads might still be vulnerable to sabotage. Moreover, with the bulk of the ammunition stored on Soviet territory, NATO's willingness to destroy nuclear ammunition would depend upon its willingness to escalate and involve Soviet territory; a step which might give the Americans pause. Whatever their vulnerability, the efficacy of transporting large numbers of warheads from Soviet territory to Eastern Europe is dubious. In a conflict the transportation of the warheads could hardly be concealed (given their signature) and might inadvertently trigger war by encouraging NATO to pre-empt.

Finally, it should be noted that whatever the mission of the SRBMs, it is a considerably different one than for similar forces in NATO. The NATO forces are a part of the flexible-response strategy and are used to deter, or if necessary break, a Warsaw Pact conventional assault. The Warsaw Pact, however, has every reason to confine the conflict to the conventional level, given their superiority. The use of chemicals or high explosives from aircraft and missiles to depress NATO capabilities would be far more efficacious if it could be done. The release authority for commanders in the field would be less complicated and the Soviets would not have to cross the nuclear threshold. While Soviet doctrine continues to state that a European war would escalate to world war, they have acquired capabilities that give them options far short of that. In fact, at least one way to view the 'no-first-use' pledge is as a serious doctrinal refinement attempting to confine the conflict to the conventional level where it is widely assumed the Warsaw Pact, not NATO, enjoys the advantage. The Soviets because of geographic proximity do not need to forward deploy longer-range forces and can afford to limit deployments of the SS-20 and SS-22 to their own territory. Nevertheless, for what seem to be blatantly political motives, they have apparently decided to deploy the SS-22 forward. This decision based not on military necessity, but on political considerations, was not the first time that the Warsaw Pact had been so used and Eastern European concerns have been heightened by the decision.

The INF Issue and Eastern Europe

If the Eastern Euorpean view of the European theatre is taken into account, it is easy to see that their view of INF is quite different from that of the Soviet Union. Indeed, because of their desire to keep the nuclear threshold very high, the INF decision of the actual stationing of weapons does not threaten the Eastern Europeans, but actually helps them. Eastern European territory has been vulnerable to American missiles all along. While Pershing IA might not have sufficient range and accuracy to strike targets deep within the Soviet Union, it is certainly capable of threatening targets in Eastern Europe. The addition of long-range forces only gives the West further military capability against Soviet territory, presumably ensuring that Soviet territory could be endangered in a European war.

In many ways the Eastern European view of 'coupling' matches that of those who argue that INF, by threatening the territory of the superpowers, raises the stakes for Moscow and Washington and makes them more circumspect about initiating a conflict in Europe. The argument could be made with particular fervour for the GDR whose first priority must be certainty that East Germany will not be isolated in a European war. The spectre of a separate peace between the Soviet Union and West Germany has always haunted East Germany's rulers. The nervousness which the Soviets have exhibited about the NATO deployment must ring hollow for the Eastern Europeans. It could not have gone unnoticed in Eastern European capitals that American forward-based systems, British and French forces, and now INF have always worried Moscow more than shorter-range nuclear weapons which endanger Eastern Europe.

On the surface, this view of the 'coupling' is entirely logical, but the Eastern Europeans have not made the argument in this way. There are presumably two explanations for this. The first is quite clear. Any public accusation that Moscow is not concerned about allied territory and is playing the 'superpower game' would be blasphemy in the Warsaw Pact. Now more than ever, there is a 'circle the wagons' mentality in the socialist alliance, both because of the onslaught of the Reagan administration and the difficulties attending the Polish crisis.

But a second explanation is that the Eastern Europeans feared exactly the sequence of events that followed the breakdown of arms control. The frontline states, Czechoslovakia and East Germany, were initially outspokenly supportive of Moscow's position on the NATO decision and of the Soviet negotiating position. Poland, understandably preoccupied with the internal crisis at this juncture, was relatively silent. Hungary and Bulgaria supported Moscow but really made little comment, while Romania pressed for mutual disarmament in Europe and pushed the Ceaușescu proposal for a nuclear-free zone. But there was an interesting twist in the statements of both East Germany and Czechoslovakia which suggested that this was Moscow's matter, as long as the Eastern European territory was not involved. They went to great lengths to point out that the non-involvement of allied territory is a principle by which the Warsaw Pact should continue to abide. For example, the East Germans boasted that the Eastern Europeans were not a threat to the West, since the Soviets (unlike the Americans) were not using the territory of the allies as a 'launching pad'.[22] The Czechoslovaks specifically reminded the West that no medium-range missiles are on Warsaw Pact territory.[23]

But as the INF talks stalemated in the autumn of 1983, it became clear that the Soviet Union intended to use Eastern European terittory as a launching pad, or more precisely as a counter-launching pad. The first hint that Eastern Europe figured in the Soviet retaliation was on 28 May when *Pravda* and *Izvestia* both carried a statement that, if the NATO deployment were carried out 'the need would also arise to carry out, by arrangement with the other Warsaw Treaty member states, other measures for the deployment of additional systems with a view to creating the necessary counterbalance'.[24] This was followed by stern warnings from Defence Minister D.F. Ustinov about retaliatory measures.[25] Another lengthy statement was made at a press conference by First Deputy Minister of Foreign Affairs G.M. Kornienko and First Deputy Chief of the General Staff S.F. Akhromeyev. Though they stated that the 'USSR and its allies will take appropriate countermeasures', he refused to say where deployments would take place, calling that information a 'military secret'.[26]

One month later an extraordinary meeting of the Committee of Defence Ministers of the Warsaw Pact convened in Sofia. The lukewarm communiqué said nothing which approached the clarity of the Soviet threat, but it was noted that the Warsaw Pact would not allow superiority to be gained over them. It was also said that the Committee had taken 'an appropriate decision'.[27]

A flurry of meetings with leaders in Czechoslovakia, the GDR and Hungary followed. Then, in October, the Soviets announced preparation of new missile sites in Czechoslovakia and the GDR. Poland was apparently too vulnerable to figure in the equation, while Hungary, inexplicably, was dropped from the plan. When the Soviets left the INF talks on 23 November, Andropov announced that the preparations had been accelerated. The counter-deployment in East Europe includes the shorter-range ballistic missiles and the SS-22 will apparently be deployed in East Germany.

It is not known whether the Eastern Europeans actually knew of the Soviet plans when they made the earlier statements that their territory was not involved. Perhaps, knowing the history of the Warsaw pact, they simply expected the retaliatory measures to involve their territory. Whatever the case, they have been a little more candid than usual about their unhappiness. On 29 November 1983, Erich Honecker implied that he would do his socialist duty even if he lacked enthusiasm for the plan.[28] The Czechoslovaks have been less forthcoming, but it is noteworthy that statements about the counter-deployment have appeared in the Soviet, not Eastern European, press.

The outcome of the INF issue is a very difficult one for the Eastern Europeans. There are so many political and economic problems for them; this one simply adds to the difficulty. Gustav Husak in Czechoslovakia has not succeeded at all in building domestic legitimacy for his regime. For him, the lending of Czechoslovak territory is a mixed blessing. He does not need to appear any more pro-Soviet than he already does if he is ever to build domestic support. Nevertheless, it is all the more important to him to be an unquestioningly loyal and useful ally for the Soviet Union. At least he can remind the Soviets that when Hungary and Poland either could not or would not respond, Czechoslovakia was there.

For Erich Honecker, the problems are more acute. East Germany is changing and remarkably a part of that change has been in reaction to the 'militarisation' of East German life. A substantial underground church-related peace movement exists there and protests have even taken place openly in Dresden. Moreover, the East German leader was engaged in his own rather cautiously independent course towards West Germany for some time. Clearly, Honecker did not set out to tread an independent course. In fact, he was brought to power because Walter Ulbricht refused to fall in line behind Moscow's policy of détente in Western Europe. But as is often the case, policies can have a momentum of their own. The co-operative relationship with West Germany is important, even critical, for the stability of Honecker's regime. He cannot afford to fall in line with Moscow's harder line toward the West.

How great is Honecker's room for manoeuvre remains to be seen. Soviet pressures clearly caused him to cancel his plans to visit the Federal Republic in the autumn of 1984. Further Soviet dissatisfaction with the East German course is evident. Reminiscent of early messages to the Czechoslovaks in 1968, articles have begun to appear about West German designs on the GDR. One states bluntly that 'revanchist' elements wish to 'gobble up' the GDR and western Poland and to alter the basic principles of Yalta and Potsdam.[29] Nevertheless, having lent his support (and territory) on the missile issue, Honecker may have secured more freedom in his policy toward the West in the longer term.

These problems were already acute for the Eastern Europeans prior to the deployment. The new tensions that developed over INF threaten to eliminate what is left of détente, a policy on which the Eastern Europeans were politically and economically dependent. The hardest hit have been Czechoslovakia, the GDR and, of course, Poland which cannot afford any further trouble with the West. This desire to preserve détente must be balanced with loyalty to Moscow; and loyalty to a Soviet leadership which does not appear to be in the mood for divergence. With Poland on one front and tensions with the West, the Warsaw Pact may feel itself virtually under seige. The Kremlin is in the midst of a war scare with references to the similarity of the present situation to the 1930s. In this atmosphere it will be difficult to obtain breathing space from Moscow on any issue.

The concerns of the Romanians are different and interesting, but they may be ultimately less important to the actual military-political balance in Europe. Ceauşescu is obviously pressing a political offensive to establish both the legitimacy of Romania's independent foreign policy line — lobbying for Washington eye — and further to decrease tensions in Europe so that Romania can continue to pursue her independent course. The recent Romanian participation in the Los Angeles Olympics and refusal to go to the 'Friendship' Games is one example. The nuclear-free zone idea, which Romania supports, did get the attention of Zhivkov in Bulgaria and Yugoslavia's leaders.[30] The initiative, though not particularly threatening to Moscow (since installations in South-Eastern Europe would be of little military interest), must be disquieting none the less. In particular, any *rapprochement* between Bulgaria, Romania and Yugoslavia would raise another set of dangers on the southern tier. If nothing else, it must have been embarrassing for the Kremlin to watch 240,000 march in Bucharest (matching exactly the numbers in Bonn) in support of mutual disarmament. However, on balance, problems on the southern tier appear far less likely and less threatening.

The Question of Leverage

This, then, raises the question of leverage. The Eastern European agenda was different from Moscow's and there was a lot at stake in INF. Clearly, the Europeans have ambivalent attitudes about nuclear weapons — sometimes expressed more fervently and less supportively of Moscow than at other times. But the fears, often taken for granted in the West as puppeteering by Moscow, should be examined more closely. Ever since the Rapaki plan, the Eastern Europeans have maintained a high profile and continuing interest in arms control in Europe. As small states in central and southern central Europe, the vulnerability of the Eastern European homeland — despite Soviet guarantees — is quite obvious. This should not surprise the Western analysts. The

Eastern European elites may be ultimately dependent on the Soviet Union for a variety of favours, including, in some cases, stability of domestic rule, but this does not mean that they are oblivious to the dangers of their membership in the socialist alliance in the nuclear age.

The position of the political leaders in Eastern Europe is particularly difficult, because political-military decisions are taken primarily in Moscow and they are obliged to tow the line in foreign policy. Any attempt to form 'national' attitudes on defence is very dangerous, for in the final analysis the Soviets assume the buffer arrangement is only sound if only the Soviet Union is responsible for military affairs in the region.

Now that the INF issue has been settled, at least for the time being, the Eastern Europeans have no choice but to go along. Nevertheless, they would have strong incentives to encourage the Soviets to relax tensions in Europe. Clearly, Moscow will take steps to secure Europe as it sees fit. But if the Warsaw Pact's co-operation is to be ensured without difficulty, the Eastern Europeans must be certain that their interests are being taken into account. Some time ago, the Soviets opted for a semi-sovereign system of socialist states, held together by at least some perception of mutual interest. That Moscow values a less overtly repressive relationship is seen in the hesitancy with which the Soviets deal out punishment for deviation.

The Soviets, of course, did not have to worry that the frontline states would have refused to go along with important military initiatives. Thus Moscow enjoyed the opportunity to play to anti-American opinion in Western Europe without analogous pressures from the socialist allies. Behind the Kremlin, however, there were nervous political clients who may now wish to 'collect' for their support; given at considerable cost to their own interests.

Notes

1. A.V. Antosiak, *Zarozhdenie narodnia armii uchastnri Varshavskovo Dorgovora* (Moscow: Izdatelstro 'Nauka', 1975), p. 76. The missions are discussed in the Report of the Central Intelligence Group to the United States Department of State (20 May 1950), 860F 113/1-145-12-13, T 335.
2. *Voyennaya Mysl'* (May 1955).
3. V.D. Sokolovsky, *Military Strategy* (New York: Praeger, 1963).
4. *Pravda*, 4 July 1955.
5. A. Ross Johnson, Robert Dean and Alex Alexier, *East European Military Establishments: The Warsaw Pact's Northern Tier* (Santa Monica: Rand Corporation, 1980).

6. The extent to which the Eastern Europeans see themselves as responsible for the Eastern territory of the USSR is highly questionable. Certainly the Warsaw Pact is, by charter, a European security instrument, and the small states are sensitive to suggestions to the contrary. See discussions of 'socialist' extension of power in *Pravda* (Bratislava), 19 May 1976.

7. Ibid.

8. Josef Hodic, *Military-Political Views Prevalent in the Czechoslovak Armed Forces: 1948-1975* (Vienna: Mulbricht, 1979).

9. Ibid.

10. Ibid.

11. Ibid.

12. Ammunition dumps were sighted in Cuba by American intelligence.

13. *New York Times*, 5 February 1982.

14. V.D. Sokolovsky *et al.*, *Military Strategy*.

15. Josef Hodic, *Military-Political Views*.

16. 'How Czechoslovak State and Military Interest are to be Formulated', *Lidova Armada* (15 February 1968).

17. Quoted in Condolezza Rice. *The Soviet Union and the Czechoslovak Army: Uncertain Allegiance* (Princeton: Princeton University Press, 1984).

18. Ibid.

19. A. Ross Johnson *et al.*, *The Warsaw Pact's Northern Tier*.

20. *New York Times*, 5 February 1982.

21. *New York Times*, 5 February 1983.

22. *ANV International News Service* (Berlin), 3 December 1981.

23. *Rude Pravo*, 15 January 1982.

24. *Pravda*, 28 May 1983.

25. *Pravda*, 31 July 1983.

26. *Pravda*, 15 September 1983.

27. *Pravda*, 16 October 1983.

28. *New York Times*, 29 November 1983.

29. 'FRG Revanchist Group seeks to 'Gobble UP GDR" ', *Tass*, 6 August 1984.

30. *Rabotchmesko Delo*, 6 May 1981 (Foreign Broadcast Information Service (Springfield, Va.), 9 May 1981).

9 WHITHER THE NUCLEAR CONFRONTATION?

Paul Doty and Gregory F. Treverton

No concluding chapter could do justice to the diverse background contained in this book. Nor could it hope to adequately extend the signposts to the future of the nuclear confrontation in Europe that these chapters contain. Yet it is useful to bring the strands together, especially so since the question of theatre nuclear forces (TNF) involves such a tight network of political and military considerations. Sorting out those strands is the first task of this concluding chapter. A second is to sketch out the arms-control issues that TNF pose; that is an issued touched on by many of the chapters in this book. Finally, as the debates of recent years testify, the future of the nuclear issues is intimately bound up with the future of NATO. Will the alliance survive in its current form? What possibilities are there for more independent European defence arrangements? How much denuclearisation is prudent? Does emerging weapons technology provide a way out? How do the nuclear alternatives affect NATO's political goals and cohesion? These questions are hardly new, but they are once again in the air, and sharply, in the aftermath of the NATO deployments of intermediate nuclear forces (INF). Previous chapters set out past episodes of such questioning and thus provide hints for the future. This chapter will assemble those hints and comment on the new stresses induced by the Strategic Defense Initiative.

Military Forces and Political Purposes

Where We Stand

The first point underscored by the analyses in this book is that the TNF issue will not go away. To be sure, the heat of anti-nuclear protest in Europe was waning even before the first cruise missiles and Pershings were deployed in December 1983. With staunch conservative governments in power in both Britain and the Federal Republic, the deployments were a foregone conclusion, even given the tension in superpower relations and the parlous state of East-West arms control that prevailed at the time.

Yet the missiles will not be fully deployed before 1988 if the entire plan is implemented. And while popular concern about nuclear weapons is now diminished in Europe, it is not dead, as Jeffrey Boutwell makes clear in Chapter 6. Nevertheless, the magnitude of the immediate political victory of deploying in Europe for the first time — over the intense objections of Moscow — missiles that could reach the western Soviet Union should not be muted. Despite its high cost, the alliance survived a severe test and the positioning of the West for subsequent negotiations has been improved.

When and how serious nuclear oppositon might re-emerge in Europe are critical qestions for the future. Will anti-nuclear sentiment fuel the quest for alternative defence strategies? So far there has been little evidence that it will, a point to be addressed later. What about the left-of-centre political parties, especially the British Labour Party and the German Social Democratic Party, that veered sharply leftward on security issues while in opposition: will they return toward NATO orthodoxy when they get closer to power, or will they propel more radical security alternatives to the fore?

The TNF issue will not go away because there will remain questions of a more strictly military sort. It is worth noting that even if NATO deployed all 572 cruise and Pershing missiles — or fewer if the Dutch and Belgians did not accept their share — the numerical balance between NATO and the Warsaw Pact in INF missiles would be no better in 1988 than it was when NATO took the December 1979 decision. At that point NATO had no land-based INF missiles (other than an uncertain linkage to the 18 French IRBMs), while the Soviet Union had deployed 120 SS-20s and still had nearly 600 of the older SS-4s and SS-SS-5s on station.[1] Even if the Soviet Union held its SS-20 deployments to the 400-odd it had by the end of 1984 and dismantled all its older INF, in 1988 it would still have some 1,200 warheads on the triple-warhead SS-20s, while NATO would have only 572 warheads on its single-warhead systems. Even subtracting the third of SS-20s based in the Far East, the European warhead balance would still be comfortably in the Soviet favour, 828 to 572.

It is true, as Gregory Treverton notes in Chapter 4, that neither the political nor the military logic of the December 1979 decision required NATO to seek a weapon-for-weapon balance in INF with the Soviet Union. The point of the deployments was to assure the credibility of NATO strategy by more visibly 'coupling' the security of Europe to the American strategic deterrent. Yet the political logic of that argument was controversial, as Boutwell outlines: to many in Europe the new deployments looked more threatening than deterring because they seemed to hint at an American preparedness to fight a nuclear war limited to Europe.

Those deployments were also faulted on military grounds, more often from the Right than the Left and in a way much less visible than the anti-nuclear protest. They seemed to some military analysts, taking into account their dubious survivability, too few to matter; others argued that the short flight time of the Pershing posed a new threat to Soviet command and control, thus inviting the Soviets to pre-empt in time of war. These military arguments will continue, and that will thereby keep the European nuclear-missile issue visible in a way that had no counterpart during the 'wilderness years' between the mid-1960s and mid-1970s.

The next issue on the nuclear agenda is likely to be shorter-range TNF. As Stephen Meyer points out in Chapter 7, the Soviet Union is now deploying with its forces on Soviet territory a new generation of shorter-range missiles – the SS-21 (120 km in range), the SS-22 (900-900 km) and the SS-23 (500 km).[2] From NATO's perspective, the SS-21 and SS-23 would not pose a significantly new military threat even if deployed with Soviet forces in Eastern Europe. The Western allies had been expecting for some years that the Soviets would replace the aging Frog-7 and Scud missiles, first deployed in the mid-1960s.

However, the longer-range SS-22 has attracted much more attention. Given its range, if it were based in Eastern Europe, it would pose much the same threat to Western Europe as does the SS-20. It was for this reason that the American negotiating positions in the INF talks included 'non-circumvention' provisions to try to ensure that limits on the SS-20 would not be negated through deployments of SS-22s. After the installation of cruise and Pershing began, the Soviet Union announced that it would carry out its previous threats to deploy corresponding new systems in 'ocean and sea' areas adjacent to United States territory as well as new 'enhanced-range operational-tactical' missiles in Eastern Europe. The latter was the more disturbing by far. NATO had expected these deployments to be the SS-21 and SS-23, but there were reports in January 1984 of Western intelligence sightings of the SS-22 in East Germany.[3]

These deployments, especially the SS-22, will clearly complicate the future of nuclear-arms control in Europe, a point raised later in this chapter. Not only will such deployments feed the disquiet in Western Europe; but they will become a centrepiece in the argument that NATO has paid a high price to 'solve' its SS-20 problem only to have it replaced by additional Soviet nuclear missiles which may in turn call for a NATO response.

Political and Military Logic

The Soviet so-called response to the NATO deployments underscored another central theme of this book: the European nuclear issue is a tangle of military and political considerations. To ask of a particular measure 'is it primarily political or primarily military?' is usually to mispose the question. The initial Soviet responses to the NATO deployments were military in form but seemed political in purpose. With the exception of possible deployments of the SS-22 in Eastern Europe, they were mostly measures that NATO had expected the Soviet Union to take in any case. They were packaged as a response, to demonstrate Soviet resolve and to try to fan anti-nuclear protest in Western Europe, especially West Germany. The immediate response did not, for instance, suggest special concern over the military implications of the Pershing II missiles.

In fact, as Stephen Meyer argues, there would be little military logic to forward deployments by the Soviets of short-range nuclear systems. Given Soviet advantages in conventional forces, the Soviet imperative is to deter NATO from further nuclear deployments. That would hardly be accomplished by short-range systems that might suggest, contrary to Soviet pronouncements, that the Soviet Union contemplated nuclear war fighting, or whose vulnerability might encourage Western pre-emption.

Politically, moreover, the Soviet response was a double-edged sword. Whatever effect it had on public opinion in the West, it also had a pronounced impact in Eastern Europe. Tension within the Warsaw Pact over nuclear issues, while muted, has been present in the past, as Condolezza Rice suggests in Chapter 8. But this time it was more visible, though still nowhere near the scale of anti-nuclear opposition in Western Europe. Romania, for example, called for a cancellation of the Soviet counter-measures in return for a withdrawal of the Pershings and cruise missiles. And there were signs of public concern in Czechoslovakia.

Most significant was the reaction in East Germany — one of the countries chosen to host the new missiles — 80 per cent of whose population can receive West German television. There was visible anxiety in East Germany over the 'counter' deployments. Before the fact, Soviet pronouncements had labelled the NATO deployments a 'palli-sade of missiles' that would divide East and West Germany. Yet in the wake of the NATO deployments, relations between the two Germanies actually improved for a time, reflected in a sharply increased migration westward and in new credits by the conservative West German government to the East. Certainly, the Soviet Union must have sanctioned East Germany's policy, or at least its general direction. But the episode illustrates again that simple predictions about the political effect of nuclear deployments are suspect.

For NATO, the mingling of political and military logic is inescapable. Deterrence is, after all, as much a political as a military concept. NATO always has confronted a fundamental paradox of geography: most of NATO's ultimate deterrent, American strategic nuclear forces, resides an ocean away from the likely point of attack or political pressure. The dilemma is also an anomaly: it crystallised the exceptional situation of the 1950s and with it the military dependence of Europe on the United States. Western Europe has become a real confederation; its nations are past the point of fighting with each other. In the decades after World War II the Western European states came to possess all the attributes of sovereignty save one: responsibility for their own defence.

For more than three decades, dramatic alternatives to the nuclear status quo have seemed either unwise, or impossible, or both. That conclusion runs through the chapters of this book. There has seemed no one-for-all solution to the nuclear dilemma. It has only seemed possible to manage it, with a combination of military deployments and alliance cohesion, backed by the presence of 300,000 American troops in Europe. Whether that will continue to be the case is the last subject of this chapter. Will dramatic alternatives hitherto regarded as impossible or unwise come to be seen as attractive? Or, conversely, will the difficulty of managing current arrangements continue to preoccupy NATO and drive out consideration of such alternatives?

TNF and the Strategic Balance

Previous chapters have underscored the connection between TNF, particularly longer-range TNF, and strategic forces. For NATO, that link is a matter of doctrine: TNF represents the connection between defence in Europe and the American central strategic deterrent, a link vital to maintaining the spectrum of deterrence needed to discourage any Soviet adventure.

Yet it is the political and psychological dimension of the strategic balance that is most critical. In the past Europeans could feel somehow that as long as the United States remained superior in nuclear terms to the Soviet Union, by however loose a definition, they could be tolerably confident that it would respond to Soviet attack on Western Europe with nuclear weapons if need be. It did not matter much that Europe became in some sense 'hostage' to Soviet intermediate-range missiles targeted against it — some 700 SS-4s and SS-5s by the early 1960s. However, when strategic parity became a fact of life, Europeans could no longer be so confident.

The military basis for the perception that the American guarantee was weakening actually came in three steps. Until about 1962 the Soviet Union could deliver less than a hundred weapons each on Europe and the continental United States. Considering the inaccuracy and vulnerability of these Soviet weapons, an American first strike could have been 'successful', leaving only a few Soviet weapons whose use might have been deterred by the American inventory that was nearing 1,500. It was both the ten-to-one superiority in weapons and the fact that the Soviet forces were so numerically small that a first strike could largely eliminate them that produced the easy reliance on the American deterrent.

A decade later not only had the American margin narrowed to two to one but the number of Soviet weapons had reached 2,000, a number that could no longer be eliminated by a first strike. Within another decade — by 1982 — both sides had MIRVed, and each side was approaching 8,000 strategic weapons on line. Although the United States had lost its first-strike option nearly two decades earlier, it had now lost its image of superiority as well by virtue of the Soviet Union pulling abreast. This, more than military analysis, made the impact on public thinking. That was true even though militarily the changes by the early 1970s were more decisive because thereafter the United States could not risk using even a few nuclear weapons without inviting retaliation on its homeland. This qualitative asymmetry has been removed and a more comprehensive parity has been put in place, whatever the pros and cons of deploying TNF in Europe able to reach Russia.

Yet, how much has changed in fact is open to question. Happily, having no tests, we do not know how Moscow would act in a nuclear crisis. Yet the Soviets insist that retaliation against America will follow any use against Russian territory — even presumably, a retaliatory use by the United States or NATO. It follows, therefore, that now, as in the past, deterrence in Europe rests on the confidence that the United States will respond with nuclear weapons if need be, despite the risk to its own cities. Indeed, if deterrence should fail, the Soviet Union would have more incentive to spare European than American cities, since it might have post-war purposes for the latter. From the European point of view, then it is not obvious that their cities are more at risk and American cities less as a result of the new NATO deployments: there probably has been no change.

What is a change is that if conventional war did break out, the new NATO ground-launched cruise missiles (128 four-missile units) and the Pershing II missiles would become high priority, time-urgent targets for conventional attack, along with all other NATO nuclear systems. But these added targets are probably more than compensated for by the hundreds of shorter-range nuclear weapons that are being withdrawn. On balance, it is hard to make a strong case that either Western Europe or America is more at risk as a result of the Pershing and cruise missile deployments. Meanwhile, the NATO deterrent probably has been marginally improved, while the increased accuracy and lowered vulnerabilty of the SS-20 force has increased somewhat the Soviet threat to Western Europe.

Strategic will continue to be a fact of life. Important as nuclear modernisations — of both INF and American strategic forces — are, they will not restore an American 'superiority' that is psychologically reassuring, let alone be of much military significance. That will continue to make the nuclear issue in Europe sensitive. It is an exaggeration, but not much of one, to say the Europeans care less about the precise details of the nuclear balance than about whether Americans are tolerably comfortable with that balance. There are analytic grounds for that: Europeans can do little about the technical details of the balance, and they are dependent, finally, on American decisions. So American confidence is critical. With continuing parity, American military planners will not be tolerably confident; in European eyes, American analysts will continue to worry about this or that technical deficiency in the nuclear balance. That worry will be vocal; politics may make it more so. Europeans, in turn, will hear that lack of confidence and make it their own.

The strategic balance and INF will interact in still more direct ways. For example, in the debate surrounding the December 1979 decision, Europeans frequently argued that if the United States was unwilling to base its MX missile on land, why should the European allies accept cruise and Pershing missiles on European real estate?

Or consider the so-called 'star wars' initiative of President Reagan in 1983. In a speech in March, the President proposed that the United States undertake a major effort to develop defences that would be so effective against ballistic missiles as 'to give us the means of rendering . . . nuclear weapons impotent and obsolete'.[4] The proposal, officially known as the Strategic Defence Initiative (SDI), was widely criticised by strategic analysts. To most, the exotic space-based systems on which it depended were simply unlikely to work effectively, at least in this century. Or worse, they could be easily counteracted, and building them would merely ratchet up the arms race at enormous expense. To arms controllers, the prospect that the 1972 Anti-Ballistic Missile (ABM) treaty, the one significant piece of superpower strategic arms control, would have to be abrogated to permit such defences was deeply disquieting.

The initiative was also criticised by Europeans across the political spectrum, although the British and German governments endorsed the research phase. Their initial reaction was dominated by politics — the sense that the United States was about to launch another cock-eyed scheme that would fuel the arms race and needlessly antagonise the Soviet Union. Yet beneath this immediate reaction there were also European interests at play, ones that will become more visible in the future depending on how the missile-defence issue plays out. Most obviously, even modest defences deployed by the Soviet Union, ones far less capable than those contemplated by Mr Reagan, could negate the independent capabilities of the British and French nuclear deterrents. What might be only minimally effective against an American arsenal of 10,000 warheads could be devastatingly efficient against a French force of several hundred. Certainly, any move to modify or abrogate the ABM treaty would be discomforting to the French and British, for the reasons that Freedman suggests in Chapter 2.

If, in the end, the United States were only able to construct population defences that were modestly effective, that would have unpredictable impacts on the situation in Europe. As so often happens with nuclear issues, strategic and political logic would collide. In strategic analysis, even modest population defences should, in principle, strengthen extended deterrence because any decision to use American central strategic weapons — and thereby to risk Soviet attacks on American cities — would be less apocalyptic, at least at the margin. Politically, however, Europeans would be likely to read modest population defences as a sign that the United States indeed intended to 'de-couple' its own security from that of Europe, that it was prepared to fight a nuclear war in Europe while maintaining the United States as a sanctuary.

Other possible results of the defence initiative would have similarly mixed effects on the nuclear confrontation in Europe. In strategic analysis, the vulnerability of American land-based ICBMs does diminish the credibility of extended deterrence in Europe, for reasons outlined by Treverton in Chapter 4. Thus, if the defence initiative eventually took the form of hard-site defence of missiles, that should be reassuring

Whither the Nuclear Confrontation?

to Europeans. Again, however, it would not likely be so reassuring in political terms, particularly not if it required abrogation of the ABM treaty. Such a development risks being seen as an indication of an American desire to decouple. That might even be the case if the defence initiative first produced an interest in anti-tactical missiles (ATM) to be deployed in Europe. Even that would probably suggest to Europeans an American desire to fight nuclear wars limited to Europe.

The proposal in 1983 that strategic defence be introduced into the East-West strategic equation even before its reality is tested or given shape, and the insistence by President Reagan in 1984 and 1985 that — contrary to the Soviet view — the search for such defences be insulated from future arms-control negotiations: these drastically altered the landscape on which arms-control negotiations take place. They brought into question the fundamental basis of deterrence that the two sides had doggedly worked out over the last three decades. Whether or not they eventually will make for a marked change introduces a new uncertainty into the final sections of this chapter.

The Question of Arms Control

TNF have had a checkered history in arms control, one alluded to in several of this book's chapters. The most recent instance — the INF talks begun in a preliminary form in Geneva in the autumn of 1980, then recommenced the next autumn after President Reagan's election, and suspended in December 1983 when the Soviet Union made good its threat to walk out if NATO began its cruise and Pershing deployments — is illustrative more of what to avoid than of what to emulate. From the beginning, the second — or negotiating — track of the 1979 double decision was driven almost entirely by political concerns. If they were to deploy new nuclear weapons, the Europeans had to convince their publics that they had first done everything they could to avoid the need to do so.

On military grounds, however, the negotiations were unpromising in the extreme. In 1980 Soviet launches numbered 600 and the warhead numbers were destined to grow as SS-20s were deployed while NATO was only to begin its deployment in late 1983. NATO was thus in the position of bargaining intentions, and questionable intentions at that, against weapons in place. It was clearly too much to expect arms-control negotiations to produce balance from such an existing imbalance.

In those circumstances it was almost a relief when the separate INF talks were suspended. That separation was, after all, an accident, not a NATO design. At the time of the December 1979 decision, the allies assumed that INF negotiations would be pursued 'in the SALT II framework' once the American Senate ratified SALT II.[5] The Soviet invasion of Afghanistan dashed that expectation and created the separate INF talks. Yet as the attention of both experts and publics to TNF remains higher than in the past, the issue of TNF arms control will remain on the agenda. In time the pause, weary and wary, provoked by the NATO deployments and the Soviet walk-out from both the INF and the START talks will be seen as just an interlude which ended in March 1985.

The Negotiating History

The paradox of geography that confronts NATO is also at the heart of the deep difference between Eastern and Western perspectives of TNF negotiations. Since America and Europe are an ocean apart, the Soviet Union can threaten American allies with nuclear weapons that cannot reach the continental United States. By the same token, Western TNF based in Europe threaten the Soviet Union in a way that Soviet TNF do not threaten the American homeland. In negotiations over strategic arms, the United States from the start sought to define 'strategic' weapons by their range. In contrast, the Soviet Union tried to label as 'strategic' any nuclear weapon that could strike the Soviet homeland, no matter where that weapon was based. Nothing short of moving non-Russian Europe to the middle of the Atlantic could resolve this paradox since only then could both sides target Europe with weapons unable to reach the other's homeland.

Thus, in the SALT I negotiations Moscow sought to include not just American intercontinental systems but also so-called 'forward based systems' (FBS) in Europe, as well as French and British independent nuclear forces.[6] At the same time, the Soviets resisted inclusion of their SS-4s and SS-5s because those could not reach American territory and because they were needed for defence against 'third countries'. With the assent of its allies, Washington resisted expanding the negotiations, and in May 1971 the Soviets relented. They did insist, however, that FBS be 'taken into account in any future agreements. The SALT I agreement, signed in May 1972, made no explicit mention of FBS, but it did allow the Soviet Union more offensive missiles than the United States. Moreover, a Soviet unilateral statement, rejected by the United States, reserved the right for the Soviet Union to increase the number of its missile-carrying submarines if French and British submarine forces grew.

TNF also figured in the Mutual and Balanced Force Reduction (MBFR) negotiations in Vienna, in the so-called Option Three offer made by NATO in December 1975. That episode is discussed in Chapter 2. It was, however, like discussions several years later of concessions the Soviet Union might make if NATO forwent deployment of enhanced radiation weapons, less a real arms-control proposal than a sweetener. In the instance of Option Three, NATO offered to give up weapons it probably needed to replace or retire anyway in exchange for Soviet concessions of another sort. Having evoked no interest this option has now been withdrawn.

TNF became an issue again in SALT II. In November 1974 the Soviet Union agreed not to push the FBS issue on the assumption that TNF would be considered in SALT III. In a very real way, as has been commented many times in this book, that omission of TNF from SALT II, given public visibility in Chancellor Schmidt's speech in October 1977, set in train the events that led to the December 1979 decision.

That December 1979 decision outlined the NATO position on INF negotiations:[7] negotiations should be bilateral, thus dealing only with Soviet and American delivery systems; they should concentrate on INF missiles, not aircraft or sea-based systems; the principle of parity should apply; limitations should be global, not just applicable to systems deployed in Europe; and any agreed limitations should be adequately verifiable. In the autumn of 1981 President Reagan made the so-called 'zero option' offer — NATO would forgo new deployments if the Soviet Union dismantled all its SS-20s.[8] Later the United States indicated that it was also willing to accept almost any number between 50 and 450, provided there were equal numbers for the two sides and provided there was some constraint on Soviet SS-20 deployments in the Far East. With regard to the latter, Washington was willing to concede the Soviets some 100 additional SS-20s in Asia, above the European ceiling, if the United States had the right to compensatory deployments of its own, a right it would not exercise unless the Soviet deployments in Asia greatly increased.

The basic Soviet negotiating position, and its purpose, seemed painfully plain. The position, from the autumn of 1979 onward, was that parity in INF already existed;[9] the Soviet purpose was to prevent NATO from deploying *any* cruise or Pershing missiles capable of reaching the Soviet homeland while using the negotiations to dissociate Western Europe from the United States. Central to the argument for parity, and thus to the Soviet position, was the inclusion of British and French nuclear systems in the INF balance. Only once did the Soviet Union even approach a willingness to agree to an outcome that would have permitted some of NATO's INF deployment to go forward. Instead, Moscow's formal position moved from reductions in European-based systems to 300 on each side, then to 162 — the number of British and French missiles — and finally to 140. The Soviet Union did move somewhat toward the American position by agreeing that warheads and not just missiles should be limited, and by accepting some limits on Asian-based SS-20s.

The only time the two sides came near to breaking the impasse was the so-called 'walk in the woods'.[10] In informal conversations with his Soviet counterpart in the summer of 1982, the American negotiator, Paul Nitze, worked out a formula: the Soviet Union would reduce to 75 SS-20s aimed at Europe (225 warheads) and would deploy no more than 90 SS-20s in the Far East; in return, the United States would not deploy Pershings and would deploy only 75 cruise missile systems of four missiles each, or 300 warheads. Each side would have equal numbers of medium-range bombers, and both numbers and quality of short-range TNF would be frozen at existing levels.

For NATO, the proposal was a nice blending of military logic and political necessity, and for that reason it is surprising that — at least according to Nitze's account —the Soviet Union considered it. In the end, however, it came to naught. Nitze says that his counterpart did not get back to him. In the meantime, Washington, initially favourably disposed, authorised Nitze to proceed only provided not all Pershings were given up — a point on which the Pentagon insisted. At this point the game was over. European leaders, not consulted during the time the formula was being devised, both resented the lack of consultation and regretted the demise of the 'walk in the woods' formula.

This most interesting episode of the Euromissile drama should provide some guidance to possible future solutions, but, alas, there is no agreed-upon analysis of the events. In the most exhaustedly researched version of the event, Talbott concludes:

> The walk-in-the-woods episode remained as mysterious as it was controversial. The principal mystery concerned what had actually happened on the Soviet side — and, hypothetically, what might have happened if the Reagan Administration had quickly and unequivocally endorsed the package deal. There is not enough evidence to concludes, or even to speculate persuasively, that the Administration

missed an opportunity to reach what would have been a very good agreement for the West, in both its political and its military consequences. On the contrary, it is at least as plausible that the package deal would have come apart and been repudiated in Moscow, regardless of how Washington responded. So Nitze himself, in his own post-mortem of the affair, came to believe.[10]

More recently, knowledgeable Soviet visitors went out of their way to insist that the formula was never at any time of interest to the Soviet Union.

Issues for Negotiations

Negotiations concerning intermediate range nuclear forces are scheduled to be one of three parts of the new negotiations beginning in Geneva in March 1985. Unsuccessful as they were, the first rounds of the earlier Geneva talks did produce rough agreement on several issues: warheads should be limited as well as launchers, (some) aircraft may be included, and Soviet missile deployments in the Far East should be somehow constrained. More fundamentally, the fact of negotiations moved the Soviet Union toward accepting the strategic unity of Europe and the United States; no longer can Soviet weapons that can reach 'only' Western Europe be left out of negotiations. Moreover, by announcing its new missiles deployments in Eastern Europe as a counter to the NATO deployments, the Soviet Union risks including them in any new INF talks.

Yet any negotiations on TNF will confront a number of issues:

How to Treat British and French Forces. This issue, one that runs back to the beginning of SALT, is bound to be pressed even more strongly in the future by Moscow because the INF talks made it the linchpin of the Soviet negotiating position. Thus far, both London and Paris have insisted that their small forces must for the time being be excluded from arms control, and certainly from any separate INF talks. In INF, the United States has insisted that the talks are purely bilateral — its position also in the START talks — and that by doctrine and posture the French and British forces are not theatre weapons. The principal weapons are submarine-launched ballistic missiles indistinguishable from those of the United States and the Soviet Union that have been routinely included in the SALT I, SALT II and START negotiations.

Until now it has also been possible for the United States to argue that those forces were relatively insignificant by comparison to superpower nuclear arsenals, constituting about 4 per cent of the strategic forces of either superpower. However, this basis of exclusions is eroding as British and French forces modernise. On current plans, the French could have as many as 750 SLBM warheads, probably MIRVed, by the end of this decade. If the British proceed with the Trident programme, they will have 512 MIRVed warheads on four boats by some time in the 1990s. Even then the British and French forces would still be about the same size in proportion to superpower weaponry as they were at the time of SALT I. There would, however, be weight to the Soviet argument that the absolute threat they posed to the Soviet Union was much greater since the marginal utility of nuclear weapons decreases as the numbers increase in the range of what the superpowers now have.

Chinese nuclear weapons pose a subsidiary issue. Surely there is no near-term prospect of Chinese participation in arms control, and the Soviets must recognise that fact. The October 1983 Soviet offer to 'freeze' SS-20 deployments in the Far East was contingent on the lack of 'changes in the strategic situation in Asia', a clear reference to China (and perhaps to American nuclear deployments in the region).

Since this issue involves the weapons of three other countries that consider their weapons strategic, it is unlikely that any agreement can be found within the TNF framework. If strategic and long-range TNF weapons are considered collectively, or the negotiations merged, the interpretation of parity becomes central. The Soviet Union will insist that parity for it means essential equivalence between its forces and all those of the other four nuclear powers since it may be threatened by all four simultaneously. The United States will insist that parity means essential equivalence between the two superpowers.

Clearly a far-reaching compromise is called for in a region where principles conflict. Since the principles do conflict, any solution will have to be somewhat arbitrary. Viewed in one way, the issue is what weight to assign to the weapons of the three smaller nuclear powers. Assigning them a weight of zero corresponds in effect to the American preference. Assigning them a weight of unity and assuming that if used they would be used against the Soviet Union is the Soviet preference. A compromise lies in somehow constructing, implicitly or explicitly, a weighting factor somewhere between zero and one.

Alternatively, if the United States and Russia could agree to substantial reductions in an agreement covering both strategic and long-range TNF weaponry, the three smaller nuclear powers might accept a contingent agreement. In the short run they might undertake to limit their forces since successive reductions by the superpowers could not be expected if the three smaller nuclear forces continued to expand. And they might agree over the longer term to keep their own forces from growing relative to those of the superpowers.

How to Treat Aircraft. Negotiating verifiable limits on nuclear-capable aircraft is the most demanding aspect of controlling TNF. The numbers are large and the types diverse, and it is hard to distinguish nuclear-capable, potentially nuclear-capable and non-nuclear-capable aircraft. NATO reckons that the Warsaw Pact has 7,500 aircraft technically capable of delivering nuclear weapons against NATO countries, while offsetting NATO forces number 3,000, not including French forces.[11] These totals break down as follows: the Soviets have 400 medium bombers, NATO none (if American F-111s are counted in the next category and the British Vulcans are completely phased out); each side has about 2,000 ground-attack fighter bombers; the Warsaw Pact outnumbers NATO in interceptors by five to one and in reconnaissance aircraft by two to one.

Of these aircraft, only about 800 on the Warsaw Pact side and 500 on the NATO side (600 with France included) are believed to be assigned to nuclear missions.[12] Yet with many of these aircraft indistinguishable from the same types assigned non-nuclear missions, there is no obvious way to count and control the nuclear-capable aircraft alone. This remains one of the central problems of arms control; it is becoming worse with the introduction of nuclear-armed and conventionally armed cruise missiles, which have flight characteristics much like aircraft.

A first cut would be to constrain only the longer-range part of nuclear-capable aircraft. If the range limit were set at about 2,500 km, then Warsaw Pact Badger, Blinder, Backfire and Fencer planes (roughly 350 nuclear-capable out of a total of 1,400) might be set against NATO F-111s, F-16s, Tornado, some carrier-based aircraft and possibly some French aircraft (roughly 350 nuclear capable out of a total of 1,200).

In September 1983 the United States did modify its opposition to including aircraft in the first phase of an INF agreement. For their part, the Soviets insisted from the start that aircraft be included. For instance, in 1981 Brezhnev asserted that the INF balance for both aircraft and missiles was 986-975 in the West's favour. In doing so he apparently included American aircraft, like the F-111, based in the United States and a larger number of US F-4 aircraft than exist in inventories, much less have a nuclear role. More important Brezhnev *included* some Western systems (like F-4s) while *excluding* Soviet systems with comparable or greater capabilities (e.g., Fencer).

On the one hand, some long-range aircraft on both sides are, by virtue of their range and performance rather unambiguously comparable to missile systems in performing INF roles, although their ability to penetrate varies because of superior Soviet air defence. Excluding them would, at best, leave a gap in any agreement; at worst, it could channel competition away from missile systems which were covered into aircraft which were not. Moreover, if NATO wanted to achieve limits on Soviet aircraft that, like Backfire, raise concerns of the sort Meyer outlines in Chapter 7, it would have to be prepared to throw some of its own aircraft into the bargain.

Yet on the other hand, the characteristics of particular aircraft are variable and hard to discern; hence their inclusion or exclusion can easily become particularly arbitrary. It is not easy for one side to know, much less to verify adequately through national technical means (NTM) exactly what portion of the other side's force of a particular plane is nuclear capable, still harder to know how many of those actually would be used in the nuclear role should a war occur, and finally to track actual numbers within the noise provided by commercial air traffic. Similarly, the range of particular aircraft is knowable only within broad margins, for it depends crucially on where the planes are based, on how much of a weapon load they carry and on the profile of the mission they actually fly.

Clearly the control of aircraft remains the most difficult of the TNF (or INF) negotiating problems. Even if progress is made on merging the strategic and INF forces under common ceilings, the problem of which aircraft are to be included remains. There seems to be no alternative to beginning with the longest-range aircraft capable of nuclear missions and negotiating global limits on a balanced short list, taking into account the non-NATO requirements of both the United States and the Soviet Union. The long-term problem would be eased if agreements could be reached to 'denuclearise' a growing number of aircraft categories, with a random inspection scheme sufficient to ensure adequate compliance.

How to Treat Sea-Launched Cruise Missiles. This issue was little in evidence during the first INF talks, but it cannot be avoided in the future because it offers a means of circumventing any simple agreement. Because of growing numbers, the issue cannot be avoided in any comprehensive agreement. The Soviet Union has since 1962 gradually deployed on naval vessels tactical cruise missiles (SLCM) with ranges up to 1,000 km. These now number about 700 and about half are thought to be nuclear armed. Their mission is primarily anti-ship but in some circumstances they could be used for shore bombardment.

With the advent of the modern cruise missiles the United States has developed a new kind of SLCM, the Tomahawk, with a range of 2,500 km. This can be used against ships or for land attack. Plans call for deploying 4,000 to 8,000 of these on submarines and ships, but only a fraction (perhaps 400) are to be nuclear armed. Deployment has already begun. Meanwhile the Soviet Union is well under way in a comparable development.

This arms-control problem may be the most difficult of all; some analysts believe it is insoluble.[13] With hiding so easy and detection so difficult and intrusive, the monitoring of production, as is now done for submarines, may be the only reliable means of control, difficult as that would be. Negotiated limitations on the platforms on which SLCMs would be permitted offers another route, but inspection would remain difficult, intrusive and expensive. A total ban on SLCMs, or on all those with a range greater than a few hundred kilometres, would be a solution that could be verified more easily.

If this issue reaches the negotiating table, conflict is certain. At a minimum, Moscow will raise this as a circumvention issue, insisting that any limits on NATO's INF not be 'circumvented' by deployments of SLCMs. NATO's interests will run in exactly the opposite direction. For it the imperative is to sustain its right to deploy *some* INF. Even if in the end it were prepared to bargain away most (or all) of its Pershings and ground-launched cruise missiles, it would still want to retain the right to deploy some SLCMs oriented toward the European area.

Should Shorter-Range TNF Be Included? There are powerful arguments, mentioned earlier, for including shorter-range systems in negotiations. Soviet SS-22s based in Eastern Europe pose much the same threat as SS-20s based in Russia, and just as SALT II dramatised the latter by excluding them, so INF talks could underscore the former by leaving *them* (and kindred systems) out.

Yet the arguments against including (many) shorter-range systems are formidable. Firstly, it would vastly complicate negotiations that already are overloaded. The talks would become negotiations over what was to be negotiated. It will be hard enough to compare SS-20s with GLCMs or with Backfire bombers; adding shorter-range systems would only compound those problems of incommensurability.

Secondly, as more short-range systems are included, the overall balance comes to be dominated by tactical aircraft whose status as theatre nuclear weapons clearly is more questionable than for longer-range systems.

Finally, it is clear that negotiating verifiable limits on the longer-range fighter-bombers, as suggested above, would be a major breakthrough. Thus, it is better to achieve that objective than risk all. Should it be necessary to proceed into some shorter range systems, then missiles, would be a more promising arena than the much more numerous shorter-range aircraft.

How to Treat Strategic Defence. As the first round of the new negotiations began in March 1985, the pace of and commitment to the Strategic Defence Initiative (SDI) on the part of the American administration, and the corresponding Soviet programmes, seemed likely to dominate the scene. With the exception of France, the major NATO governments voiced support for the SDI research programme of about $30 billion over five years. Since there is wide agreement that research cannot be controlled and since the Soviet effort is comparable now to that of the United States, this was a relatively easy decision. In addition to demonstrating allied solidarity, it kept the door open for allied participation in this next generation of military high technology, with its presumed economic spin-offs.

Yet in the long run, European opinion and government position may be quite different. Suppose, for example, development and deployment required modification or abrogation of the ABM Treaty (SALT I). Or suppose the Soviet strategic defence effort threatened to nullify the British and French strategic forces. Or, deployment might threaten to produce a range of effects from an increased instability, to a 'decoupling' in NATO doctrine, to a reopening of conventional arms races of even to a greater likelihood of conventional war itself.[14]

For their part, the Soviets have both sensed opportunities to divide the alliance and worried about engaging in a high technology race in space with the West. They have sought to nip SDI in the bud. Tactically, stopping SDI before it accelerated has replaced the earlier campaign against deployment of NATO missiles. As the latter led to a Soviet walkout from negotiations, so the current round might founder if the United States insisted on moving forward with SDI. Nor is it hard to imagine negotiating scenarios that would produce considerable strain in the

NATO alliance. Suppose, for example, that Moscow was prepared to agree to deep reductions in strategic and INF warheads but only in return for restraints on the American defence initiative. European governments might be prepared to accept such a deal, but the United States might resist, all the more so since 'European' concerns so far have taken a back seat to the more general strategic appeal of SDI for Americans.

How to Verify an INF Agreement. Verification obviously will be a serious problem, for reasons that are familiar from SALT and START but worse in this case: most of the systems under discussion are mobile, many are small and thus easy to conceal, and there will be the need to distinguish between nuclear-capable and conventional versions of the same system in a way that can be verified. The central point is that verification will become more of a problem, and be more likely to hang up the negotiations, the more ambitious an agreement is sought. For example, the United States verifies the number of SS-20 launchers with satellite photography, much as with Soviet ICBMs. It does so by observing the activity at SS-20 bases, often without actually seeing an SS-20 launcher. That would provide tolerable verification of numbers of SS-20 *launchers*, but if agreements sought to constrain numbers of *missiles* with launchers, additional verification procedures probably would be required.

Similarly, if agreements go beyond missiles to include aircraft, it will be necessary to design ways, verifiable to the other side, to distinguish nuclear or nuclear-capable versions from those that are purely conventional. That will in any case be necessary for cruise missiles.

Verification will be a joker in the negotiating deck. In technical terms, while the problems of verifying, say, cruise-missile deployments are severe, they are not insurmountable. SALT and START provide some precedents. Yet, as with SALT II, if INF agreements are controversial for other reasons, much of the currency of that opposition will be verification.

Form of Negotiations

The ending of the first INF negotiations (at the end of 1983) was inevitable. The separation from the strategic talks was an accident in the first place. Having committed themselves so strongly to preventing any NATO INF deployment, the Soviets had no more attractive recourse than to break the talks and retain their original demands until another opening arose. Moreover, Soviet incentives to engage in arms control are stronger in the strategic realm, given the momentum of American strategic programmes. So it is no surprise that INF is to be negotiated separately, but linked to the START talks, as one of the three tables under the umbrella, as agreed at the Gromyko-Schultz meeting in January 1985.

There were — and are — a number of arguments for some merging of INF and START. Doctrinally, NATO stresses the continuum of nuclear deterrence. In particular, the December 1979 decision on new deployments was taken explicitly to reinforce the link between the European theatre and central American strategic nuclear forces. The link that NATO plans forces to sustain should not be weakened by arms-control approaches that seemed to separate — 'decouple', in the jargon of the trade — strategic forces from their closest doctrinal kin, INF. Logically, it never made much sense to proceed far with INF talks while the future of limits on central strategic forces was unclear. Why, after all, strive for limits on the Soviet SS-20 if the Soviet intercontinental forces, which can reach European targets as well, might be left unconstrained?

Linked negotiations would ameliorate, though hardly solve, the problems of numerical asymmetry in INF and of British and French forces. What are large asymmetries between the INF forces of the two sides would become less dramatic in talks comprising both INF and strategic systems. Similarly, British and French forces would loom less large numerically in such linked talks.

European analysts have in the past expressed interest in fully merged INF-START negotiations, and that interest will recur. Certainly that approach would underscore the doctrinal unity between INF and central systems. For instance, the SALT II aggregate limit for missile launchers of 2,250 might be raised to 2,650 to include INF, with both sides given freedom to determine the precise mix between INF and central systems.[15] Constraints on warhead numbers might be achieved by including INF systems under SALT II sub-ceilings on MIRVed launchers, perhaps expanded somewhat.

The degree of merger will become a pivotal issue as negotiations proceed. Loosely merged negotiations raise the prospect that one side or the other might hold agreement in one working group hostage to progress in another. By contrast, tightly merged talks might be more complicated than the process could bear. SALT II took seven years to negotiate; the INF talks have complexities, discussed earlier, that run beyond even those of SALT. Putting the two together simply might bring the entire process to a standstill.

Far from sustaining the link between the European theatre and

American central forces, tightly merged negotiations might strain NATO politics. In tightly related or merged negotiations, it would be especially tempting for the Soviets to target proposals where the interests of America and Europe seem to diverge, as suggested above with regard to SDI. Suppose, for example, that the Soviet Union accepted the principle of deep cuts in strategic forces, but only on the condition that the Soviet Union (and NATO) forgo deployment of the 572 Pershings and cruise missiles. An American administration committed to deep cuts and focused on the strategic balance might be tempted to agree. Yet that would look to Europeans like trading European interests for American ones, thus provoking a row in the alliance. Nothing would prevent the Soviet Union from making proposals of this sort even in separated negotiations – indeed they are predictable – but tightly linked negotiations would make them easier.

Moreover, until now the process of consultation within NATO have been different for INF than for START. On INF, the United States has consulted its allies closely and in detail in the Special Consultative Group (SCG) set up in the wake of the December 1979 decision. That process gives the Europeans a real say in the INF negotiations, tantamount to a veto. By contrast, the process for START has been looser, with Washington briefing its allies on the process of negotiations. If the talks were fully merged, the Europeans surely would insist on no less than the role they have with regard to INF. That no doubt would be resisted by the United States, accustomed to more freedom in the strategic talks and disinclined in any event to concede its allies that much influence over American strategic programmes. Thus, fully merged negotiation would pose NATO hard choices over how it does its business. Certainly, suggestions that the Europeans participate directly in the INF portion of negotiations – like Henry Kissinger's 1984 proposal – are premature; it is not in any case for Americans to make them.[16]

Nuclear Weapons and the Future of NATO

It is hardly a surprise that the management of nuclear weapons, and in particular nuclear deployments in Europe, has been and continues to be an index of NATO's cohesion. As many chapters in this book illustrate, that has been so almost since the beginning of NATO. By geography, by doctrine, and by the emotive politics of nuclear weapons, TNF as the link between European defence and the American deterrent is bound to be sensitive. Nuclear issues have been and continue to be a barometer of the state of European-American issues. When Europeans are tolerably confident in the United States, nuclear issues recede; when they are not, nuclear issues come to the fore as symbols of larger disquiet.

As NATO approaches its fortieth anniversary, its future is once again being debated, for reasons that have much to do with nuclear weapons. These questionings are hardly new; quite the contrary, as the chapters herein underline. Yet there are reasons for thinking the questioning may be more serious this time. Assessing the reasons for this would go beyond our purposes here, but at the root of much of the questioning seems to be a sense that the degree of European dependence on the United States reflected in current arrangements simply cannot continue. It seems to many no longer compatible with Europe's political and economic stature by comparison to the United States, and it seems to require a degree of American consistency — not to say benevolence — that is no longer in the cards.

Radical Alternatives

The dramatic alternatives to something like NATO in its current form have changed little in several decades, as Ireland points out in Chapter 1.

European Self-reliance. Now, as in the 1960s, one logical alternative to existing arrangements is a dramatic increase in European co-operation, including in the nuclear realm and perhaps extending to the creation of a European nuclear force. On that score, General de Gaulle's logic is compelling: if Europeans fear that America will not push the nuclear button, then they need buttons of their own with nuclear weapons to match.

If the logic is both familiar and compelling so are the obstacles: the political difficulty of Anglo-French cooperation, and the much greater problem of how to include Germany. A European nuclear force would hardly be credible without a German finger on the button, but will continue to be politically impossible with it. It is hard to imagine that half-way measures, such as some form of 'dual-key' arrangements within Europe, would suffice. If Germans doubt the willingness of the United States to use *its* force in their defence, even with dual keys, they could hardly believe that Britain or France would commit *their* much smaller forces. Moreover, as presently constituted, both French and British forces are quite independent in character, last-ditch deterrents against attack on British or French soil.

Talks in the early 1980s between France and Germany about

Whither the Nuclear Confrontation? 225

increasing their military co-operation illustrated the difficulties: the French sought to convince the Germans that French nuclear weapons protected them, while the Germans were more eager to beef up the French conventional presence in Germany. The French security debate of the mid-1980s has been a lively one, in significant part because of French anxiety over political developments in Germany; perhaps new possibilities will emerge. It may be that some greater 'European' orientation of both French and British nuclear forces could serve not as a substitute, but rather as a complement to the American nuclear guarantee. However, what that would mean and whether it would diminish or increase the second-class status of the Federal Republic with regard to nuclear weapons: the answers are by no means clear. Most likely, European interest in 'European' defence arrangements will increase, but the obstacles to dramatic change will remain for the foreseeable future.[17]

Nuclear Defence. NATO is even less likely to move in the opposite direction — towards nuclear defences that economise on manpower. Again, the logic of nuclear defence is as old as the alliance; NATO could have broken its dilemma by acknowledging frankly that no conventional defence was possible within foreseeable levels of spending, given Soviet conventional capabilities. The alliance would then have built its defence around the threat to use nuclear weapons at the very start of any conflict. Its forces would be structured accordingly, and might be much smaller and cheaper than at present.[18] Such strategies would explicitly decouple the American strategic arsenal from the immediate defence of Europe. They would aim to deter attack by presenting unacceptable odds on the ground, not by the risk of escalation.

NATO has never accepted such strategies, and they were specifically abandoned when the doctrine of flexible response was adopted in the late 1960s. Yet they persist. The growing Soviet arsenal of short-range systems, coupled with the conclusion that NATO could well be worse off after an exchange of battlefield nuclear weapons would appear to make such strategies less and less attractive on military grounds. However, a nuclear defender dispersed for nuclear combat could retain some of the advantage of the defence, and a variety of means of making the early use of nuclear weapons credible has been suggested, for instance by creating or preparing to create in time of crisis a depopulated border zone on the intra-German frontier and an increased reliance on mobile, guerrilla-like, harassment units.

However, responsible political leaders in the West simply will not authorise the use of nuclear weapons early in a conflict (unless the other side fires them first), or delegate responsibility for firing weapons to anyone else (much less to field commanders). Politics in NATO Europe are strained enough by current nuclear issues. They could not bear the weight of strategies that relied on the early and extensive release of nuclear weapons, even if those strategies had the virtue of a clarity that current NATO doctrine does not. Indeed both public and official temper is moving towards further delaying the first use of nuclear weapons.

That conclusion is not fundamentally altered by the impact of new nuclear technology. Technology will not solve NATO's nuclear dilemma. The most that can be said about enhanced radiation weapons (ERW), for example, is that under certain specific, and transitory, battlefield conditions, they would be marginally more effective against Soviet tank formations than NATO's existing tactical nuclear weapons.[19] That marginal gain hardly outweighs the problems with their use or of their cost. ERW are, after all, nuclear weapons, with all the inhibitions surrounding their use. To make a military difference, they would have to be used early and in large numbers. Even if we could convince West Germans that ERW could be used on their territory without devastating it, they could not be convinced that the Soviet Union would play that game. Indeed, the Soviets would have reason not to do so. And given the fragility of command and control arrangements, especially in Europe, no one could have any confidence that a nuclear war could be contained once dozens of even 'small' nuclear weapons are being exchanged.[20]

Conventional Deterrence. If dramatic nuclear alternatives are beyond the pale, the opposite possibility, greater reliance on conventional weaponry, merits more consideration. Again, the logic is compelling: if deterrence through the threatened resort to nuclear weapons is less and less credible, then raising the nuclear threshold through better conventional defence is preferable. Certainly, there is no shortage of proposals on the table. And just as surely, NATO badly needs to work on conventional defence.

The obstacles are of several sorts. Most obviously, better conventional defence is likely to be expensive, both in money and probably in manpower. The European countries, deeply worried about the structural competitiveness of their economies, will be hard pressed to maintain defence-spending increases of the order of recent years while making drastic social changes, such as increasing productivity by shortening vacations. And all of them, but especially the Federal Republic, will face the need to recruit or draft larger and larger fractions of diminishing age cohorts in the years ahead. Even if new technology can substitute for manpower, that technology is likely to be expensive. And, to boot, most of it will be American, raising the spectre of even greater technological dependence on the United States.

Secondly, some of the current enthusiasms — such as for deep interdiction strikes with precision-guided weapons well behind the front lines, or even for NATO counter-attacks into Warsaw Pact territory — will raise political problems in Europe.[21] NATO always has had some capability for deep interdiction strikes, so at the margin innovations can be useful. But sharp changes in NATO doctrine or practice are likely to remain politically difficult, especially for West Germans. Many of those innovations in conventional technology, such as conventional cruise missiles, will also bedevil nuclear-arms control.

Thirdly, even if NATO could markedly improve its conventional forces and convince its publics that it had, it would still confront the abiding European horror of a conventional war in Europe. In European eyes, if better conventional defences make a resort to nuclear weapons less likely, the Soviets may in a crisis be *more* tempted to risk such a conventional war. For Europeans, at least in governing establishments, the nuclear threshold should be high but not too high.

Finally, even with better conventional defence, NATO would still confront an opponent with nuclear weapons. Hence NATO would need nuclear weapons of its own to deter those of the other side. To be sure, that nuclear posture might comprise many fewer weapons than at present, and those that remained would be much more sensibly deployed. But it is far from obvious that the change would reassure European publics enough either to diminish the heat of the nuclear issue or to call forth the requisite increases in spending for conventional forces.

Despite the imposing magnitude of these obstacles, some modernisation of NATO forces will continue. The choices range from uncoordinated marginal changes through Air-Battle 2000 to a technological revolution, dubbed ET (emerging technologies), in conventional weapons systems of such promise as to rival 'star wars' in space.[22] The arguments range from urging priority for reserves, ammunition, spares and logistic support, forgoing all of ET, to embracing ET as the only way to cope with declining manpower pools, to raise the nuclear threshold and to keep Europe apace with advancing technology. NATO has always faced hard choices in allocating scarce funds.

What is changing is the range of choice: it is broadening as never before.

However, the European NATO members are not well positioned to meet the challenge of those choices: economic integration has slowed, productivity is sluggish, military forces and weapons development are not well integrated, and Europe seems to be gradually falling behind in high technology. The high technology gap in the military arena is an inevitable consequence of the fact that the United States invests about 10 times as much in military research and development as does NATO Europe. No amount of 'sharing' can wipe out this difference. The result is that ET in Europe is destined to be largely American-made unless the high technology gap can be narrowed. To generate a sustained modernisation in NATO forces that will provide a more credible, less nuclear-prone deterrent in Europe will require nothing less than the modernisation of Europe. That awesome task seems bound to be achieved at best in part. What, then, are likely NATO options?

Likely Futures

As usual in human affairs, the future of NATO and of nuclear weapons in the alliance is likely to look much like the past. NATO is not about to collapse, nor is it likely to reach agreement on a dramatic change in strategy and doctrine. Many of the current debates in NATO have parallels in the past: we have been through this before. That is especially striking for nuclear issues, as Timothy Ireland in particular makes clear in Chapter 1. Yet the current enthusiasm, especially in the United States, for improving NATO's conventional forces in order to diminish reliance on nuclear weapons has much in common with the efforts of the Kennedy administration in the early 1960s, efforts which led to NATO acceptance of the doctrine of flexible response in 1967. It is tempting to say that NATO is in crisis and always has been.

Yet some things have changed. Current debates are not exact replicas of their predecessors. Sorting out what has changed from what only seems to have changed is one of the purposes of this book. Certainly the temperature of the nuclear confrontation in Europe will remain higher in the future than it was during the wilderness years of 1965 to 1977. That is assured by nuclear parity between the United States and the Soviet Union, and the consequent debate among experts over what it takes to sustain deterrence and extend it to Europe in those circumstances. We conclude by sketching two illustrative futures, one distinctly possible, the other more probable.

Increasing Disarray. NATO is not about to collapse, but there are reasons for thinking that this 'crisis' is more serious than those the alliance has weathered in the past. In particular, strains over a number of issues could coincide and accumulate, raising the risk of a serious break in alliance arrangements. Firstly, for example, the temperature of the nuclear issue will remain high, hence both the difficulty of managing it and the costs of maladroit handling will be higher. Suppose East-West nuclear-arms control remained blocked for some time, and NATO confronted the next round of nuclear modernisation — either of short-range systems or of mid-range systems, shorter than INF but longer than most of NATO's current inventory. The domestic consensus on security issues in critical European countries could come even further apart.

Secondly, little may come of the current enthusiasm for better conventional defence. Suppose the initiatives collapsed with considerable bad feeling on both sides of the Atlantic: Americans feeling that Europeans were unprepared to provide for their own defence, with the United States being asked to run unacceptable nuclear risks on Eruope's behalf; and Europeans feeling pressed to spend more than they could afford, and to bolster the American lead in high technology industries in the process.

Thirdly, issues outside Europe, especially in the Persian Gulf, will be a focus of continuing strain. Suppose a crisis more serious than Iran arose. Even short of a crisis, American feelings, already evident, that they are being asked to shoulder the burden of defending access to oil that is more important to Europe than to the United States could become much more salient politically. For their part, Europeans could feel they were being badgered to support policies, not just in the Persian Gulf but also in Central America, that they found questionable, even dangerous.

Fourthly, economic strains will bedevil the alliance. Suppose European economies remained stagnant. The nuclear issue would be harder to handle, and Europeans would remain sensitive to the cost and technological implications of efforts to improve NATO conventional defences. Over the longer term, Europeans will continue to feel that they lag behind America and Japan in high technology, hence will remain reluctant to rely more on military technology that is made in America. European exporters will also be tempted to look harder at markets in the East, thus raising the prospect of more inter-allied strains over trade with Eastern Europe and the Soviet Union.

The list could be extended. If accumulating strains led to a crisis, that crisis could be touched off by an American decision, taken in frustration and no doubt driven by Congress, to withdraw American forces from Europe. Calls to do so run back to Senator Mike Mansfield in the mid-1960s; then, those who made them were predominantly 'liberal', but similar pressures in the American Congress now run across the political spectrum. In June 1984 Senator Sam Nunn, certainly no enemy of NATO, proposed that American forces be reduced gradually if Europeans did not meet a series of specific defence improvements. His amendment, opposed by the Reagan administration, did not pass, but it illustrated the American sentiments. Even Europeans who were sympathetic to the specific improvements Nunn proposed found the measure irritating in tone: a single American senator setting conditions for European defence efforts.

If some future Nunn Amendment passed, NATO might be trapped in a self-fulfilling prophecy. American sponsors of the move surely would not regard the intent of the measure as hostile; they would see it as a goad to Europeans to do more. Just as certainly, however, European states would find it difficult to do more, in other than cosmetic ways. They might instead seek fresh arms-control or other negotiations with the Soviet Union, leading Americans to feel that their worst fears of Europe's 'finlandisation' were coming true. Even absent such European efforts to cut their own deals with the Soviets, if American troops began to leave and Europe did not move to fill the gap, Americans could then argue that their remaining forces in Europe were under too much risk. And so the pressure for further withdrawals could grow.

Muddling Through. Such a dire scenario, or others that could be painted, are far from out of the question. More probably, however, NATO will continue to muddle through, in a way that fully satisfies no one but does not lead to any sharp break in current arrangements. There will remain considerable consensus on both sides of the Atlantic that NATO is necessary. Europeans and Americans will agree on the need for *some* military insurance against Soviet military power, even if they do not agree on any detailed assessment of the Soviet threat, or on how much insurance, or in what form.

Flexible response, for all its frayed edges, will remain the core of NATO strategy, less because of enthusiasm for it than because the alternatives are unappealing. 'New approaches' will amount to tinkering at the margins, though experts will sometimes hint at, and publics will often hope for, more. Those tinkerings are important; efforts to make NATO's nuclear posture more credible by withdrawing most short-

Whither the Nuclear Confrontation? 231

range warheads and by doing what can be done to improve conventional defence are essential to managing NATO's nuclear dilemma. But they are ways to manage a messy *status quo*, not once-and-for-all resolutions of the dilemma.

By the same token, NATO will be able to manage the nuclear confrontation in Europe mostly because dramatic alternatives to current arrangements are in the end so unattractive. But it can be managed also because goverments have relatively greater control over the issue, over timing and tactics, than is the case for other issues in transatlantic relations. For example, fewer loose words in public on nuclear issues from the Reagan administration and demonstrable movement on arms control of any sort would have done much to undercut anti-nuclear protest in the early 1980s, in Europe as well as in the United States. The evolution of the nuclear-freeze movement in the United States is a case in point. What emerged from Congress in 1983 were freeze resolutions that merely exhorted the Executive to negotiate mutual and verifiable freezes with the Soviet Union. That was true despite the prospect of major new nuclear deployments in the United States and Europe, deep scepticism about the administration's commitment to arms control, and occasional official talk of superiority', 'prolonged nuclear war', and 'war winning'. Better handling of the issue, especially in public, probably would have pre-empted even the watered-down freeze resolution that eventually ensued.

Such a reading is reinforced by deeper features in the public perception of nuclear issues. From the viewpoint of the early 1980s, public anxiety about nuclear weapons seemed a phenomenon that suddenly and mysteriously sprang up from the grass roots, or dropped full-blown from the sky. Certainly it was hard to know exactly why concern emerged when it did, rather than earlier or later, unless the anti-nuclear power groups formed a base which could gravitate to nuclear weapons issues. Even the combination of factors — stalled arms control, lack of confidence in the American administration, imminent new nuclear deployments — does not add up to a satisfactory explanation. It may be simply that about once a generation nations must come to grips anew with nuclear weapons, and that exactly what touches off a particular period of soul-searching is inherently unpredictable.

It is in one way a mistake to view the early 1980s as an aroused public opinion, preoccupied with the threat of nuclear war, forcing foreign policy elites to heed it. In fact, the process seems more nearly the other way around. What occurred is that the rough consensus on nuclear issues among experts or foreign-policy elites broke down during the late 1970s. Leaders of the anti-nuclear movement became fully up to debating the intricacies of nuclear strategy or weaponry with the commander of the Strategic Air Command. And so, contending experts sought to mobilise public opinion. Or the fact of the debate increased concern among the public at large – 'if there's a debate, perhaps I should be worried'. Various public opinion surveys, granting all the caution with which they must be treated, suggest considerable stability in basic public views. As Boutwell suggests in Chapter 6, those basic views contained internal contradictions – the American commitment to both peace and strength, for example, or Europeans' attachment to NATO coupled with their allergy to nuclear weapons.[23] Basic views, including the contradictions, have changed little; the 'face' that is politically apparent *has* varied over time.

That process is easier to understand in light of another aspect of public opinion: for most people the threat of war, and with it the salience of security issues, remained relatively low. When Germans, for example, were asked in the early 1980s what problem was most important to them, economic and domestic issues continued to receive over 80 per cent of the nominations.[24] Among foreign policy problems, 'maintaining peace' consistently has been held to be most important, but overall the percentage of Germans citing it declined during the 1970s. Fear of war did increase in the early 1980s but not by much across whole populations.

The relatively low salience of security issues was also suggested, in an impressionistic way, by the German and British elections of 1983. Deciding what determines election results is fool's play, but in both cases the opposition party sought to emphasise the nuclear issues, especially the impending deployments of INF. In both bases the emphasis seemed to hurt, rather than help. Both parties seemed to pay a price for attempting to shift the electorate's attention from the economic issues which were its primary concern. In fact, long before the cruise and Pershing missiles began arriving in Europe, in December 1983, their deployment was a foregone conclusion. The peace movement, frustrated, was also exhausted, and the attentions of the media and their public audiences had moved to other issues.

In that context the apparent paradox in public attitudes on security issues is more understandable. On one hand, large majorities in every NATO country save France continue to deem NATO 'still essential' to their security. For example, a March 1981 poll produced the following majorities: 70-15 in Britain, 59-28 in Italy, 66-21 in Norway, and 62-15 in the Netherlands. Yet at the same time polls record considerable opposition to particular defence arrangements, especially nuclear deployments like INF. Given that security issues are not at the top of most people's concerns, what seems likely is that they react in a generally favourable way to the notion of buying some security insurance through participation in the NATO alliance. Yet when pressed further to contemplate unpleasant scenarios which they had not previously thought much about — like using nuclear weapons in their defence or having them stationed in their neighbourhood — people retreat from the prospect. That paradox is less surprising on second thought.

These features of public perception carry both positive and negative implications for managing the nuclear issue. On the negative side, they suggest that efforts at public education on the nuclear issue are likely to fail. Most people will continue not to want to think about the issue and generally feel they do not need to. And so the public debate will ebb and flow; it will be frequently passionate but usually ill-informed, despite the efforts of the contending experts and elites.

More positively, there does seem space to manage the issue. The image of the public having reclaimed the nuclear issue from their leaders is wide of the mark. Some people have become more concerned, but most have resisted being drawn too far into the unpleasant details of the issue. They are less confident that the nuclear dilemma is being well managed. But the evidence hints that public attitudes provide room if national leaders are more sensitive in handling the issue.

In managing it, campaigns to 'educate' the public at large, while worthy, will be less successful than attempts to re-establish a minimum consensus on nuclear issues among the experts and attentive public. If there is rough consensus there, the public mood will moderate, and rival elites and experts will be less able to mobilise public opinion. The experience of the Scowcroft Commission established in 1982 by President Reagan to examine American strategic forces is instructive. Its report patched together a political compromise: several Democrats in and out of Congress agreed to support the MX missile in exchange for a presidential commitment to strategic arms control and the development of a small, single-warhead, ICBM. In the process, the Commission ratified across a relatively broad spectrum of defence experts a set of propositions which had been disputed within that community, especially by the political right at the fringes of the Reagan administration — that there is no 'window of vulnerability', that strategic arms control should focus on stability rather than numbers, and that single-warhead missiles are preferable to those with multiple warheads.[25]

In fact, the compromise began to unraval almost as soon as it was stitched together. Exacerbated by the Soviet shooting down of the KAL aircraft, the climate for superpower arms control was inhospitable as the Soviet Union left the START talks at the end of 1983, and the Reagan administration's START position remained, at best, confused, leaving the Democratic authors of the compromise feeling they had been deceived in agreeing to support the MX. Yet, with better luck and more sincere commitment on the part of the administration, the Commission might have succeeded in narrowing the agenda of the nuclear debate in the United States.

These comments suggest that there is space for NATO to manage the nuclear confrontation in Europe. Whether it *will* be tolerably managed is another question. Managing it will require limiting expectations about what the alliance can accomplish and limiting claims the NATO partners make on each other. It will require special caution about proceeding with projects — such a nuclear modernisation — over which the ostensible experts in the alliance are disagreed. These lessons are not new. They have been, and will continue to be, easy to state but hard to accomplish. The NATO alliance and the governmental machines that comprise it are blunt instruments. The domestic politics surrounding the alliance often increases the bluntness even as it impels allied governments to engage each other in complicated projects and to make their fulfilment a test of loyalty or cohesion.

Yet with a modest amount of sensitive management and a little luck, NATO at fifty, or even sixty, may not look much different from how it looks today. The lack of attractive alternatives frustrates the search for radical change, but it also provides time for incremental adjustments, such as improvements in conventional capabilities. Thus, even if NATO looks on the surface much the same several decades hence as it does not, beneath the surface the change might be considerable. NATO might, in those circumstances, serve the interests of both Europeans and Americans at least as well as it does today and provide a stable environment in which Europe may become less divided.

Notes

1. From International Institute for Strategic Studies, *The Military Balance 1979-1980* (London: IISS, 1979).
2. International Institute for Strategic Studies, *The Military Balance, 1984-5* (London: IISS, 1984).

3. *New York Times*, 26 January 1984.
4. *New York Times*, 24 March 1984.
5. In NATO Press Communiqué M2 (79) 22 (12 December 1979).
6. On the FBS issue, see Stephen M. Millet, 'Forward-Based Systems and SALT I', *Political Science Quarterly*, vol. 98, no. 1 (Spring 1983), pp. 79-97; and Gerard Smith, *Doubletalk: The Story of SALT I* (Garden City, NY: Doubleday and Co., 1980), pp. 90-8, 123-30, 192-7.
7. NATO Press Communiqué M2 (79) 22.
8. In a speech to the National Press Club in Washington, 18 November 1981.
9. Soviet leader Brezhnev used numbers asserting parity in an interview in 1981 with the German magazine *Der Spiegel*. It is reproduced in English in Foreign Broadcast Information Service, *Daily Report, Soviet Union* (2 November 1981) p. G8; and the relevant portions are excerpted in English in *The Guardian*, 23 November 1981. He disaggregated the Western figure in the original interview and provided additional information on the Soviet number during his visit to Bonn, reported in *The Times*, 25 November 1981.
10. The most complete account of the 'walk in the woods' is contained in a *Deadly Gambits* (New York: A.A. Knopf Inc., 1984). Strobe Talbott. Nitze has described the episode in many interviews. See, for example, 'Missile Talks Doomed from the Start', *Science*, 223 (February 1984), pp. 566-70.
11. *NATO and the Warsaw Pact: Force Comparisons* (Brussels: NATO Information Services, 1984).
12. R. Kennedy, Chapter 7 in R. Kennedy and J.M. Weinstein (eds.), *The Defense of the West* (Boulder, Colo. and London: Westview Press); International Institute for Strategic Studies, *The Military Balance 1983-84*.
13. Richard K. Betts, *Cruise Missiles and U.S. Policy* (Washington, DC: The Brookings Institution, 1982).
14. P.E. Gallis, M.M. Lowenthal and M.S. Smith, *The Strategic Defense Initiative and U.S. Alliance Strategy* (Congressional Research Service, The Library of Congress, 1 February 1985).
15. This idea had been suggested earlier by some German and British analysts. For an interesting proposal along those lines, see Lawrence Freedman, 'The Dilemma of Theater Nuclear Arms Control', *Survival*, vol. 23, no. 1 (January/February 1981), pp. 2-10.
16. For one European suggestion along that line, see Christoph Bertram, 'The Implications of Theater Nuclear Weapons in Europe', *Foreign Affairs*, vol. 60, no. 2 (Winter 1981/82), pp. 323 ff. Kissinger's proposal is in his 'A Plan to Reshape NATO', *Time*, 5 March 1984, pp. 20-4.
17. See, for example, Pierre Lellouche's argument for a broadening of the role of British and French nuclear forces, in 'Europe and Her Defense', *Foreign Affairs*, vol. 54, no. 4 (Spring 1981), pp. 813-34; Hedley Bull's explicit call for more European co-operation, including nuclear, in 'European Self-Reliance and the Reform of NATO', *Atlantic Quarterly*, vol. 1, no. 1 (Spring 1983), pp. 25-43; and a similar though more tentative argument from German Social Democrats, in Wilhelm Bruns and Christian Crause, 'Reflections on a European Peace Order' (Friedrich Ebert Stiftung, December 1982).
18. W.S. Bennett, R.R. Sandoval and R.G. Schreffler have done the most work on such proposals. See their 'A Credible Nuclear-Emphasis Defense for NATO', *Orbis*, vol. 17, no. 2 (Summer 1973).
19. Kent F. Wisner, 'Military Aspects of Enhanced Radiation Weapons', *Survival*, vol. 23, no. 6 (November/December 1981).
20. For a strong argument about the difficulty of controlling nuclear war, see Desmond Ball, *Can Nuclear War Be Controlled?* Adelphi Paper no. 169 (London: IISS, 1981).

21. See, for example, Senator Sam Nunn's report, *NATO: Can the Alliance Be Saved?* Report to the Senate Committee on Armed Services, 97 Cong., 2 sess. (13 May 1982); and Report of the European Security Study, *Strengthening Conventional Deterrence in Europe: Proposals for the 1980s* (1983); F. Hampson, 'Groping for Technical Panaceas: The European Conventional Balance and Nuclear Stability', *International Security*, vol. 8, no. 3 (1984) pp. 57-82; and S. Huntington, 'Conventional Deterrence and Conventional Retaliation in Europe', *International Security*, vol. 8, no. 3 (1984), pp. 32-56.

22. The British Atlantic Committee, *Diminishing the Nuclear Threat: NATO's Defence and New Technology* (London: 1984); International Institute for Strategic Studies, *Strategic Survey: 1983-84* (London: IISS, 1984), pp. 12-17.

23. For interesting evidence on this point, see Philip P. Evert, 'Public Opinion on Nuclear Weapons, Defense and Security: The Case of the Netherlands' in Gregory Flynn and Hans Rattinger (eds.), *The Public and Atlantic Defense*, forthcoming from the Atlantic Institute for International Affairs, Paris.

24. Hans Rattinger, 'The Federal Republic of Germany: Much Ado About (Almost) Nothing' in Flynn and Rattinger (eds.), *The Public and Atlantic Defense*.

25. See *Report of the President's Commission on Strategic Forces* (Washington: April 1983).

NOTES ON CONTRIBUTORS

Jeffrey D. Boutwell is staff associate for international security studies at the American Academy of Arts and Sciences and adjunct research fellow at the Center for Science and International Affairs, Harvard University. He is co-editor of Weapons in Space, to be published in 1985 by W.W. Norton, and author of the forthcoming *Nuclear Weapons and the German Dilemma* (Cornell University Press).

Paul Doty has been the Director of the Center for Science and International Affairs at Harvard University since its founding in 1973. Although a biochemist, he has long been active in international security matters and arms control. He founded the quarterly journal *International Security*, co-authored *Living With Nuclear Weapons* (Harvard University Press, 1984) and as Aspen Senior Fellow has co-chaired annual summer conferences in Aspen and Berlin on arms control and European security issues. Professor Doty also served on the General Advisory Committee on arms control of the President's Science Advisory Committee.

Lawrence Freedman is Professor and Head of the Department of War Studies at King's College London in the University of London. He previously held research positions at Nuffield College, Oxford and at the International Institute for Strategic Studies before becoming Head of Policy Studies at the Royal Institute of International Affairs. Professor Freedman is the author of *US Intelligence and the Soviet Strategic Threat* (Macmillan, 1977), *Britain and Nuclear Weapons* (Macmillan, 1980) and *The Evolution of Nuclear Strategy* (Macmillan, 1981). He is a co-author of *Nuclear War and Nuclear Peace* (Macmillan, 1983) and the editor of *The Troubled Alliance* (Heinemann, 1983).

Timothy Ireland was assistant Professor of Political Science at Tufts University when this book was written. He is the author of *Creating the Entangling Alliance* (Greenwood Press, 1981).

Stephen M. Meyer is Associate Professor in the Political Science department at the Massachusetts Institute of Technology. He is a consultant to the U.S. Department of Defense and the Central Intelligence Agency and author of *The Dynamics of Nuclear Proliferation* (University of Chicago Press, 1984).

Condoleezza Rice is Assistant Professor, Political Science, and Assistant Director, Center for International Security and Arms Control, at Stanford University. She is the author of *The Soviet Union and the Czechoslovak Army: Uncertain Allegiance* (Princeton University Press, 1984).

Gregory F. Treverton is Lecturer in Public Policy at the Kennedy School of Government, Harvard University. Formerly, he served on the directing staff of the International Institute for Strategic Studies in London; before that, he was staff member for Western Europe on the National Security Council in Washington, D.C. He is the author of the recently published *Making the Alliance Work*.

INDEX

Acheson Committee report 19
Adenauer, Konrad 24-5, 28-30, 38, 69, 147
Agnew, Dr Harold 57
Agt, Andreas van 153
Ailleret, General 26, 122-3
aircraft, nuclear-capable
   Great Britain 116
   NATO 74-7, 101
   Soviet 91-2, 171-8
   treatment of, in negotiations 217-18
   vulnerability of 92, 106
   Warsaw Pact 194-5
air-sol moyenne portée (ASMP) missiles 75, 127, 130
air-to-surface (ASM) missiles 177
Akhromeyev, S.F. 198
Alford, Jonathan 101
Andropov, Y. 198
anti-ballistic missile (ABM) systems 99, 209-10
Anti-Ballistic Missile Treaty (1972) 210-11, 220
anti-submarine warfare (ASW) 179
anti-tactical missiles (ATM) 211
arms control
   and deployment 148, 152
   and NATO military logic 107-10
   see also INF talks; MBFR; negotiations; SALT; START; treaties
Atlantic Nuclear Force (ANF) 37
atomic demolition munitions (ADMs) 50, 58, 80, 101
Atomic Energy Act (1946) 9-10, 12-13, 22-3
Atomic Weapons Research Establishment (AWRE) 120
Aurillac, Michel 128

B-52 bomber 74-5, 77, 104
Backfire bomber (Tu-26) 71, 172, 174, 177-8, 217
Badger aircraft 217
Bahr, Egon 70, 148-9
balance between superpowers *see* parity

Barre, Raymond 127
battlefield nuclear weapons 49, 78-80, 94-6, 101-2, 105, 116, 122-3
   and China 132-5
   Soviet 172-3
Beaufre, General 26
Belgium 17, 143-5, 152-5, 204
Bermuda agreements (1957) 13-14
Blinder bomber (Tu-22) 172, 174, 217
Blue Streak missile 23
Boutwell, Jeffrey H. 67, 141, 203-4, 232
Bowie, Robert 33-4
Brandt, Willy 148-9
Brezhnev, L.I. 168, 217-18
Britain *see* Great Britain
Brown, Harold 81
Buccaneer bomber 75, 77, 118
Buchan, Alastair 39
Bulgaria 197, 200
Bundy, McGeorge 82
Buteaux, Paul 53

Callaghan, James 157
Canada 143, 159
Carte Blanche war-game 10, 28, 94
Carter, Jimmy 70, 78, 144, 157
Carter administration 67, 70-1, 81, 144-7
Ceauşescu, N. 197, 200
China 132-8, 216
Chirac, Jacques 125-6
Choca, General Boleslaw 190
Christian Democratic Union (CDU), FRG 28, 38, 150
Christian Social Union (CSU), FRG 28
Churchill, Winston 26, 115
circular error probable (CEP) 175, 177
Clifford, Clark 51-2
Cohen, Samuel 128
collective forces in NATO 32-9
command, control, communications and intelligence (C3I) 93, 104

239

240 *Index*

167-72, 177
Conservative Party, GB 26, 37, 232
control of nuclear weapons
   NATO 13, 21, 95-6, 104-5, 119-20
   Warsaw Pact 179-80, 186, 192-4
conventional forces
   and China 133
   and defence of Europe 7, 20-2, 28, 94-6, 99, 229
   and flexible-response 21, 94, 99, 122
   as deterrence 226-8
   conflict with nuclear-capable systems 101, 106
   Long-Term Defence Programme 61, 67, 70-2, 147
   NATO inferiority in 20, 70-1, 99, 105, 146, 196
   nuclear threshold 46-8
   Soviet view of 169-71, 182
   Warsaw Pact 186-7, 194, 196
Corporal missiles 9, 21, 116
Cossiga, Francesco 155
Council for Mutual Economic Assistance (COMECON), E. Europe 188
'counter-vailing' strategy 81
coupling 17, 57, 204
Craxi, Bettino 156
credibility of NATO's deterrence 101-2, 147-8
cruise missiles
   as targets 209
   campaigns against 117-18
   European deployments of 1, 17, 73, 83, 87, 145-51, 204, 223, 232
   ground-launched 73, 79, 180-1
   sea-launched 73, 103-4, 218-19
   Soviet view of 167
   survivability of 92
Cuba 18, 167, 192
Cultural Revolution, China 133, 135-7
Czechoslovakia 180, 189-94, 197-9, 206

Davignon, Etienne 154
decision-making in NATO 141-6
de Gaulle, Charles 24-7, 32-9, 69, 110, 121, 124-6, 131, 147, 193, 224
delivery systems 62, 171-2, 177, 189-90
   see also aircraft
'demonstrative' use of weapons 52-3, 58
Denmark 17, 143, 145, 158
dependence of Europe on USA 2, 5, 20, 48, 207
deployments, missile
   in Eastern Europe 71-2, 108, 180-1, 189-94, 204-6
   in Western Europe 203-5; cruise and Pershing 1, 17, 73, 83, 87, 145-51, 223, 232; opposition to 15-16, 83, 107, 149-50, 160, 204; Thor and Jupiter 5, 14-17
deterrence
   and first use 50-5, 60
   conventional and atomic 47-8, 226-8
   denial and punishment 56-7, 97-8
   flexible-response 19-20, 97, 170
   mutual 26
   NATO view of 7, 87-110
   proportional 27, 123
   Soviet view of 170, 181-2
   TNF 170
   US v. European view of 88-91, 98
Doty, Paul 1, 203
Douglas-Home, Sir Alec 37
dual-capability
   aircraft and artillery 74-7, 101
   missiles 195
dual-key systems 13, 21, 116, 118, 224
Dulles, John Foster 9-10, 12, 15, 116

Eastern Europe
   formation of Warsaw Pact 187-8
   leverage in 200-1
   nuclear Warsaw Pact 188-93
   pre-Warsaw Pact 186-7
   Soviet deployments in 71-2, 108, 180-1, 189-94, 204-6
   Soviet view v. other WP members 194-200
economies, national 229
Eco-peace movement, FRG 150
Eden, Anthony 7
'education campaign' 30, 233
Egypt 12
Eichenberg, Richard 153
Eisenhower, Dwight D. 7-13, 22, 32
Eisenhower administration 7-19,

Index

46-7, 116
emerging technologies (ET) 227-8
enhanced radiation weapons (ERW) 70-1, 98-9
  and France 128-30
  and FRG 144, 226
  and NATO 61, 67-8, 71, 88
  US production of 78
Enthoven, Alain C. 49
Erhard, Ludwig 38
escalation 51-5, 94-6
  Soviet view of 166-8, 173, 180, 196
  see also threshold
Euromissiles 70-4, 214
Europe
  dependence on USA for defence 2, 5, 20, 48, 207
  independent national nuclear programmes 22-7
  national nuclear forces 12-13, 20; *see also* France; Great Britain
  self-reliance 224-5
  view of TNF 88-91
European Defence Community (EDC) 7-8
European Economic Community (EEC) 24, 51
European Security Study (ESECS) 83

F bombers 73-7, 217
Federal Republic of Germany (FRG)
  aircraft 76
  and ERW 144, 226
  and first use 58
  and France 124-5, 130-1, 224-5
  and GDR 3, 147-8, 151
  and independent nuclear programme 24-5, 28-32, 35
  and MLF 37-8
  cruise and Pershing deployment in 83, 146-9, 232
  Mace deployment in 21, 29, 31, 143
  internal politics 146-52
Fencer aircraft 217
'fire-break' between nuclear and conventional war 46-50, 63, 171
first use 50-5, 60
  see also no-first-use policy
flexible-response doctrine 18-21, 68, 82-3, 94-100, 168, 230-1
  and France 27

and FRG 30
  criticism of 96-100, 122
forward-based systems (FBS) 74, 189, 212-13
forward defence strategy 7
France
  aircraft 75-6
  and deterrence 121-2
  and Europe 6-8
  and FRG 24, 36, 38, 124-5, 130-1 224-5
  and missile deployment 24
  and MLF 37-8
  and NATO 39, 91, 142, 145, 232
  and negotiation 215
  and Suez 12
  and 'theatre' concept 113-14
  and weapon-sharing 12-13
  independent nuclear forces 23-7, 35, 113-14, 121-32, 216, 224-5
  TNWs 124-9
Franco-German Treaty (1963) 24, 36, 38
Freedman, Lawrence 4, 44, 69, 97, 113, 210
FROG (SR) missiles 135, 189-90, 192, 195, 205

Gallois, General 26
Geneste, Colonel Marc 128
German Democratic Republic (GDR)
  and FRG 3, 147-8, 151, 197, 206-7
  and Warsaw Pact 197-8
  Soviet deployments in 180, 189-91, 199
  Soviet nuclear storage sites in 180, 195
Germany 6-8
  see also Federal Republic of Germany; German Democratic Republic
Giscard d'Estaing, V. 126-8, 157
González, Felipe 159
Goodpaster, General 56
Great Britain
  aircraft 74-5
  and EEC 24, 51
  and MLF 37-8
  and NATO 232
  and negotiations 215
  and Suez 12-13
  and weapon-sharing 12-13

cruise and Pershing deployment in 83, 146-9, 232
Healey-Schröder report 51-2
independent nuclear programme 22-6, 35, 114, 118, 216, 224-5
Thor and Jupiter deployment in 14-17
TNWs 115-21
Greece 16-17, 143, 158-9
Green Party, FRG 149-50
Gromyko, A.A. 222
ground-launched cruise missiles (GLCMs)
see cruise missiles
guidance, precision 58

Hades missile 130
Haig, A. 81
Hassel, Kai-Uwe von 31
Healey, Denis 51-2, 97, 117
Healey-Schröder report 51-2
Hernu, Charles 128-9
Herter, Christian 34
High-Level Group 61, 72-3, 146
Holland *see* Netherlands
Honecker, Erich 3, 151, 198-9
Honest John missiles 9, 31, 62, 78-9, 101, 116
Howard, Michael 46
Hsieh, Alice Langley 135-6
Hungary 197-8
Husak, Gustav 199

Iceland 16, 143, 145, 159
intelligence-gathering 143-4
see also command, control, communications, and intelligence (C31)
inter-continental ballistic missiles (ICBMs)
Chinese 134, 137
Soviet 14, 171, 174, 177
US 11, 20, 89-90
vulnerability of 90-1, 99, 210
intermediate-range ballistic missiles (IRBMs) 11
Soviet deployments 14
US deployments 14-17, 40, 48-9, 89
intermediate-range nuclear forces (INF)
and W. European politics 145-59
NATO 67, 71-2, 108
negotiation on 1, 83, 211-15

Soviet 71-2, 108
talks 1, 83, 145
verification of agreement 221
International Institute for Strategic Studies (IISS) 71-2, 136, 146-7
Ireland, Timothy 5, 44, 50, 228
Israel 12
Italy 17-18, 40, 76, 143, 155-7, 232

Jaguar aircraft 76-7, 118
Johnson, Lyndon B. 37-8
Joint Chiefs of Staff, USA 8
Joint Committee on Atomic Energy (JCAE) 12-13, 37, 57
Jupiter IRBM
European deployments 5, 11, 14-17, 40, 48-9, 89
vulnerability of 16-17, 40

Kaufman, William 102
Kekkonen, Urho 158
Kennan, George 82
Kennedy, John F. 19, 23, 30, 34, 36-7, 167
Kennedy administration 17-27, 30, 33-4, 228
Killian, James R. 11
Kissinger, Henry 52-3, 69, 159, 168, 223
Kohl, Helmut 130, 150
Komitet Gosudarstvennoi Bezopasnosti (KGB) 179-80, 191
Kornienko, G.M. 198
Krushchev, N.K. 12, 18, 188-90, 193
Krylov, Marshal 174

Labour Party, GB 38, 83, 121, 160, 204
Laird, Melvin 53, 57
Lance missiles 78-9, 101, 118
land-based missiles
NATO systems 79, 102-4
v. sea-based systems 17, 81, 103-4
launchers, strategic 39
Lee, Admiral Richard 36
Legge, J. Michael 51-4, 61
Liberal Party, GB 121
Limited Nuclear Test-Ban Treaty 37
limited nuclear war 52, 117
Soviet view of 166-9, 193
US view of 81-2
Lisbon force 7-8

Index

Longbow MRBM 73
long-range aviation (LRA) *see* aircraft
Long-Term Defence Programme 61, 67, 70-2, 147
Lubbers, Ruud 152-3
Luxembourg 143, 145, 159

McGiffert, David 72-3
MacMahon Act (Atomic Energy, 1946) 9-10, 12-13, 22-3
Macmillan, Harold 13, 22-3, 37
McNamara, Robert S. 19-20, 36-7, 47-9, 59, 82, 134
Mace cruise missile 21, 29, 31, 40, 48, 62, 143
Mansfield, Senator Mike 59, 230
Mansfield Amendment 59
Mao Tse-tung (Zedong) 134, 137
Maoist doctrine 133-4
Marshall Plan 6
Martens, Wilfred 154
Martin, Laurence 58
Mason, Roy 60
Matador missiles 91, 21, 29
Mauroy, Pierre 129
medium-range ballistic missiles (MRBMs) 15, 32-3, 73
Mery, General Guy 126-8
Meyer, Stephen M. 164, 205-6, 218
MiG aircraft 174-5
military doctrine and strategy, Soviet 165, 169, 173
military logic of TNF 87-110, 207-7
  and arms control 107-10
  and flexible-response 96-100
  and political objectives 110
  differences between European and US views 88-91
  escalation 94-6
  guidelines for posture 100-7
  NATO's posture 88-91
  problems 91-4
'mini-nukes' 58, 61
Minuteman ICBM 20, 167
Mirage bomber 75-7, 123, 130
Mitterand, François 129-30, 156
Monnet, Jean 6
Montgomery, Field Marshal Viscount 116
Multilateral Force (MLF) 33-9, 48-9, 87, 89
Mutual and Balanced Force Reductions (MBFR) 44, 56, 62, 108, 213

Nasser, Gamal Abdel 12
negotiations 211-23
  aircraft 217-18
  British and French forces 215-17
  form of 221-3
  history of 212-15
  issues for 215-21
  short-range TNF 219-20
  SLCMs 218-19
  strategic defence 220-1
  verification of agreement 221
  see also MBFR; SALT; START
Nerlich, Uwe 49
Netherlands 16-17, 59, 143-5, 152-5, 204, 232
neutron bomb 67-8, 70-4, 128-30
'New Look' strategy 8-10, 116
'New New Look' 10-11
Nike missiles
  Ajax 21, 29
  Hercules 21, 48, 80, 101
  Zeus 31
Nitze, Paul 214-15
Nixon, Richard M. 51
no-first-use (NFU) policy 82-3, 106-7, 138, 196
Non-Proliferation Treaty 37, 45
Nordli, Odvar 158
Norstad, General 5, 15, 29, 32-3, 89
Norstad plan 32-3
North Atlantic Treaty (1949) 6
North Atlantic Treaty Organisation (NATO)
  1950-1965 5-41; collective forces 32-9; FRG 28-32; from Sputnik to flexible-response 10-22; independent nuclear programmes 22-7; pre-Sputnik 6-10
  1965-1977 44-64; debate 1970s 55-60; first use 50-5; new technologies 60-3 role of TNWs 46-50
  1977-1985 67-84; coping with parity 67-70; doctrine questioned 80-4; neutron bomb and Euromissiles 70-4; TNF structure 74-80
  and arms control 107-10
  C31 93
  control of weapons 13, 21,

95-6, 104-5, 119-20
  dependence on USA 2, 5, 20, 207
  flexible-response doctrine 18-21,
    27, 30, 68, 82-3, 94-100,
    168, 230-1
  future 223-34; conventional
    deterrence 226-8; disarray
    228-30; European self-reliance
    224-5; nuclear defence 225-6
  military logic and politics 87-110
  politics and weapons 141-61;
    composition of Alliance
    142-5; decision-making 141-6;
    differences in viewpoint
    141-2; W. European politics
    145-59
  third country nuclear forces
    113-38
  TNF posture 88-96, 100-7
  TNF structure 74-80, 100-1
  see also Nuclear Planning Group
Norway 17, 143, 145, 157-8, 232
nuclear delivery vehicles (NDVs) *see*
  aircraft; delivery systems
Nuclear Planning Group (NPG) 38-9,
  143-5
  and first-use 50-4, 57
  and TNF 72
  studies of new technologies 60-1
Nunn, Senator Sam 56, 230
'Nunn Amendment' 230

Obrona terytorium krajni (OTK) 190
operational art and tactics, Soviet
  165, 170-1, 173
Ostpolitik 3, 147-8

Papandreou, Andreas 158
parity between superpowers
  coping with 67-71
  INF 213-14
  strategic 1-2, 5, 18, 89-90,
    146-7, 168, 208-9
Partial Test-Ban Treaty 45
Patriot SAM 80
peace movements 83, 107, 149-50,
  160, 232
'pentomic' division concept 9, 21
permissive action links (PALs) 21,
  93, 195
Pershing missiles 21, 31, 48
  I 78-9, 92, 101, 196
  II 73, 209
  deployment in Europe 1, 17, 73, 79,

83, 87, 145-8, 204-5, 223, 232
  Soviet view of 167
  survivability of 92, 209
Pincus, Walter 78
Pleven, René 7
Pluton missiles 78-9, 101, 124-5, 130
Poirier, General Lucien 127
Poland 189-91, 194-9
Polaris SLBM system 11, 18, 20, 92
  and GB 23, 118, 121
  in NATO 34, 36, 38-9
politics
  and military logic 87-110, 204,
    206-7
  NATO 141-61
  Soviet 164-82
  W. Europe 145-59
Pompidou, Georges 38
Portugal 17, 143, 145, 159
Poseidon SLBM system 39, 62, 92,
  95, 167
Programmes of Co-operation (POCs)
  143
public opinion 231-3
  and deployment 144
  confidence in deterrent 97-8,
    102, 105-7
  peace movements 83, 107,
    149-50, 160, 232

Radford, Admiral Arthur W. 11
Radford Plan 11, 28
Reagan, Ronald 78, 81-2, 108,
  209-11, 213, 233
Reagan administration 80, 91,
  233-4
  and European defences 230
  and sea-based systems 104
  ERW 70-1, 92
  SDI 1, 81-2, 209-11, 220-1
  (zero option) 108-9, 213-14
Redstone missile 21
Regulus missile 9
Reorganisation Objective Army
  Division (ROAD) 21
retaliation, massive 9, 116-17, 122,
  129
Rice, Condolezza 185, 206
Rickover, Admiral Hyman 36
Rogers, General Bernard 82-3, 105
Romania 185-6, 193, 197, 200, 206
Rosenberg, David Alan 18
Rubbi, Antonio 155
Ruehl, Lothar 62

Index

Ruiter, Jacob de 152-3
Rumsfeld, Donald 61

Sagebrush war-game 10, 28
Sandys, Duncan 14
satellite reconnaissance 221
Schelling, Thomas 93
Schlesinger, James 56, 58-60, 63, 69
Schmidt, Helmut 29, 69-72, 81, 83, 90, 144-52, 157, 213
Schröder, G. 51
Schultz, George 222
Scowcroft Commission 233-4
SCUD missiles 190, 192, 195, 205
sea-based missile systems 17, 38-9, 62-3, 81, 92, 103-4
 see also submarines
sea-launched cruise missiles (SLCMs) *see* cruise
second-strike capability 19-20
Segal, Gerald 138
Sergeant missiles 21, 31, 48
short-range ballistic missiles (SRBMs) 174, 196
short-range TNF
 and negotiations 219-20
 NATO 76-80, 88, 94, 100-1
 Soviet 1, 94, 174
'signalling' 51-3, 131
Simpson, J. 119
Skybolt missiles 23
Slessor, Air Marshall Sir John 25
Smith, Gerard 36, 82
Smith, K. Wayne 49
Social Democratic Party, GB 121
Social Democratic Party (SPD), FRG 28-9, 83, 148-51, 160, 204
Sokolovsky, Marshal V.D. 168, 192-3
Soviet Union
 aircraft 91-2, 171-8
 and China 133-8
 and conventional warfare 169-71
 and flexible-response 168
 and limited nuclear war 166-9
 and negotiations 211-13
 and nuclear theatre warfare 171-3
 and SDI 220-1
 and US IRBM deployment 15-16
 command and control 179-80, 186, 192-4
 deployment of TNF 71-2, 108, 180-1, 204
 ICBMs 14
 IRBMs 14, 91

SRBMs 1, 94, 174
TNF capabilities 15, 174-9
TNF doctrine and strategy 165-73
Warsaw Pact 185-201
 see also parity; SS-4, *etc.*
space-based systems 209-10
Spain 143, 145, 159
Special Consultative Group (SCG) 154, 223
'special relationship', GB and USA 13, 22-3
Sputnik 14
SS-4 IRBM 14, 29, 89, 108, 171, 175-7, 192
SS-5 IRBM 14, 29, 89, 91, 108, 175-7, 192
SS-11, SS-12, and SS-19 ICBMs 171, 174, 177
SS-20 IRBM 71, 91-2, 108, 171, 174-7
 deployments of 71, 196, 204
 limitations on 213, 221
 threat to NATO 1, 71, 106, 109, 144, 147, 155, 176-7, 219
SS-21, SS-22, and SS-23 SRBMs 92, 94, 109, 174, 180, 195-6, 205, 219
Stalin, J.V. 187-8
'star wars' 209, 227
 see also SDI
Stehlin, General 26-7
Stoltenberg, Thorvald 158
storage sites for tactical warheads
 NATO 92-3, 172, 177
 Soviet 179-80, 191-2, 195
Strategic Air Command (SAC), USA 7-8, 18
Strategic Arms Limitation Talks (SALT) 1, 44, 56, 74, 90, 113, 145-7, 219-23
 I (1972) 212-13, 215
 II (1974) 71, 109, 213, 215
Strategic Arms Reduction Talks (START) 1, 83, 215, 221-3, 234
Strategic Defense Initiative (SDI) 1, 81-2, 209-11, 220-1
strategic nuclear forces
 and TNF 48, 58, 90, 113, 207-11, 222
 defined 212
 parity in 1-2, 5, 18, 89-90, 146-7, 168, 208-9
Strategic Rocket Forces (SRF), Soviet 171-2

Strauss, Franz Josef 28-9, 31-2
submarine-launched ballistic missile (SLBM) systems
   NATO 39, 62, 92, 103
   Soviet 171-2, 174, 179
Suez crisis 12-13
Super-Etendard aircraft 76-7, 130
Supreme Headquarters Allied Powers in Europe (SHAPE) 15

tactical nuclear delivery vehicles (TNDVs) *see* delivery systems
tactical nuclear weapons (TNWs)
   1950-1965 5-41
   late 1960s 46-50
   1970s 55-9
   Chinese 135-8
   first use of 50-5
   see also later theatre nuclear forces (TNF)
Talbott, Strobe 214-15
talks *see* INF talks; MBFR; negotiations; SALT; START
tank warfare 62, 172
technologies, new 226-7
theatre nuclear forces (TNF)
   and strategic forces 48, 58, 90, 113, 207-11, 222
   deterrent role of 96-100
   Great Britain 115-21
   NATO: 1950-1965 5-41; 1965-1977 46-64; 1977-1985 67-84; doctrine 80-4; military logic and political purpose 87-110; structure 74-80, 100-1
   Soviet Union 164-82; capabilities 174-9; doctrine and strategy 165-73, 182
third-country nuclear forces 113-38, 215-16
   and 'theatre' concept 113-15
   China 132-8
   France 121-32
   Great Britain 115-21
Thor IRBM
   European deployments 5, 11, 13-13-17, 40, 48-9, 89
   vulnerability of 16-17, 40
threshold
   conventional-nuclear 46-8, 88, 94-6, 99, 171, 196
   tactical-strategic 48, 58, 90, 113
Tomahawk SLCM 219
Tornado bomber 75-7, 118, 120, 217

treaties
   Anti-Ballistic Missile 210-11, 220
   Franco-German 24, 36, 38
   Limited Nuclear Test-Ban 37
   Non-Proliferation 37, 45
   Partial Test-Ban 45
Treverton, Gregory F. 1, 87, 203-4, 210
'triangular' division configuration 21
Trident missile system 121
Truman, Harry S. 6-7
Tupolev bombers 71, 172, 174, 177-8
Turkey 15, 17-18, 40, 158-9
'two battles' doctrine 125

Ulbricht, Walter 199
United States of America (USA)
   aircraft 74-5
   and control of weapons 13, 21, 95-6, 104-5, 120-1
   and independent European forces 22-7, 40-1, 119-21
   and MLF 34-9
   and NATO 6-7, 32-3
   and negotiations 211-13
   and new technologies 60-3
   Army 8-9
   Carter administration 67, 70-1, 81, 144-7
   conventional forces 20-1, 46-8
   differences from European views 88-91, 142-4
   Eisenhower administration 7-19, 46-7
   ERW 70-1, 144
   Johnson administration 38
   Kennedy administration 17-27, 30, 33-4, 228
   Navy 11, 18, 36
   Nixon administration 51
   Reagan administration 1, 70-1, 80-2, 91-2, 104-9, 209-14, 220-1, 230-4
   SDI 1, 81-2, 209-11, 220-1
   storage of warheads 92-3
   TNW policy 56-9
   Truman administration 6-7
   view of TNF 88-9, 142
   vulnerability of 90-1
use of nuclear weapons
   demonstrative 52-3
   first 50-5, 60
   follow-on 54

Index

no-first- 82-3, 106-7, 138, 196
USSR *see* Soviet Union
Ustinov, D.F. 180, 198

Vance, Cyrus 67
Vandenberg Resolution 6
verification of agreements 221
Vietnam 134, 136-7
Vogel, Hans-Jochen 150-1
Vulcan bomber 75, 118-20, 217
vulnerability
   aircraft 92
   ICBMs 90-1, 99, 210
   land- v. sea-based systems 17, 81, 103-4
   SLBMs 92
   Thor and Jupiter 16-17, 40
   'window of' 81, 233

war-games 10, 28, 94, 117
Warsaw Pact/Treaty Organisation 185-201
   formation of 187-8
   in the nuclear age 188-93
   leverage 200-1
   policies 142
   Soviet deployments 198-9
   Soviet domination 186-90
   tension within 189-94, 198-9, 206
   TNF posture 194-6
Wehner, Herbert 148-9
Weinberger, Caspar 195
Western European Union (WEU) 7
Wilson, Harold 38

Xu Baoxi 137

Yugoslavia 200

'zero option' 108, 213
Zhivkov, T. 200
Zuckerman, Sir Solly 117

For Product Safety Concerns and Information please contact our EU representative GPSR@taylorandfrancis.com
Taylor & Francis Verlag GmbH, Kaufingerstraße 24, 80331 München, Germany

www.ingramcontent.com/pod-product-compliance
Lightning Source LLC
Chambersburg PA
CBHW071823300426
44116CB00009B/1413